DE'LURE PUBLICATIONS PRESENTS

TAKE MY BREATH

SAVE ME FROM MY PAST

TAKE MY BREATH AWAY 3

DE'LURE

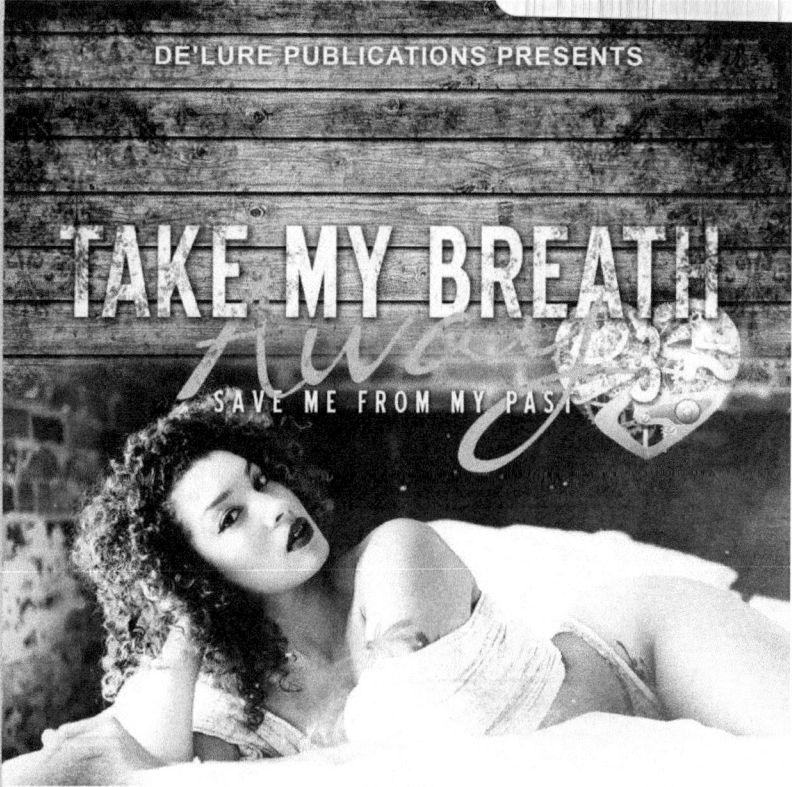

INTERNATIONAL BESTSELLING AUTHOR

DE'LURE

De'Lure
Publishing

Author Quotes

"I will die a dreamer... A dreamer with the heart and the talent to realize their dream is more powerful and blessed than the richest man on the planet..."

De'Lure

"Once you recognize the fact that NOTHING in your past be it lies or truth, can discount your present accomplishments, or the things you will achieve in the future, life becomes much simpler."

De'Lure

"We are taught to believe that our names and our images are everything... If so that's a good thing because we are in control of all of the above..."

De'Lure

"To read my work... is to peek inside of my very heart and experience my vivid rainbow of imagination"

De'Lure

"When people can't compete with your present, and they fear your future, they have no choice but to bring up and attempt to distort your past"

De'Lure

"We are not who THEY say we are... but exactly who we choose to be"

De'Lure

"If we let the ghosts of our past affect our present and our future... well then we were much better off dying, along with those nagging ghost of long ago..."

De'Lure

"FOREWORD"

What can I say about a passionate writer such as De'Lure... someone who has reunited me with the love of reading. I've only known De'Lure for a short period of time, but I definitely see his ambitious drive. The way his words flow from page to page sounds like a beautiful written melody. You know like the one that you want to keep on replay. Juicy to say the least from beginning to end, you will never really want it to end. The way he lets his reader into his creative mind, bringing us along for his imaginative ride. Reading any of De'Lure's masterpieces will have you on a wonderful, twisted, articulate lyrical high. Take my breath away series is a force to be reckoned with. If you're beginning with TMBA3 I can guarantee you that you're missing out. Get ready to be wowed by this powerful young author he will definitely leave you gasping for air.

Twaneshia Powell

"DEDICATION"

I dedicate this book to all of my wonderful friends/readers/investors. I love you all very much, and besides my passion for the art of storytelling you are the main reason I wake up and write every single day. Thank you and I love you all eternally.

"If you're scared of becoming great just attach yourself to somebody who already knows how to fly. You'll never learn how to soar until somebody shows you how to grow your own wings..."

M.L. De'Lure

ACKNOWLEDGEMENT

I want to acknowledge God first always, without my Lord and Savior none of what I do would matter or even be possible. I definitely traveled the road less traveled to reach where I am in every aspect of my life. Honestly as horrific as my past was at times it's all worth it to me now. All glory to God. I also want to acknowledge Twaneshia Powell, Valerie Olivier, and Carol Burton who all worked very closely with me in the editing process of Take My Breath Away 1, 2, and now 3, as well as my other published novels. I thank you all eternally and you mean more to me than you'll ever know.

Personal De'Lure Investors

Regina Kennedy

Chantay Calhoun

Nneka Henry

Kela King

Twaneshia Powell

Rita Lowry

Charita Leak

Audreka Everett

Valerie Olivier

Syreeta Powell

Katrice Brown

Brandilyn Hayes

Edna Rowell

Geri Patterson

Brittney Thrasher

James Bryant

Martenia Shyne

LaShonda Barton-Koonce

George Odom

Jordan Aune

Kriss Mitchell

Tondalaire Ray

Patrick BigRev Milton

Lamar Jones

These events and the characters you are about to read about are all fictional. The things I write about are always born through pure imagination.

(The End of Take My Breath Away 2)

Chapter 22
We will follow God...

(Pastor White's final appeal)

Pastor White has so much on his heart and mind this Sunday morning. As he finishes his sermon, and prepares to leave the pulpit he offers his final appeal.

"I have loved you with an everlasting love. Before... time began, I knew you. For years you swam around in a sea of meaningless, searching for love, hoping for hope. All that time I was pursuing you, aching to pursue you in My compassionate arms. I lifted you out of the sea of despair and set you down on a firm foundation. Sometimes you felt naked... exposed to the revealing Light of My Presence. I wrapped an ermine robe around you: My robe of righteousness. I sang you a love song, whose beginning and end are veiled in eternity. I infused meaning into your mind and harmony in your heart. Join Me in singing My song. Together we will draw others out of darkness into My Marvelous Light."

Pastor White steps down out of the pulpit and walks down onto the floor directly in front of his congregation. "Jesus... is calling you people of God. He is calling you right now, and he wants to hold you and wash all your painful tears and sins away."

Pastor White pauses briefly to smile comfortingly at little Jazemene on the second row, and now he smiles and nods to the rest of her family.

"Some are called" Pastor says, "some are sent, and some just packed up and went." he laughs comfortingly.

"We are all ministers in some shape form or fashion," he continues, "But if you want it... you may not be the one. Let me say that again. If you want it... you may not be the one. See God... often times, calls people who don't want to be called. We come here to church to worship, praise, and glorify Him. We don't come in here to be seen, and glorify ourselves or each other. We, People of God... are not in show business... we are in the soul business. And now together we all have a Goal to go home with Jesus. In Heaven... there is no Westside or Eastside of Heaven. There is no white or black side of Heaven... no racial or economical barriers between us. All of the blood is red and its purity will make us all as white as snow. God is calling you right now... The ball is in your court. Make your move People of God. I love you all, be eternally blessed."

"EPILOGUE"

Jaze is living with Whitney and Charlie Breeze for the summer. Her baby brother K.J. is in Brazil with his father Love, on an amazing two-month South American excursion. Tyrone's theme park is doing very well to say the least. He and Osiana have a huge new house together in Miami, and they plan to get married in a few months at Pastor White's church. Jay has released several successful mix tapes. And now that his fan base has gotten freakishly big, he is considering releasing his first full length album later this year. His main focus now though musically is producing and managing new young talent in the Miami and Orlando area. He and Jaze's teacher Cidra Bell are still dating but nothing too serious.

(Cam)

Lying here in his arms, in our bed I finally know what true happiness is. I will never in my life forget that I owe every ounce of my joy to my handsome brother in law, Lance Orlandis Vinson, B.K.A. Love. The moment my dead twin lifted her gun and aimed it at me that last time, my entire life flashed before my eyes. Love walked in a second before she tried to shoot me, and when I swung that old rusty screwdriver at that bitch, he shot her in the back of her head. Luckily not much blood got on me or my gorgeous dress. After he shot her, he told me to go find my husband and he would take care of everything else.

Cam rolls over and passionately kisses her husband's big soft lips. "Goodnight Mr. Keldrick Jermaine Cole Sr." she says.

He smiles knowingly at her. "I don't know exactly what happened, and I probably never will," K.C. admits, "but know that I know exactly who you are. I can tell the difference. Goodnight... Mrs. *Cameron* Jiles Cole." Cam's heart stops... and then she smiles with her flushed face dug deep into his strong chest.

THE END
"Bonus Chapter"

He rarely comes here anymore. In fact, the city itself rarely crosses his mind ever. Jet-setting around the world has become common place to him. Being gone is his only comfort zone now. The unknown is the only welcomed constant component in his life at this point.

Nothing can stand in the way of the level of freedom his mind, body, and soul know now. He has been to each end of the spiritual spectrum and back again. He has been the deepest darkest demon the world has ever known, and he has been a saver and protector of the weak, a loving brother and uncle, as well as the primary care giver to his beautiful son.

None-the-less he's back in the city now. This could very well be his last time in Orlando, Florida ever. He didn't want to come back at all but a promise is a promise, and a deal is a deal.

One thing that comforts him is the fact that the only people that know he's the "Florida Finisher" are all dead. Well, all except for his family members of course, and they would never tell a soul. The Florida Finisher, they actually gave him a name and everything.

After Osiana Blue left the force the chief eventually dropped the case completely. Chief Tiago Splitter knows the only person he had who was capable of finding a killer of Love's magnitude was Detective Blue. The day she resigned, he already decided in his mind that the case of the Florida Finisher would never be solved.

A bright red Camaro pulls up in front of the Orlando police station. "I'll be right back." he says looking over his shoulders. He checks his large pants pocket, to make sure his silencer is already attached and ready to go.

He says a short mental prayer, and then takes a deep breath before stepping out of his gorgeous car adorned with brand new gold rims and a matching gold grill in the front.

He's dressed in a black loose fitting polo collar shirt, designer jeans, and concord 11 retro Jordan shoes laced tightly. His long dreads are pulled back into a rigid ponytail, and he has dark tinted black Ray Bans on his face.

Even as he gets closer and closer to the front door he realizes just how insane this last mission is, even for him. But for some reason that makes it all the more exciting to him. His adrenaline is pumping fiercely and maintaining an all-time high now.

As he grabs the handle to the front door he feels so powerful. He feels as if he could pull the entire door completely off its hinges.

As he walks in he's greeted by several friendly officers who speak and keep walking as if he's not the monumental threat that he is to all of them. Looking around Love tries to decide which way he thinks the Chief's office is.

"May I help you?" an ugly young clerk asks him from behind. Love spins around quickly trying not to make his panic, and surprise too obvious. "Excuse me..." he says to her, as he wipes the new sweat from his brown brows.

X

"Wow," she smiles an unpleasant toothy smile, "you are pretty aren't you?" Love returns an uncomfortable smile. "Um yeah... thanks." he replies.

"May we help you with something," she's blushing now, "do you need to file a report, or do you need to report a *Florida Finisher* sighting maybe? We've been getting them all week." she laughs.

Love wrinkles his brows, crosses his arms, and settles into a comfortable posture. "What's funny miss..." he asks.

"Well," she explains, "the whole *Florida Finisher* case right? The reason they can't find him... and the reason nobody really knows what he looks like is because the mother fucker doesn't really exist." she tells him. "Is that so?" Love inquires.

"You're damn right its so," she confirms, "and what a weak name right? The *Florida Finisher,* like that's the best they could come up with?" she laughs.

"But you think this guy doesn't exist at all though?" Love asks. "If he does exist he's definitely *a gay*." she says.

Lance feels his blood beginning to boil rapidly. As the ugly young woman continues to unknowingly bash him to his face he can no longer hear a word she's saying. Her lips are moving but absolutely no sound is reaching Love's yellow ears.

"Where is Chief Splitter's office?" he interjects coldly. "Its... right down that hall, third door on the left," she turns around to point, "he's in there now. I actually just left his office moments ago. Do you have an appointment with him?"

"Yeah," Love replies blankly, "hey can you uh show me where the bathroom is?" he asks. "Sure is right over..." she starts.

"No, I want you to take me..." he interjects with a sick sexy smile. "Oh... Oh my," she returns his smile, "you wanna have random hot sex with me at my job don't you?" She blushes bright red.

"I work at the police station," she whispers, "that would be *so epic*... and *so wrong*. Oh to hell with it, you only live once right? And you are just too gorgeous to turn down. Come on..." she takes him by the hand.

As they walk Love notices that no one seems to be paying them any attention. When they reach the door she turns around to see if anybody is watching. Love quickly grabs her by the head and pushes her inside.

After stepping inside the bathroom himself he walks her into an empty stall. She immediately drops down to her knees and opens his zipper. After she licks his shiny head twice, Love pulls his gun out, pushes her back hard towards the toilet stool behind her, and shoots her twice in the face.

The blood on his dark shirt is barely noticeable. He quickly exits the bathroom and makes his way to the Chief's office. He walks in without knocking.

"Who the hell are you?" Chief Splitter demands. "I'm Love," he says, "well technically I'm Lance right now but..."

"Love," Splitter repeats, "so you're the sorry son of a bitch that's been playing on my phone all damn day... trying to meet me somewhere?"

"You know," Love smirks, "I am actually **the son of a bitch**, but she's dead now and I killed her. Wow… it feels so good to admit that." Love looks all around him trapped inside his own new amazement.

"And in a police station none-the-less," Love continues, "I killed Patterson the correctional officer, Ligetti my old scumbag landlord, my brother's father Paul, my childhood shrink Bruce Granger. Man the list just goes on and on." Love's smile is growing larger.

Splitter stands up on two shaky feet, with his eyes as wide as they have ever been before. "You… you're the **Finisher**?" the chief stutters.

"In the flesh you fat, sexist, son of a bitch," Love says," and if I knew who your mom was… I'd kill that ugly, old, brown bitch too sir." Love laughs in perfect rendition of an evil genius.

"Why me?" the chief asks. "All your victims were connected," Splitter continues, "everybody you killed wronged you in some way. I've done my research, there was always a connection. I don't even know you, hell I never even met you." the chief reminds Love.

"You, sir," Love smiles as he pulls out his loaded weapon, "Owe your dark fate to a pretty young lady by the name of Osiana Blue. Oh, and you also stopped answering my phone calls Chief Splitter… see that's my biggest pet peeve."

"Detective Blue," the chief asks, "so you're working for a bitch? You little faggot…" he says. Love lifts his gun.

"And that sir," Love says, "is my other huge pet peeve. Gay is a sexual act that I have never willingly participated in."

With supreme satisfaction Love shoots the chief twice, once in the head, and once in the chest. Walking around the desk Love kneels down close to his limp body.

Chief Splitter's cold eyes are staring up into Love's eyes as he devours his soul. With gloved hands he locks the chief's door from the inside and walks out as calmly as possible.

After jumping back in his car Love drives off slowly. "What took you so long Daddy?" a voice says from the back seat. Love turns around as he drives off to gaze at his handsome little boy.

"It's over now son," Love tells K.J. "Daddy is never gonna leave you like that ever again. I promise..."

Take My Breath Away 3 (MOMENTS) "SAVE ME FROM MY PAST" by De'Lure

Prologue
(Jazemene Cole)

I am the archetype of loveliness. But I am much more than my beauty and my femininity. I am more than strong, I'm undeniably powerful… I am more than capable, I am masterful… and I am more than confident, I am completely convinced that I am an untouchable entity of unadulterated perfection. These are the things every young woman should train herself to believe, especially in a situation like mine. I'm 21 years old, and the daughter of the wealthy ex-pro football star Keldrick "Kool Hands" Cole. I live in a one-bedroom apartment in downtown Miami with my baby brother K.J. who just turned 16, and my boyfriend an asshole named Bleek. His real name is Dewey De'Mario Galloway. His long dark dreads carry my very heart at their pitch black tips, the tone of his raspy voice when he speaks with his harsh Miami street slang is like soothing waterfalls surrounding everything I am, and in his eyes I thought I could see forever. That was before my black eyes became a staple in our relationship, if you wanna call it that. I once met a man who told me the self-hatred southern, light skinned black women have for themselves tickled him. He claimed, girls like me are taught from a very young age to hate ourselves, and that we are taught to feel bad about being beautiful and having fairer skin. He further said that we are brainwashed, raised, and ultimately trained to date unattractive men as opposed to dating men who look more like us. He continued by saying that he believes there are plenty of very attractive brown, and dark-skinned men, but the majority of the women he encountered were with men who meant them no good, and weren't even pleasant to look at in the least. He told me we grow to feel comfort in the company of less intelligent men as to not feel as much of a possibility to get game ran on us. This he says is the dumbest part, because street thugs are the innovators of modern day "game". He says that men... men like my Bleek are more powerful than they should be. He says we as women give these men the power they have by publicly condoning and promoting the ignorant fuckery they do. In closing he said although we think less attractive, less intelligent men are a better option as not to be hurt or heartbroken... the truth he says is these men because of their deeply embedded insecurities cheat and mistreat us more than any confident man would ever dream of. I see truth in what that man told me, every day of my life. But I still haven't left, so that says more about me and my black ass eyes, than it could ever say about my Bleek. I am so tired of living from paycheck to paycheck... my father is a billionaire. I know he loves me, but he disowned me six months ago, took all my credit cards, and froze all three of my bank accounts when I stood up to him and told him I was dropping out of the University of Miami and choosing to be with Bleek. My baby brother K.J. left with me, I don't know why but the closer he's gotten over the past eleven years with his biological father my Uncle Love, the more he's changed and grown emotionally detached from my father Keldrick. I had another baby brother that we never talk about; Kelmeron was just six years old when it happened. God the pain is still fresh and very real. Like dad and Cam, I find it easier to just block him from my mind completely. Anyways back to my other little brother K.J. who thinks he's a man now, he tells me as much everyday... it's cute. I kinda wish he would move back home, he shouldn't be struggling trying to be loyal to his stubborn and lost big sister. Now about Bleek, he doesn't work right now, but he does hustle as best he can. I work three minimum wage jobs, and K.J. is a delivery boy for Domino's. We make ends meet, but I'm tired of struggling now. Since age 10, I grew up the princess of a true Black American king, and I honestly miss my old lifestyle. I can't go crawling back to my father now, because that would be admitting defeat. I don't know what I'm going to do, but I gotta figure out something fast... I need you Mama Cole.

As the new tears begin to rush her face Jazemene continues to cry out to her deceased grandmother, Mama Cole...

Chapter 1
12

I wonder sometimes how I allowed myself to fall so far down. My self-esteem is at an all-time low. After my dad got married eleven years ago he eventually decided he wanted me to go to public school, bad move. It was really that bad. From the moment I set foot inside that school, the girls there were very mean to me. My father was going through so much I didn't want to worry him. He was transitioning from being the best active NFL football player to a powerful business mogul and true off the field star.

His marriage to my step mom Cameron Jiles was still new; I knew they needed alone time to get readjusted to each other and their new lives together as husband and wife. My father also missed my mom Whitney, but he didn't dare let Ms. Cam know as much.

Every single day I went to school was pure torture. Man, it was like living through the day my former best friend Josiah and I got in a fight with that bully Mariah at my old school, Key Point Academy every damn day. I thought the private school kids were bad; the ones in public school were unbelievably worse. They all hated me. The only person I could talk to about it was my stepmother Cam; she's my best friend now. She helped me a lot over the years. Although, her *childhood struggles were different from mine; she gave me some much needed advice and I used it to survive the best I could.*

Josiah Bell and I haven't been best friends for years now; once I changed schools we grew apart rather quickly. God I miss that boy! If you're going to understand how I ended up in my current situation... I'm gonna have to take you back to when I was just 12 years old. That's when it all started; I remember the pain like it was yesterday.

I was at the park with Josiah, and I had just gotten the news from Dad that I was changing schools. I remember it was so hot that day at the park, loud kids and families were everywhere, and Jojo had no idea why I texted him and asked him to meet me there...

(At the park)

Side by side the two of them rest on brand-new mountain bikes equipped with gears to ride at top speed. Jaze's bike is green with pink flakes throughout it. Her mother Whitney, the ultimate Alpha Kappa Alpha sorority member had the bike customized for Jaze a few weeks back. Jaze wasn't too partial to the overtly feminine look of her made over bike, but she pretended to love it because her mother was obviously excited about it. On her feet

Jaze has on authentic size 6 Bred 11 Jordan shoes, red Jordan basketball shorts, a black tank top, and a red sports bra that is showing just a little bit. On her left leg she has on a red Nike wristband, as her entire outfit matches her red and black retro Jordan shoes. Her long curly brown hair gently accented with blonde highlights is pulled back into a tight ponytail.

Jojo's bike is black with lime green wheels. He's wearing light brown cargo shorts, Vans shoes, and a Hollister tank top.

"Why you looking so sad Jazzy..." Jojo nudges Jaze gently, as the two of them rest on their bikes near the edge of the park.

"What did I tell you about that Jojo?" she grimaces.

"I know the other kids at school let you boss them around Jazzy," Jojo looks at her with no regret, "but I'm not them, I'm your best friend... and you do not get to pick my nicknames for you."

They share a laugh.

"Besides you call me white boy," Jojo reminds her, "***Jazzy*** can't be worse than that."

"Everybody calls you white boy Jojo..." Jaze hits him on his left arm harder than she intends to.

"Ouch," Jojo rubs his left arm to relieve some of the stinging pain from the punch, "and what did I tell you about hitting me?"

"I'm sorry Jo..." Jaze reaches for his hand.

Jojo pulls away from her leaning his bike in the opposite direction. "I hate when you hit me," he reminds her, "And you know that crap Jaze."

"I said I'm sorry bro." Jaze tells him.

"Sorry isn't good enough **bro**," Jojo says harshly, "It's like every day, you're trying harder and harder to be a boy."

"Wow," Jaze frowns, "Thanks Jojo. God, you didn't have to say all that, I said I was freakin' sorry..."

Jaze fights back familiar tears.

Jojo looks over at her intently. "And you better not start crying." He says.

Jojo lays his expensive bike down on the ground and approaches the silent Jazemene. He reaches for the seat of her shorts.

Jaze knocks his hand away. "What the hell are you doing Josiah?

"Just making sure you didn't piss yourself again..." he tells her.

Jaze quickly dives off her bike tackling Jojo to the ground. Luckily they're far enough from the park that no one can see the struggle between the two; it would easily draw a huge unwanted crowd.

Jaze punches Jojo in the face twice. With strength he didn't know he had Jojo rolls Jaze off of him and starts choking her as hard as he can.

Jaze uses all her power to continue to punch at him as if she has no need to breathe. With a swift upward motion Jaze knees Jojo in his groin area.

With his eyes tripling in size Jojo rolls off of her and onto his back writhing in pain.

"I should beat the hell out of you," Jaze stands over her prey with pure malice in her eyes, "but you ain't worth it Josiah."

Jaze turns to retrieve her scratched bike.

"Yeah I bet..." he mumbles still rolling back and forth.

Jaze rushes back to him without thinking twice. Sitting on his stomach Jaze begins to choke him the exact same way he was choking her before.

"***I hate you Josiah Bell***!" she spits venomously.

He doesn't respond, mostly because he can't breathe. The pain in his groin area has left his mind as now he just wishes he was able to take in air again.

"I hate your freakin' guts," she continues, "You tell me to stop being creepy when you know ***damn*** well I'm in love with you... So, I start acting like one of the guys so I can still be around you and not have to feel awkward the entire time. I worship the ground you walk on. I live just to smell your sweet sour skittle breath and it kills me anytime I go too long without hearing your ***freakin'*** voice!!! Uh oh, there I go being ***honestly*** creepy again."

Jaze lets go of his neck just before he loses consciousness. Looking down at his reddened face it takes everything inside Jaze to not proceed with taking his life.

The vivid almost natural killer instinct inside of her scares Jaze at first, then it quickly fades into a feeling much like euphoria.

"What the hell Jaze!!!" Jojo tries to stand up.

"You..." Jaze starts.

"I what," Jojo interjects finally making it to his shaky feet, "I what, tell me what the hell I did to deserve all this? I checked to see if you were having a panic attack like you have so many times in the past. I pay very close attention Jaze, that look on your face before I checked your shorts was the same distant look you get every time you're having one of your pissing spells. Yeah, I pay attention even when you think I don't."

"Why..." Jaze holds back the tears.

"Why," Jojo yells, "Why the hell not? Maybe because I care about you or *cared* about you before you just tried to kill me!!"

"Sure you cared about me Jojo..." Jaze puts a hand on each hip.

"You're my best friend Jazemene," he exclaims, "Do you have any idea what the hell that means?"

"I know it'll never mean what I want it to mean," Jaze admits, "I know it will never mean what I need it to mean."

"Jaze please don't start being creep..." Jojo starts.

"***Jaze please don't start being creepy***," she mocks, "Damn it Josiah! Do you have any idea how bad that shit feels when you say that to me? Why is it that all those ugly, skinny, pimply faced white and Asian chicks at school can fawn all over you, but as soon as my ***black ass*** says anything I'm a creep?"

"Don't talk like that Jaze," Jojo sits on the curb near his bike, "You know I don't consider you as ***black***."

"Gee thanks Josiah," Jaze laughs, "Is that supposed to be a compliment?"

"Well yeah," Jojo looks down at his feet and then back up at Jaze, "You know how blacks can be really tacky sometimes..."

"Thanks Jojo that made it better." Jaze reaches down to pick up her bike.

Jojo stands up and dusts himself off.

"You know what the truth is?" Jojo asks reaching down for his own bike.

"No, but I'd love to hear it Jim Crow." Jaze tilts her head to the side.

"The ***truth*** is," Jojo pauses, "The truth is... maybe I don't just... wanna be your best friend forever. ***Maybe*** I like you too, maybe I love the way your breath always smells like Juicy Fruit gum, and the way you light up whenever you say my name... maybe I never go a second without thinking about your caramel eyes and your perfect curly hair. But I could never be your boyfriend Jazemene... seriously though?"

"What because I'm black," Jaze spits, "You do know my people are *free* now right, and its legal and safe for interracial couples to date?"

"No," JoJo says, "You don't understand."

"I understand *very* clearly," Jaze drops her bike and approaches Jojo, "I understand that you're a freakin' *racist* bigot, who finally admitted he... could *at least* be physically attracted to me *a black girl*, but you wouldn't dare make that black girl your *actual public girlfriend*. No, that's *waaay* too embarrassing. As long as everybody knows I'm just your token black best friend that's okay, but you have to make damn sure nobody thinks anything else could possibly be going on between the two of us because of the color of my *damn* skin! The sickest part is with that weak ass tan you have now; you're almost *darker* than me Josiah..."

Jaze stands face to face with the only boy that can without moving a muscle regulate her very heartbeat.

"Are you finished little girl?" Jojo smiles at her.

"Josiah Aiden Bell," Jaze puts her nose to his, "I am so close to beating you up again. Boy you have no idea..."

"So what," he smiles again, "you hit like a girl anyway. Now if you're finished being tacky I can tell you what I meant by what I said. Do you mind or do you have some more ignorant crap to say?"

"No." Jaze steps back.

"Are you sure," Jojo asks, "because I can sit back down on the curb and listen to a few more minutes of that stupid shit if you want me to..."

"Ugh," Jaze groans, "Will you just say what you were gonna say Josiah?"

"Fine," he slowly runs his fingers through his longish blonde hair, "the reason I can't be your boyfriend Jazemene... is because of your father."

"***Good job Josiah***," Jaze wrinkles her brow, "**Yes,** my father is black as well, are there any other Negroes that I'm connected to that you'd like to blame for not dating me or is my daddy's big black ass enough to foot that bill?"

"Shut up Jaze," Jojo furrows his own brow as his face begins to redden, "You talk so damn much! You talk but do you ever listen?"

"I'm listening Josiah, but you're not..." Jaze starts.

"Then listen and shut up!" Josiah barks.

Jaze doesn't know why, but it felt good for Jojo to speak to her in a demanding tone.

13

"The reason your Dad is in the way, of me ever wanting to date you," Jojo hesitates, "Is because he knows full well that my mother is head over heels in love with him."

"Ms. Cidra," Jaze gasps, "Is really in love with my dad? My mom told me that at the wedding, but I didn't really believe it was that serious."

"What wedding?" Jojo inquires.

"My dad's wedding." Jaze replies.

"Right," Jojo growls, "the one I had to watch my mom cry her freakin' eyes out afterwards **all damn night**!"

"I didn't know Josiah." Jaze pleads.

"Why the hell would that idiot invite us to that monkey fest of a wedding ceremony," Jojo barks, "Knowing full well how my mom feels about his black ass?"

"Watch your mouth Jojo," Jaze says, "Maybe my dad doesn't know."

"He knows!" Jojo exclaims.

"*I didn't know*," Jaze claims, "So what would make you so sure that my dad knows?"

"Because of all the nights I heard him use the key my mom gave him to our house," Jojo sheds a few tears, "and he would come in..."

"Wait a second Jojo," Jaze holds up both of her hands, "Why do I feel like I've heard this story before..."

"That asshole," Jojo continues to speak in a trancelike state, "Would waltz into my house... into my mom's room at any time of the night he chose and *lie* to her, and then lie to her *some more*... over and over again about the possibility of them having a real relationship together one day... and then he used her until he got what he came for and left her to cry herself to sleep *again... Any night he chose!"*

"Wait, how could you..." Jaze steps towards him.

"We don't live in a mansion like you famous Coles' Jaze," Jojo cries, "Our walls are very thin. I heard everything! *That man*, your dad is a *jackass*, a *pervert*... and he has *no* shame *period*!"

"I'm sorry bro," Jaze reaches for his shoulder, "I've never seen you cry before."

"I'm not your bro Jaze," Jojo spits, "you're a girl... *act like it*. And I am not crying I'm just *mad as hell* that my mom could be so... *damn stupid* to fall in love with a..."

"With a what, Jojo," Jaze interjects, "Go head and say it so I can knock all your pretty little teeth out your mouth..."

"He's a street thug!" Jojo exclaims.

"You *fake ass* Justin Bieber *wanna be*," Jaze growls, "What are you *sixty years old*? What kid says street thug? You need help."

"*I* need help," Jojo laughs drying the still visible tears from his face, "My mom is the only thing I have in this world, and it's my job to protect

15

her. So when *she's* in pain *I* hurt too. But you, your lame ass is in love with me and everybody in school knows how obsessed you are with me... And I never *ever* wanted to even touch you. Who needs more help *me or you*?"

Jojo picks up his bike and rides off into the distance.

Until this very moment Jazemene Cole never really knew what it meant to be all alone. Standing here with a cool breeze at her back, she realizes without him she means nothing. She means nothing, because she believed that everything she is or will ever be is buried inside of him. Her knees are weak, her arms feel heavy, and her head is pounding harder than it ever has before. As a few warm salty tears enter in through the left corner of her mouth, Jaze can feel the familiar warm liquid running down her left leg. She quickly stops herself before too much damage is done. Almost scared to do so, Jaze strategically checks her surroundings. Once she's sure the coast is clear she hurriedly picks up her bike and pedals away towards her father's mansion.

"*STUPID*," Jaze screams out loud, "Stupid, stupid, stupid!!! Why do I keep wasting my time? At least forty boys asked me to the last school dance, and I turned them all down without hesitation. I turned down some really cute boys because they didn't meet my qualifications. It

16

wasn't fair to them, because my standards are impossible to meet. The only qualification any boy at my school needed was to somehow transform into Josiah Bell. None of them could pull that trick off, so I turned them all down. Jojo ended up taking some redheaded girl with way too many freckles on her face to the dance. I stayed home and ate ice cream as usual. The dance was supposed to be over at 8:30; Jojo was at my house by nine. We sat in my room for the next hour while he told me everything the little redheaded freckle faced girl did wrong at the dance. Did I really want to hear about it? Hell no, but he's my best friend so I had to listen. Would he have sat there and listened to me talk about some guy that I went out with? Probably not, but then again he'd never have to because I'd never go out with another guy."

As Jaze approaches the front gate of her father's mansion she can see her baby brother through the gate pacing back and forth frantically. She quickly enters the gate code and rides through as the large iron gate closes behind her.

"K.J...." Jaze rushes to her baby brother's side.

Seven-year-old Keldrick Cole Jr. is wearing gray sweats and a Miami Heat T-shirt. His long curly hair fits his thoughtful yellow face well.

"She's gone Jaze," he looks up at her with his father's piercing green eyes, "it's over with she's..."

"Wait what the hell are you talking about K.J.," Jaze looks behind him towards the front door, "Where is dad?"

"I don't know Jazemene." K.J. whimpers.

"Is she," Jaze pauses, "Are you sure she's..."

"She's dead Jazemene," he cries, "I'm a kid not a **retard,** I know what dead is..."

"Oh my God," Jaze covers her mouth with both hands as a few tears begin to roll down her yellow face, "And you... you found her?"

K.J. nods his head up and down.

"Damn it," Jaze cries, "Where's dad, this is gonna kill him..."

"**My dad** is in Tampa today looking at property," K.J. tells her, "I haven't seen **your** dad all day."

"Damn it," Jaze yells pulling her smart phone out of her gym shorts pocket, "Not right now Squirt! I don't have time for that right now. I have to call my dad."

"Why?" K.J. asks.

"What do you mean why," Jaze puts her left hand on her hip looking like a twelve-year-old version of her beautiful mother Whitney, "**Unless**... is this some kind of joke little boy?"

"No Jaze," K.J. screams, "She's really dead, but I don't understand why you're calling your dad, he never liked her anyway."

"What are you talking about Squirt, my dad loved her." Jaze tells him.

"Stop calling me Squirt I'm almost as tall as you are," K.J. insists, "And he did not, your dad hated her. He never talked to her or spent any time with her at all."

"Are you crazy K.J.," Jaze has both hands on her hips now, "Those two went through hell and back. My dad would die just for her to live!"

"Whatever," K.J. says wiping his old tears away, "Rico is out back with a shovel he's gonna bury her behind the pool between two of the trees."

"Behind the pool," Jaze screams, "Between two trees? My dad is gonna kill everybody in this house when he gets home."

K.J. smiles a sick smile.

"**My dad** is a **real** killer," K.J. proclaims, "Your dad is just all talk."

"Get the hell out of my way," Jaze pushes her baby brother down to the ground as she approaches the front door, "You and your crazy ass dad probably killed her. Poor Cam…"

Jaze pushes the already ajar front door open completely. She walks through the front room and then into the kitchen to find a woman humming as she cooks. Even from the back she knows who this woman has to be.

"Are you Megan," Jaze cries, "I thought you died… What did you do to Cam?"

The lady turns around with a peculiar look on her dark face.

"What do you mean?" the woman asks.

"I know she's dead, my brother already told me," Jaze steps closer to her, "You might as well kill me too, because if you don't I'm gonna kill you! *I swear to God on my life I will kill you Megan*!"

"Jazemene," the woman says, "Look in my eyes baby…"

"*Cam*…" Jaze cries.

"Yes baby," she smiles, "my twin sister Megan is dead, and she's never coming back baby… Are you okay Jaze, what's wrong baby girl?"

Jaze rushes into her stepmother's loving arms.

"Oh Cam…" she cries.

"Are you feeling okay baby?" Cam asks as she rocks side to side hugging Jaze tightly.

"No," she cries, "K.J…. He played a terrible joke on me outside… he said you were dead. He was crying, and he said he found your body."

"Oh baby," Cam kisses her on the forehead, "I'm not going anywhere. How can I, who wouldn't want to see your beautiful face all day every day?"

"Josiah Bell." Jaze mumbles under her breath.

"I couldn't hear you Jaze speak up." Cam says turning around to finish cooking.

"Nothing Cam," Jaze says, "I'm just glad Rico the gardener isn't about to bury you behind the pool, between two trees. You're like my *real* mom… You understand me better than Whitney."

20

"Well I love you too..." a soft but confident voice says from the rear.

"Mommy Whitney," Jaze blushes at the sight of her mother, "I didn't mean..."

"It's okay," Whitney interjects, "I understand completely. You spend way more time here with Cameron than you do with me at my tiny little house in the hood."

"Whit," Cam laughs, "*Girl*, you do not live in the hood."

K.J. enters the kitchen and walks directly to the fridge.

"You little jerk!" Jaze tackles him quickly.

Cam and Whitney quickly break the two up.

"Ouch Jazemene," K.J. rubs his throbbing back, "What was that for?"

"You said Cam was dead," she screams, "You said you found her dead body... and Rico was in the back yard burying her behind the pool in between two trees!"

K.J. frowns harshly at his big sister. Then he storms off towards one of the large kitchen windows. He snatches the drapes to the side revealing Rico the gardener digging a hole in the ground behind the pool in between two trees.

"Sophie died Jazemene," he yells, "*Not Cam*, you dummy!"

"Sophie," Jaze frowns, "your dog..."

"Well," her mother puts a hand on each of her perfect hips, "technically Sophia was *your* dog Jazzy."

"Don't call me that Mommy Whitney," Jaze tells her, "And I know you bought Sophie for me but I'm not..."

"Really a dog person..." K.J., Whit, and Cam interject in unison.

"Oh shut up," Jaze smiles, "So what happened to Sophie?"

"Her name was *Sophia*," her mother corrects her, "And apparently she wiggled out of that inept iron prison gate your rich father has out front... and when Cam went out looking for her, she couldn't find her. When she finally spotted her through the gate across the street, she called her name. Then Sophia tried to run across the street and a car hit her and just kept going."

"Damn." Jaze says.

"Watch your mouth little girl." Cam and Whit say together.

"And stop calling me *Mommy Whitney*," Whit continues, "I'm mommy *period*. You came out of *my* body, no one else's. Now I *love* Cam to death but she is not your mother."

"Wait," Jaze pauses to look at the shocked face of her little brother and then back at her mother, "What do you mean you *love* Cam Mommy Whit... I mean Whit... *Damn, dang, Mom* I mean..."

22

"Young lady I'm gonna wash your pretty little mouth out with soap in a minute." Whit tilts her head to the side to look at her little look alike.

"Answer the question mom." K.J. says.

"What question?" Whit's face reddens as she looks over at a silent Cam.

"I said," Jaze steps towards her mother, "What do you mean you love Cam, you kind of put emphasis on the word *love*..."

"I did not," Whit wipes her damp brow before looking at Cam again, "Did I?"

"Look," Whit continues, "Charlie is waiting on me outside so I have to..."

"Mommy," K.J. steps forward, "I'm only seven but I know something weird is going on."

"Mom," Jaze grabs her hand gently, "How come you haven't just said Cam and I are close friends and she takes care of my kids so I love her for that? You got all weird and started stuttering and sweating... Oh *and* looking at Cam."

"Jazzy..." Whit looks down in a mirror vision of her own eyes. It's much harder than she thought to lie to her own eyes.

"Stop calling me Jazzy, *Mommy Whitney*." Jaze taunts her mother.

"*Do not* call me *Mommy Whitney* again Jazemene..." her mother demands.

"Fine," Jaze replies, "now please tell me how you, a grown woman first of all sat back and watched another woman marry her lifelong

23

boyfriend? **Now** you claim to not just tolerate that woman but you **love** her? And when asked you can't even **define** that love…"

"Little girl where did you come from?" her mother asks through an awestruck smile.

"Just answer my question Whitney." Jaze sighs unimpressed with her mother's admiration of her line of questioning.

"Sweetheart," Whit looks at Cam and then down at her daughter again, "Cam and I… and Charlie, we sometimes…"

The front door opens.

"Honey I'm home…" K.C. yells.

As he walks into the kitchen wearing one of his nicest three piece suits and a fedora he can feel something isn't right, but he's getting older now and he knows when he's tired and not in the mood to be bothered he shouldn't pry in business that has not been openly made **his business**. He bends down and kisses both Jaze and Whit on the cheek, and then makes his way to K.J.

K.C. opens his arms to the boy, but K.J. instead extends his hand for his legal father to shake instead. After shaking the boys hand with an obvious look of dismay on his strong black face, K.C. makes his way over to his wife Cameron.

"I know mama bear is happy to see me." K.C. growls as he leans in to kiss her neck several times.

"Hey baby," Cam smiles before kissing K.C.'s full lips twice, "How was your day?"

"I'll tell you about it later my love, after I shower." Without another word K.C. leaves the kitchen in pursuit of a piping hot shower.

Whit is still standing face to face locked in on Jaze's eyes as if K.C. never said a word.

"You and I will talk later on little girl," Whit whispers to Jaze, "Now, are you still spending the night at my house tonight?"

"Yeah mom..." Jaze sighs.

"Well hurry up," Whit spanks Jaze on the bottom; "I wanna stop and get us some ice cream on the way home. My man said I'm losing weight..."

K.J. and Jaze leave the kitchen together headed to her room.

"Losing weight," Cam says with a smile, "You look fine to me baby..."

Whit licks her lips and approaches Cam with a sensual swagger in her step.

"You know Cameron," Whit whispers with her lips pressed to Cam's left ear, "You're welcome to come spend the night too baby, Mama been missing your little sexy black ass."

"Oooh," Cam moans as Whit rubs her print, "That sounds nice baby but I don't think I can get out tonight."

"You can..." Whit licks her lips again.

"But I won't..." Cam says before kissing Whit twice.

25

(Later that night at Whitney and Charlie's house)

The last two years have been very good to Whitney and Charlie. Cam has made very sure her two gorgeous lovers have been very well taken care of.

Her husband K.C. made it clear that after the first year Whitney and Charlie needed to begin paying their own rent and bills. The last thing Cameron Jiles Cole ever wanted to do is undermine her husband's better judgment, but her loyalty and affection for Whitney is stronger than even she thought it was.

Her love for Whitney is almost powerful enough to destroy her marriage. Cam knows deep down if she lost her marriage and ultimately her access to K.C.'s cash, she would lose Whitney as well. It's not that Cameron doesn't love Keldrick; she loves him with almost all of her heart. The problem is there is a significant part of her heart that Whitney Powell stole years ago on Carlos' island, and whether Whit cares or even notices, that part of Cam will always belong to her.

(Whit)

As Whitney's huge wall mounted flat screen television stares back at her she's trying to sort through the various thoughts flying in and out of her mind. The reality of love; pain, revenge, and the idea of acceptance of defeat and circumstance are all screaming at her subconscious to act and not remain silent and dormant. Whit shakes her head several times as she smiles an unhappy smile.

De'Lure

I have them all fooled. Charlie, Keldrick, Cameron... even my babies. But I can't fool myself, even though I've tried time and time again to do so. I am now and will forever be in love with Keldrick Jermaine Cole. He was... is my everything. Years ago Carlos explained to me that my heart, is just a decaying organ in my body, and my soul is eternal energy. He told me if I want to love anyone for a lifetime I needed to then learn how to love them from my soul not my heart. I couldn't understand what that meant beyond the surface of the obvious until this very moment, and now that I understand the genius in what he was trying to convey to me I couldn't agree more with his sentiments. Dr. Sanchez never truly loved me or Cameron, in my mind I believe his obsession with the two of us was born by way of his powerful hatred for Keldrick. He wanted us; the two women he knew K.C. loved the most to both choose to spend our lives in exile with him on his dream island, thereby leaving Keldrick back here alone in the states to die from a bleeding broken heart. Truth is, if Cam and I had stayed with Carlos on that island, K.C. probably would have died.

"Hey mama..." Jaze bounces inside from playing basketball with Charlie on the regulation goal outside their backdoor.

"Hey baby," Whit smiles looking more fatigued than usual, "Who won?"

"I did." Charlie boasts with a full smile closing and locking the back door behind him.

27

"Charlie Breeze you beat my baby in basketball," Whitney smiles with wide eyes as Charlie sits in the reclining chair across from her, "And you came back in here bragging about it?"

"Well..." Charlie starts.

"So you not only beat a child in a game of one on one Charlie Breeze, but you **proudly** beat her..." Whitney looks from Charlie to her silent daughter.

"Hell yes," Charlie reiterates, "And yeah I'm proud of it. This little thing ain't normal..."

"*This little thing...*" Whit wrinkles her brow.

"Baby," Charlie smiles, "You told me the girl could play but damn, she may look like you but she plays like she's Steph Curry in a little girl's body."

"That good huh..." Whit smiles at the red faced Jaze.

"That's my baby," she continues, "come give mama a hug little girl."

"Good...," Charlie laughs as the two hug, "Hell no, she's better than good Whit. That girl ain't going near the WNBA; she's gonna be the first girl to enter the **NBA** draft."

"I wish..." Jaze mumbles.

"Well in any event," Whit looks at Charlie with a playful scowl painted on her face, "Charlie Breeze you better not be out there beating my baby anymore, don't make mama bear have to come out there and protect her little cub against the mean old man."

28

"Whit, this little girl don't need no help." Charlie laughs.

"Oh, and she's cocky as hell too," Charlie stands up still laughing as he places the ball on the floor beside the chair, "she got *a lot* of Whitney Michelle in her, that's obvious. So, I had to beat her a few times to bring her and her fly mouth back down to Earth."

Jaze looks at her mother sitting beside her on the sofa with an unimpressed look on her face.

"Mama Charlie won one game," Jaze claims, "the last game… because I let him…"

"I let you win the other seven games Jaze." Charlie lies with a smile.

"Well I'm gonna hit the shower ladies," Charlie stretches his sore back and legs, "I'll leave you two to girl talk."

"Oh no," Whit laughs kissing Jaze on her cheek again, "I love my baby to death, but before we do any girl talking tonight she's gonna go *hit* the shower too. Hit it hard baby…"

"Really mama…" Jaze squints her eyes and puts a hand on her right hip.

"Yes baby," Whit laughs, "I can smell your… work ethic sweetheart."

"Whatever lady," Jaze smiles, "Are there clean towels in the guest bathroom?"

"Should be baby," Whit thinks, "Um, if not come back in here and I'll go get some from my room."

"Okay mama." Jaze turns to leave the room.

"And Jazemene..." Whit says.

"Yeah mama..." Jaze turns back around to face her mother.

"That is not a guest bathroom baby girl," Whit looks intently at her little twin, "that is **your** bathroom. You're never a guest here; this is your house Jazemene. It makes mama feel some type of way when you say things like you're just here visiting. I... Charlie and I want you here; we love it when you come to stay with us. And if you ever want to move..."

"Daddy needs me mama," Jaze interjects quickly, "He will **always** need me."

"I know..." Whit smiles, while looking solemnly down at her feet.

"But every Summer I'm all yours mama bear." Jaze promises with a new smile before rushing off to her bathroom.

(Jaze)

So that night my mom and I never did have that talk about her and Cam. Maybe it's for the best though, I'm not sure I'm ready to know any more deep dark family secrets. I know a lot more than my parents think, I know. I've read several telling text message between the two of them while snooping through my dad's cell phone; I've even heard despicable late night phone conversations between them with my back pressed against the wall outside of the kitchen at home. After I would finish being nosey, I'd make my way back up to my room and beat myself up for not having a life of my own. I'm a teenager, why should my parents' personal lives be such a huge concern of mine? It should be the other way around. They should be doing the snooping and secretly diving deep into the unknown world that is my young teen life. Who knows, maybe they have snooped around behind my back, but if they have I'm sure they quickly became bored with it all, and realized I have no life and I'm still obsessed with one boy... the same boy.

Chapter 2
14

(Jaze)

On my 14th birthday my dad announced his official retirement from the NFL to the world. It was sposed to be my day, but Dad's the star right? Not me. It's cool I'm sure he didn't plan it that way, at least I hope not. I cried a lot that day. I love my dad way too much to ever purposely let him know when he's hurting me. He's been through so much in his life and overcome impossible adversities. He deserves this beautiful life and all the many glorious moments he's lived along the way. But, I guess it would kind of be cool to have him treat his baby girl like the world treats him at least on my day. I only get one special day a year. And sense I do only get one day a year, I'd prefer not to share it with my world famous father.

Jaze hears a knock at her door.

"Come in..." she wipes her red face quickly.

"Why are you up here in your room all alone on a beautiful day like this princess?" K.C. walks in and sits next to his baby on her bed.

Jaze hides her face from him.

"I uh," she stutters, "I'm just tired dad..."

"Jazemene Argelle," he frowns, "you know damn well you can't lie to me little girl."

"I'm fine dad..." she lies.

"You're not fine Jaze..." he interjects picking her up and securely placing her in his lap.

She frowns up at him.

"What," he looks right back at her, "I don't care how old you are, you'll always fit in my lap, and you'll always be my baby."

Jaze exhales loudly.

"Yep," K.C. laughs, "so you can wipe that Whitney Powell look off your little pretty yellow face."

"She can't be that pretty." She mumbles.

"What did you say...?" K.C. leans forward to see his daughter's reddened face.

"Nothing dad," she huffs, "What did you need?"

"You said your mother can't be that pretty," K.C. asks, "Why, because I'm not married to her? You think that because I'm married to Cameron that in some way discounts your mother? You think I chose Cam because she's prettier than your mother..."

"Well I hope that was part of the reason..." Cam says from the door with wrinkled brows.

"Hey baby." K.C. smiles briefly.

"You okay Jaze?" Cam asks in a concerned motherly tone.

Jazemene doesn't respond.

"She'll be fine," K.C. smiles at his worried wife, "You need me now?"

"Yeah," Cam replies, "the lawn guys are here babe…"

"Handle it for me baby, I'm busy right now." K.C. requests.

Cam nods her head.

K.C. looks back at Jaze as Cam leaves closing the door behind her.

"Jazemene…" K.C. waits.

"What dad," Jaze whines, "Leave me alone. Don't you have some award show to go to or some movie to flex your breast in? Damn…"

"Baby," K.C. sits Jaze back on her bed and turns her towards him gently holding both of her shoulders, "What has gotten into you? Whatever the problem is we can fix it…"

"Oh," he continues, "ok… is it that time of the month?"

"No!" she screams. "It is not **that** time of the month! You have no clue who I am or about anything going on in my life dude!"

"Jazemene…" he says standing up.

"*Jazemene*…" she mocks him with a hideous look on her teenage face.

"I don't know what I did but I know I…" K.C. stutters.

"No, you don't know!" she interjects storming away from her bed.

She turns to look back at him.

"You really don't know shit dad," she continues, "You're so wrapped up in yourself you forget the rest of us even exist! I raised my damnself, you do realize that right? I had no mother and when you weren't drunk, you were too busy with your whores, and flying off to your stupid games to be a dad!"

K.C. drops his head as the warm salty tears streaming down his dark face enter the left side of his quivering mouth.

"Are you crying sir...?" Jaze tilts her head with a satisfied grin to get a better view of her father's disheveled face.

"Classic," she laughs, "the rude inconsiderate bastard breaks down when finally confronted and he becomes the victim. Real original dad..."

K.C. lifts his head and approaches his angry daughter.

"Little girl," he says through watery eyes, "You're like your mother in more ways than I can appreciate. I won't argue with you or punish you for your tone or foul language because in some ways you're absolutely right. I haven't ever been the perfect dad, but you know damn well I've tried and I've got much better... And for you to sit in here and talk to me like..."

"Whatever." Jaze interjects.

WHAP!!!

Jaze hits her floor before she even realizes her father slapped her.

"Damn it Jazemene!" K.C. yells.

"You hit me..." she cries from her bedroom floor.

"You will not disrespect me!" he kneels down in front of her.

"You never hit me before..." she cries.

"And you've never disrespected me like this before!" K.C. stresses.

"I hate you!" Jaze wipes tears from under her left eye.

"Hate me forever," he offers, "And you know what... hell yes I have won *a lot* of awards, and flexing my *breast* in movies, and flying to my *stupid games* has ensured that you'll *never* want for anything as long as you live! Yes, I apologize for not being there when you were younger, I apologize for putting your future before our past and present, and I apologize for not being perfect... but *damn it* you tell me when you find a man who is!"

K.C. picks himself up and storms out of his daughter's room obviously hurt, but angrier with himself than he could ever be with her.

After he leaves Jaze stands to her unsure feet. She violently snatches her light switch down and then rushes to her compassionate bed to cry until sleep comes to rescue her from the night.

As K.C. enters the kitchen downstairs he makes sure not to make any eye contact with his busy wife.

"So, what's going on with Jaze babe?" Cam asks.

"Well," the large man sighs sitting down at his exquisite kitchen table, "besides the fact that she hates my guts... I'd say she's perfect."

"Oh baby," Cam wraps her arms around him from behind, "Don't say that baby..."

"Well its true Cameron." K.C. contends.

"No, it's not." Cam insists.

"Yeah it is," K.C. confirms with a strong sniff, "And who the hell am I to tell her not to hate me?"

"Oh baby," Cam steps around in front of her handsome distraught husband, "Why would you say that Keldrick?"

"It's all true," he says nodding his head weakly, "it's all very true Cameron and I know it. I could have... no I should have been here more."

"You were an NFL superstar and a business man," Cam reminds him, "you were the face of a major NFL franchise and an entire city. Not to mention, the major endorsement deals that you had to be on call for with commercials and print ads. You were busy baby, that's all. There's a lot of responsibility that comes with being world famous, Jaze is not a child anymore, she understands way more than you give her credit for.

"None of that makes what I did okay Cameron." K.C. looks up at her.

"And what did you do that was so bad Keldrick Cole?" Cam says pulling a chair in front of him.

"You don't know Cam..." he claims.

"No, I don't know," she admits, "that's why I'm asking you."

"I wasn't the perfect parent..." he starts.

"Neither was my dad trust me... or my mom for that matter." Cam interjects.

"Let me finish Cam," K.C. says, "I was the worst possible dad. The things that I held dear to me, all the bull shit that I allowed my life to be consumed by always left me unsatisfied and utterly empty."

"I want to know everything." Cam tells him.

"Why?" K.C. asks.

"Because you're my husband," she says, "I thought we didn't have any secrets... but clearly there are things you've yet to tell me about our blind years..."

"*Our blind years*," K.C. scoffs, "is that what you're calling the years that you left me alone to die?"

"Just tell me K.C.," she begs, "now is not the time for us to fight; I want to get closer to you with this conversation. Your happiness and peace mean the world to me."

"Okay..." K.C. sighs.

"Okay?" Cam replies.

"Yeah," he starts, "so I had different women in and out of this house every single night, I was a true alcoholic... there's so much more, but you know I think the worst part.is the fact that I knew Jaze saw things she shouldn't have been seeing, but I was so blown out of my mind I just didn't care. It was my job to protect my daughter and her innocent eyes..."

"You have given that girl a life most kids only dream about." Cam says.

"That doesn't make it right Cam." K.C. says.

"I'm not in any way condoning the things you've done baby," Cam assures him, "but at the end of the day your choices may have scared Jazemene a bit emotionally, but you have set the rest of her life straight no matter what she does short of dying or going to prison for life."

K.C. puts his face in his hands.

Cam stands up and climbs into her husband's lap

"Hold me big daddy," Cam says, "you're everything I'll ever need or want."

Chapter 3
16

(Jaze)

Near my house there's a basketball gym I hoop at on a regular basis. I'm one of the only girls, but it's cool because I'm the only girl they respect on the court like one of the guys.

I hate to lose... I've always hated to lose. So since I hate the feeling of losing, I make sure I never do. Even though I believe and prove on a regular basis I'm better than every boy my age in this city, sometimes it's hard. I'm usually quicker than the other boys that play point guard like me, but they're usually bigger and stronger than me and they always jump higher. I shoot better, my ball handling skills are superb, and because I'm so low to the ground I'm a lock down defender as well.

Ever since my daddy taught me the correct defensive stance years ago I've been able to guard any boy or girl who dares dribble the ball in front of me. I feel like a super hero when I'm hoopin', but especially when I'm playing defense. I just break all the way down, knees bent, arms out wide, and I position my body at an angle to force the ball handler to go the direction I want them to go. I pressure them hard, then I fall back, then as soon as they relax I strip the ball away and sprint down the court full speed for an easy layup.

I've been playing for about three hours straight today and my body is more than tired. This is my last game today. We're playing to 24 points. My team has 19, our opponents have 22, and they have the ball. My team; consisting of me, two twin boys Ronald and Donald, a Hispanic kid named Freddie, and my big man Johnny Black. Johnny Black is seventeen years old and he's 6'8, he's the biggest kid I've ever seen in person. He always picks me to be on his team because he loves the way I deliver perfect alley-oops for him to dunk all over our competition.

Ok lock in Jaze. We need the ball back now, if they score on this possession game over. My perfect undefeated gym record would end as soon as one of these boys makes a shot.

I reach for the ball twice; I can't get it, not yet. My man passes the ball; I quickly follow him as his sprints through everybody to the other side of the court. As I chase behind him I'm watching his body language, I'm almost sure he's going to get the ball back.

I'm at least three steps behind him; damn his legs are long. He reaches his spot and quickly turns around in the corner behind the three-point line. I'm watching his eyes, they just doubled in size, the pass is already headed towards him, I'm sure of it. I quickly jump to my left with my left hand outstretched; as soon as I feel the ball on my left hand I tap it up one time to control it, then I clutch it to my chest. I make sure no one is behind me and then I take off full speed towards our goal at the other end of the court. Three members of the other team are ahead of me, but I'm not scared and I refuse to stop. I want these two points way too bad.

As I approach the first two defenders standing side by side I push the ball to my right, as they both reach to steal it, I quickly control the ball with my right hand and dribble it behind my back as I spin back to my left.

As I regain my composure I still have a full head of steam and one man left to beat. I rush towards the 6'2 light skinned power forward Raheem, or as all the girls at school call him Raheem "The Dream".

I fake to my left and then go right; Raheem doesn't bite on the fake, so I quickly go up on my tips toes with the ball raised high. After I see him leave the ground I know I got em', after he flies out of bounds after falling for my pump fake I put up the easy shot.

My team is down one now, and we need at least one more defensive stop. I quickly hustle back to the other end of the court. Just before I *reach half court I notice the guy on the other team making a long pass down court. I know if I can run fast enough I can intercept the pass. Let's go... Almost there, jump... got it. I got one man to beat, I could take em' to the hole, but I'm good at the three-point line.*

If I hit this shot, we win. I set my feet, square my shoulders to the basket. I jump, my elbow is perfectly straight. At the peak of my jump I release the ball making sure to follow through. As soon as the ball left my hands I knew we had won the game. SWISH!!!!

"Good game." One of the boys from the other team says patting Jaze on her bottom. His dreads aren't long but they're long enough to be considered dreads. She doesn't know what it is but there's something almost amazing about his dark chocolate eyes. He took his shirt off a couple games ago, and it took everything in Jaze to not stare at his ripped stomach and chest.

"Thanks man." she replies looking down at his stomach involuntarily. He licks his dark lips and smiles at her obvious awe.

"Damn man," one of his overweight teammates grunts, "whose team you on fool?"

"Shut up dude." the dread head boy replies glaring at his teammate.

"Nah," the chubby boy says, "This bitch kicked our ass like five times and you over there being friendly with her ass."

"Bitch..." Jaze quickly pulls her hair back into a tighter ponytail.

"Watch your mouth bruh," the dread head tells his friend, "The girl beat us, she's good. It's all good. Come on fool let's go smoke."

"Na bruh, look at the lil dike she's squarin' up like she wanna fight me..." the asshole says.

"So what you gon' do," the dread head boy clinches his fists and steps nose to nose with his friend, "You gon fight a girl? That's what you do now?"

"Nah." his friend replies stepping back.

"I know," the dread head says, "Cause if you touch her, I'ma beat your fat ass! Now go sit yo cryin' ass down!"

The asshole obeys but continues to mumble inaudible things as he makes his way to the bleachers on the far wall.

"What's your name lil mama?" the dread head asks.

"Me..." Jaze replies looking down trying not to blush or panic.

"Yeah you," he smiles again revealing a shiny bottom grill, "My name is Bleek... What's yours boo?"

Bleek... His name continues to echo through Jaze's mind.

"Are you okay..." Bleek taps Jaze on her left shoulder.

"Oh yea," Jaze hesitates, "I'm fine..."

44

"Yeah you definitely fine as hell lil mama," Bleek grins, "but what's your name? Walk me outside, I'm bout to smoke."

"Jazemene." she smiles following behind him as her cheeks redden despite her defenses against it.

"Jazemene," Bleek repeats returning her smile, "Yeah. Yeah, I think I like that. Yeah, yeah I might let you keep that name boo."

Jaze laughs. "What do you mean *let* me keep it," she asks, "It's *my* name. What does it have to do with you?"

"Oh shit," Bleek says turning to look at her, "you ain't know?"

"Know what?" she asks with her left brow furrowed.

"Yeah, you gone be my girl." he assures her.

"What," Jaze laughs, "What do you mean? How do you even know you're my type?"

"I'm King Bleek baby," he flashes his bottom grill again; "I'm every girl's type."

"Is that right?" Jaze can't stop smiling as he pushes the gym door open to let her walk out first."

As she steps out into the sun Jaze can almost feel the sun's rays smiling down on her replenishing all of her energy.

"Damn lil mama..." Bleek growls from the doorway.

"What **now** King Bleek..." Jaze turns to smile back at him.

"How you got **all** that booty in them **big ass** basketball shorts?" he asks.

Jaze looks down behind her with her with both brows wrinkled.

"I don't know..." she starts.

"Yeah, yeah," Bleek interjects, "So, I got one more question for you?"

"I'm scared to ask what it is..." Jaze says taking a seat on the curb in front of the gym.

"That's a no go lil mama," Bleek tells her, "You **ain't** scared. You ain't **never** scared round King Bleek; I'll never let nobody hurt you."

"What was your question King Bleek?" Jaze looks up into his confident black eyes.

"Can you please tell me," he starts, "How the hell you stole that ball from my partner Roland without even looking at the ball?"

They both laugh.

"It was kind of easy," Jaze admits, "I was a few steps behind your boy, and by the time I caught up to him I just watched his eyes. I could tell exactly where the ball was and that it was coming to him. So, I stepped in the passing lane and stole it."

"Damn lil mama," Bleek's bottom grill is shining brighter than ever, "Yeah, yeah... I think I'm gone like you."

De'Lure

(Josiah Bell)

Deep down every kid wants a dad. Every boy and girl wants and needs a father. There's something quite amazing about the comfort and power a kid feels in the presence of his dad. If the father sticks around long enough... that feeling of power and comfort stay with a kid even when he's not around his father. I know because, that's the way my dad used to make me feel. I wanted to be more than like him, I wanted to be my dad. I am a junior so I guess I have a right to feel like I am my dad. I don't know maybe that's weird but it works for me, well it used to anyway. That feeling existed way back before my dad ran away. I don't get it I thought kids were supposed to be the ones that ran away not parents, but just about every kid I know only has one parent... or worse one parent and a lame ass step parent.

My best friend Jazemene's dad K.C.'s best friend Jacody, Jay Milli Mulah... or whatever he calls himself now is dating my mom. I honestly didn't think it would last all these years but it has. He's not a bad dude but sometimes he just tries way too hard to be cool, and to be my father. My father is not here, so I don't need his ass to try to be something he's not. He's not my father, hell he's not even a father period. He's in his mid-thirties and has no kids. Well not yet at least. Between his and Keldrick Cole's activities in my

mother's bedroom that I can hear every other night one of them is bound to get her pregnant soon.

"Lil Jojo…" Jacody knocks on Josiah's closed door.

Jojo exhales deeply.

"That ain't my name **dude**." Jojo says from the foot of his just big enough bed.

"Boy open the door," he knocks again; "I wanna talk to you."

"About what…" Jojo groans.

"Damn it!" Jacody growls from outside the still closed door.

Jojo unlocks his door. Jacody opens it from the outside and walks in closing it behind him.

Jojo sits down on his bed and Jacody sits next to him.

"Wassup lil… I mean Jojo…" Jacody stutters.

"I don't know you tell me." He replies.

"You got a smart mouth boy." Jay wrinkles his brow.

"Would you rather I had a stupid mouth **Jacody Requinton**?" Jojo laughs.

"Don't you **ever**," Jay pauses, "How the hell you know my middle name any damn way?"

"Mom told me." Jojo admits.

"Whatever kid," Jay shakes his head, "You gotta start growing up a little bit."

"Right…" Jojo scoffs.

"I'm serious boy," Jay stresses, "Now your mom told me to talk to you about..."

"No," Jojo interjects, "That's a lie you're about to tell me so let me stop you before you tell it. I think my mom didn't tell you shit. I think she's lonely and vulnerable... and because of those facts she puts up with your bullshit! So when you go to her and make suggestions she doesn't agree or disagree with you, she just lets your stupid ass talk so she doesn't have to be afraid that you might leave her too... just like my dad did."

"Hey man," Jay tries to hide his emotion, "I'm not going anywhere. Hell yes I'm hard on you because maybe my parents weren't always as hard on me as they should have been. My parents loved me so much they didn't want to come down on me when I fell short. That was a gift and a curse but I know..."

"You don't have to do this Jay." Jojo interjects forcing a hard grimace on his handsome young face.

"Damn it!" Jay exclaims. "Just listen son," he continues, "I want to be here, I want to do this and talk to you about good things, bad things, and uncomfortable things."

"You make a lot of damn money now Jacody." Jojo crosses his teenage arms.

"I do." Jay agrees.

"So why the hell is my mother still struggling?" Jojo asks.

"All that's about to change..." Jay claims.

"Oh yeah and why is that?" Jojo asks.

"Well son it has to... when she becomes my wife." Jay smiles at Josiah.

"Are you serious?" the teen lights up like a Christmas tree.

"Hell yeah kid," Jay vows, "I can't be a playa for life. Well I could the ladies *love* me... but nah I want what Jazemene's dad has with Cameron. I wanna feel complete."

"Sounds good to me Jay..." Jojo respectfully holds his hand out to his apparent future stepfather.

"What you too cool to hug boy..." Jay smiles genuinely hugging the young man tightly.

"Jay..." Josiah says.

"Yeah son..." Jay replies.

"Why don't you have any kids?" Josiah asks.

"I do," Jay tells him, "a son Cody Jr."

"Well I wanna meet him." Josiah says.

"You will son," Jay says standing to leave, "you will."

(Hours Later)

As Jacody arrives at K.C.'s mansion his smile is still intact on his pleasant light brown face.

Jaze is practicing shooting free throws with one hand. Her baby brother is holding her right elbow in place as instructed by her father, who is

50

standing beneath the basketball goal shirtless with a whistle hanging on a gold chain around his neck.

"Bend your knees Jazzy…" K.C. barks.

"They're bent…" she claims.

"No they're not!" K.C. exclaims.

"You want more time;" he continues, "you want strict athletic structure and training from your **NFL**, **All-Pro**, **Dad** right… That's what you said! Now bend your knees Jazemene!"

"Whatever…" she mumbles taking another almost perfect shot.

"No discipline," K.C. declares as he snatches the made basket out of the bottom of the tight new net, "Hit the shower."

"You said two hundred shots," she puts a defiant hand on each hip, "that's only one hundred and thirty-seven."

"I'm glad you can count, that may be the only thing I taught you that you still remember." K.C. snaps walking past his daughter towards his friend Jacody.

"God I hate you!" Jazemene storms inside the house.

"What the hell was that Kel?" Jay asks.

"She's growing up Jay," K.C. shakes his head, "And it scares the hell out of me."

"Every single time I…" K.C. pauses noticing the look on K.J.'s face.

"Go check on your sister son." K.C. tells K.J.

"Yeah," K.J. scoffs, "She's my sister because of Whitney, but I told you Keldrick you ain't my dad."

"Boy get yo lil' yellow ass in that house now!" K.C. demands.

K.J. obeys reluctantly.

"And stop talking to my sister like you crazy..." he says just before slamming the door behind him.

K.C. looks at Jacody.

No words.

"Awkward." Jay breaks the silence.

"These kids man..." K.C. walks towards his Olympic sized swimming pool just beyond the regulation basketball goal Jaze was just practicing on.

"Look at the bright side..." Jay smiles as they both sit down on a comfy bench looking out of the clear blueness of the immaculate pool.

"Oh yeah," K.C. replies, "And what is that bro?"

"You're rich," Jay pats his old friend on the knee twice, "I mean I got money now too thanks to you, but nigga you are **filthy rich**. So, no worries everything is much easier when you got money."

"Not true Jay," K.C. shakes his head, "**You're rich** cannot always be the answer. Money doesn't ease true pain and discomfort in a man's life Jay."

"You are probably absolutely right bro," Jay admits, "But I'm honestly kinda flying high right now and don't wanna lose the feeling..."

"What you smokin' on fool," K.C. asks, "You don't look high..."

"Nah bro," Jay laughs, "I'm high on life... I'm high on my life, just like you told me to be. I came over with some good news and I don't want to get cold feet now because of the drama at the Cole mansion..."

"Cold feet," K.C. interjects with a curious smile, "Did you just say cold feet... I know damn well you not bout to settle down bro..."

"Well I'ma need you to know better than that..." Jay pulls a small beautiful red box out of his pocket.

"Damn," K.C. exclaims happily taking the box in his hand, "Are you serious bro?"

"I'm dead serious fool." Jay tells him.

K.C. opens the box then squints hard thinking maybe his aging eyes are playing a trick on him.

Nope they're not.

"Jay..." K.C. says looking at his smaller friend.

"What up bro." he replies.

"Man ain't nothing in this box bro." K.C. hands it back to Jay.

"Is this some kinda joke," K.C. continues, "and who would you be proposing to anyway?"

"Well," Jay starts, "There's no ring because my best friend and best man a ***ring picking*** specialist hasn't helped me pick one out yet..."

"Uh huh," K.C. wrinkles his brow, "And the other question I asked you..."

"Who else K.C...." Jay smiles at him.

"I don't know," he replies, "But I do know damn well you're not talking about my Cid."

"What the hell?" Jay stands up pushing the box back in his pocket.

"You might wanna sit back down lil bro." K.C. warns Jay.

"Nah fool Ty is your ***lil bro***," Jay snaps I'm not your bro. Now what the hell do you mean ***your Cid***?"

"Come on fool," K.C. laughs, "You know ***damn well*** that white girl belongs to me, be serious right now. You found her on my Facebook page, with your stalking ass. Now, you want me to help you find a ring to propose to a woman I'm fucking on the regular?"

WHAP!!!

Jay slaps K.C. hard across his strong black face.

Cameron pulls into the driveway in her new purple drop top Mustang GT.

"I'ma let that slide." K.C. rubs his stern jaw.

"Why, because you know you're a piece of shit!" Jay exclaims.

"Hey boys..." Cam yells waving from the driver's seat.

"Nah," K.C. stands up, "because I don't want my lady to see me absolutely slaughter yo ass."

"Are you guys hungry?" Cam calls out grabbing a couple of grocery bags out of the passenger seat.

"Not right now baby." K.C. smiles and waves back at his pleasant wife.

Jay turns to watch Cam walk inside the house.

"You confuse the hell out of me Keldrick." Jay tells him.

"How's that..." K.C. inquires.

"How can you have a fine black woman like that and damn near everything this world has to offer and still not be pleased?" Jay asks.

"Oh I'm pleased," K.C. explains, "but I'm never satisfied. I don't get tired Jacody."

"Actually you do..." Jay walks away without looking back.

As K.C. makes his way towards the back door to his monstrous house he contemplates exactly how Cidra Bell marrying Jacody would make him feel.

"Baby..." Cam croons as he steps in the house.

"Yes love." He replies sounding to her like a sweet chocolate baritone waterfall.

"I have a surprise for you..." she grins wide with bright eyes and both hands behind her mysterious back.

"You know I don't like surprises baby..." K.C. reminds her.

"Oh, I know baby," she whines playfully, "But you'll like this one."

"Okay baby whatever you say." He tries to act excited.

"Sit in that chair over there," she points to one of the chairs at the kitchen table, "and close your eyes."

He obeys.

With his arms crossed and long legs spread wide K.C. awaits his surprise.

He hears her steps coming close to him.

He smiles.

"Where are the kids..." she whispers close to his tingling ear.

"Upstairs, probably plotting to kill me again..." he laughs.

"Not again," Cam laughs, "oh well. Now, are you ready for my tasty, sexy, mind blowing surprise?"

"Yes baby..." he moans as she kisses the back of his strong black neck.

After lacing the back, sides, and front of his neck with delicate kisses Cam makes her way around in front of her handsome husband.

He can now feel one of Cam's small hands on his right knee.

"Open your eyes Daddy..." Cam whispers.

Down on her knees in front of him K.C. finds his wife licking her full, capable lips, and clutching a white and pink book in her left hand baring the name De'Lure.

"What's this?" he asks.

"This, my love," she hands him the book, "Is *"Passion Absolute"* by De'Lure. I want you to start back reading baby... You were much happier when you used to read. And you need to catch up, De'Lure has about ten books out now and they're all **breathtaking**. I swear sometimes I feel like that man's words **created** me, he gives me so much life baby."

"Should I be jealous?" K.C. smirks. "Probably," Cam teases, "No baby, De'Lure understands us women a little too well he's *obviously* gay."

"You think so," K.C. looks at the back of the book, "I don't know babe. When I read him, I sense that he's definitely straight, but he can see life so clearly sometimes it's scary."

"Maybe..." Cam says as she pulls the strings of K.C.'s gym shorts to untie the knot in them.

"What are you doing Cameron...?" K.C. quickly looks out towards both doors that lead into his massive kitchen.

"Start reading the book Keldrick," she pulls his shorts down just far enough, "a good man should never have to ask for these pleasures, don't mind me."

"Yeah baby, but not in the kit..." she engulfs him before he can finish his plea.

(A couple months later)

(Jaze)

I can't sleep. My boyfriend Bleek is locked up and he won't even tell me why. He calls three times a week, but it's never enough. This is so hard! I don't know how to feel pretty or relevant without that boy in my life. People pay attention to me at times, but nobody talks to me like my Bleek, and everybody judges me and hates me because of who my father is. Bleek sees the good in me and the good in being the daughter of "Kool Hands" Cole. He values me, my life, and our future together. He says I'm his pretty little meal ticket. That always makes me laugh; I know he's only kidding.

Bleek would never just use me for my dad's money. I put a hundred dollars on his books down at the jail every week, not because he demands that I do, but because I'm his first lady and that's what a good bitch is supposed to do. When Bleek talks I always feel like class is in session.

Oooh he's just so rough and real. His mentality is perfectly street he ain't scared of nothing! I truly believe that boy would kill or be killed for me, the complete opposite of my dad. Dad claims he used to be street. Whatever, I can't tell. I miss my boyfriend so much. He's

**the one locked up and I'm sitting in here crying like I'm
the one going through hell...**

As soon as her Nick Jonas ringtone goes off on her
phone Jaze knows who the text is from.

Josiah: Wassup buddy...

Jaze: So we're buddies now?

Josiah: Don't start that emo shit Jazemene

Jaze: Haha you can spell my whole first name...
Wow

Josiah: Really... yea whatever. Why aren't you
asleep

Jaze: Because I'm awake. Why aren't you asleep...

Josiah: Can't...

Jaze: Why aren't you at that chick's house... the
one that looks like Taylor Swift you keep posting about

Josiah: Stalker much...

Jaze: No sir. Not stalking, but it's hard not to notice
your little gay ass statuses every ten minutes. Question...

Josiah: answer

Jaze: Why doesn't she ever post about you
anymore...

Josiah: How's your dad...

Jaze: He's great, why doesn't Taylor post about
you?

Josiah: Don't wanna talk about it. Are you like
naked...

Jaze: um... why? Are you asking for a nude pic
Josiah Aiden Bell...?

Josiah: answer the question

Jaze: Nah... I have on sweats and a jersey...

Josiah: Is your dad up?

Jaze: I doubt it. Jojo it's like 2a.m.

Josiah: Kool. Does your window open?

Jaze: yes... why?

TAP TAP...

Jaze quickly looks out from under her covers to find Josiah at her large bedroom window overlooking her bed.

"What the hell..." Jaze whispers.

She jumps out of bed and races to the other side of her room to close and lock her door. After quietly unlocking her window Jaze opens it and stands back as Josiah climbs in.

Now sitting side by side on her bed the twosome is lost in an extremely awkward silence.

"Jojo..." Jaze whispers.

"Yeah." He whispers back looking in the depths of her eyes.

"Why are you here..." she starts.

Before her question is done leaving her lips, Josiah's lips are pressed against hers. Jaze's open eyes are locked in on the pale closed lids of his. Her heart and brain are both erupting simultaneously with joy, pain, and wonder.

His awkward arms are moving behind him as he tries to figure out what exactly to do with them. His left leg is shaking, but he doesn't think she can tell.

Jaze puts a hand on his left knee to steady it.

Jojo opens his eyes wide as he continues to kiss her soft pink lips.

Jaze reaches for her phone, and turns on her Pandora music app to the *Trey Songz* station. Maxwell's song *"This Woman's Work"* comes on.

Jaze's lips instantly curl up at the ends as she enjoys Josiah's soft lips while reminiscing about her favorite movie *"Love & Basketball".* In the movie, this is the exact song *Q* and *Monica* made love to for the very first time Jaze thinks to herself.

For some reason the music makes Jaze's kisses taste even sweeter to Josiah.

As their lips part ways slowly they can hear each other's hearts beating clearly. Same beat, same volume... perfect tandem.

Jojo stares deep into his best friend's beautiful dark eyes. As she stares back at him she prays that wasn't her last time ever feeling his touch in such an intimate way. So many confusing unanswered questions are swelling up inside her teenage mind.

"Jaze..." he whispers.

"Yes Josiah..." she whispers back trying hard not to have a panic episode.

"I've always wanted to do that." He admits.

"Me too..." she agrees just before he leans back in pressing his lips softly against hers again.

Jaze takes both of his arms and wraps them around her back. Then after basking in the simple adolescent perfection that is Josiah Bell for a few more precious seconds, Jazemene Cole closes her eyes to further enjoy her deepest and dearest dream finally come true.

Alone in his room Keldrick Cole Jr. is contemplating his eleven years of life on earth thus far.

(K.J.)

I don't want to hate my legal father K.C., but knowing the things he allowed my biological father to endure as a child is hard for me to forgive and forget. I honestly do miss the relationship I used to have with K.C. when I was younger, but he's just not my real dad. The problem is as time goes on my real father Love, seems to be slipping into more and more bouts of depression. My dad goes weeks at a time without even calling to check on me. No matter what, I never stop thinking about my dad and trying to contact him.

As he lies in his bed listening to his phone ringing away on speaker phone K.J. awaits, knowing full well his father isn't going to answer the phone.

"Damn it!" K.J. hangs the phone up and then calls one more time.

He pulls one of his large pillows down tight on his yellow face as the phone begins to ring again.

"Hello..." Love answers finally.

"Hello," K.J. throws the pillow across the room, "Dad, hello dad... are you there?"

"K.J.," Love mumbles, "What's wrong? Is everything okay?"

"Yeah dad," K.J. confirms, "everything is fine, but I haven't heard from you, dad. Why don't you call me sometimes?"

"I will son," Love lies, "I was going to call... I'm just in a bad..."

"You're just in a bad place right now," K.J. interjects, "Well I am too dad! I need you... Hello. Dad, dad... I'm sorry dad. Hello, dad..."

His bedroom door opens.

"Yeah son..." K.C. says from the hallway outside K.J.'s room.

"Not you." K.J. replies coldly.

"Then who are you talking to Junior," K.C. asks, "I don't see anybody else... I was coming down the hall and I heard **you**, **my son**... specifically calling out to me."

"**No**, I was on the phone calling out to my **real dad**." K.J. corrects him.

"How is my baby brother?" K.C. asks.

No response.

"K.J. did you hear me..." K.C. asks.

"You know what," K.J. explodes, "Call me L.J. from now on, I'm *Lance* Jr.! My eyes are green not black, my skin is light not crispy... I'm **Love** Jr., **not** Keldrick!"

"Why, do you hate me so much, son?" K.C. steps closer to the boy.

"I'm **not** your son," he spits, "and I will always hate you for what you did to my dad! He's a **freakin'** psychopath because his big brother was a **pussy**, and didn't **protect** him! Can you please leave me alone?"

K.C. drops his head and turns to leave K.J.'s room.

Chapter 4
Senior Prom

(Jaze)

So it's the night before prom and I'm still a nervous wreck. My boyfriend Bleek didn't want to take me because he said real niggaz don't go to dances. I begged him for months and he finally gave in. Or I guess I did. I promised Bleek he could be my first on prom night. I'm eighteen years old now, a senior in high school, and I'm still a virgin. I take... I took pride in that up until about three weeks ago. Bleek explained to me that once you become an adult, and at eighteen I guess I am an adult, if I'm still a virgin it's no longer something to brag about its just corny. He said once you're as old as me, if you're not getting any it's because nobody ever wanted it bad enough. That hurt, that hurt real bad. Mostly because I know full well if Josiah Bell had ever tried it I would have given in with no commitments, no questions, no nothing. But he never did. Well he did that one night, but nothing really happened beyond sweet magical kisses. I wish.

Jaze's door opens and in walks both of her parents. Whitney is wearing a thoughtful green dress, laced with exquisite white floral print, and white Louis Vuitton sandals to match. Her tinted hair is already neatly spun around her beautiful head for the night under a black hair wrap. K.C. has on a tight black Polo V-neck, dark fitted denim jeans, and stunning black Hermes slides on his large feet.

"Jazemene, baby," Whitney starts, "Could you please kindly tell your arrogant father that you are getting picked up for the prom from my house."

"You tell him," Jaze continues looking down at her phone, "he's right there."

"This is ridiculous," K.C. contends, "Why would you not want to be picked up from *a castle* on your prom night princess?"

"Maybe I don't feel like a princess anymore," Jaze explains, "I'm more like Cinderella's ugly ass, minus the evil step sisters."

"Baby..." Whitney sits next to Jaze on the bed and pulls her gently into her warm chest.

"That's not true," K.C. raises his voice, "You'll always be my princess no matter how many times we fight or disagree. And I spent a fortune on this prom..."

"We know dad," Jaze groans, "Hell the whole school knows. You know they actually have a picture of you outside the ballroom at the hotel where the prom is going to be held now. But, I guess that's what happens when you offer to pay for the entire prom."

"You're welcome," K.C. nonchalantly picks a few pieces of lint off of the front of his tight black Polo shirt, "So you have to get picked up from here baby girl... plus that boy ain't got no car. Aren't you taking my new limo? And by the way Cinderella was never ugly."

"My baby knows she's not ugly," Whit interjects looking down into her eighteen-year-old daughter's eyes, "You look just like I did at your age, and I was the most gorgeous girl at my prom. The world hasn't changed that much in twenty years little girl. My fine **back then**, is **still fine** today."

"My daughter is pretty not fine." K.C. corrects Whit.

"Well you used to describe me at eighteen a little different than that sir," Whit smiles at her ex, "but that's another story for another time. Bottom line, have the limo pick Jaze and Blip up at my house tomorrow night at seven sharp..."

"**Bleek**," Jaze corrects her mother, "his name for the hundred thousandth time is **Bleek**."

"Blip, Bloop, Bleek... whatever baby, if you're happy mama's happy for you." Whitney vows.

"Yeah well," K.C. frowns, "what about daddy?"

"Daddy is downstairs in the car..." Whit teases.

"Not that dread headed fool Charlie," K.C. says, "I'm talking about me. I don't like this Bleek character. Didn't he just get out of jail *again*… and Whitney why the hell doesn't Charlie's corny ass ever want to come inside my house? Is he *that* insecure?"

"First off father," Jaze stands up with her arms crossed next to her mother in almost an identical pose, "Yes, my Bleek *did* just get out of jail again. But I don't think you should judge him since you are just recently no stranger to a cell yourself."

"And another thing," Whit chimes in, "hell no Charlie ain't insecure at all. He just prefers not to be around *arrogant assholes*."

Whit looks down at Jaze, who's still staring at her father's stunned face.

"Wait, wait, wait… little girl did you just say this fool was in jail *recently*?" Whit asks her daughter.

"It's not like that Whitney…" K.C. claims.

"So tell me *Kool Hands* what is it like?" Whit asks. "And why I never heard a thing about it," Whit continues, "how much did you have to pay the powers that be to keep this out of the news?"

"Seriously…" K.C. wrinkles his newly moist brow.

"How much Keldrick?" Whit asks again.

"Fifty large," he admits, "But it was just a simple DUI, I didn't want to startle any of my new investors, so I made it go away."

"Beautiful," Whit says dryly, "Are you ready to go Jaze?"

"I thought you'd never ask." Jaze grabs a decent sized Louis Vuitton duffle bag and follows her mother out of her room.

After they exit K.C. stands there silently with closed eyes waiting to hear the front door of his mansion open and close. On regretful legs he makes his way to his daughter's bed to take a much needed seat. As his thoughts begin to rush his mind the superstar tries hard to ignore them.

(K.C.)

I just can't seem to find the constant peace I should have at this point in my career and my life. I'm owed that peace, football is over... forever. As hard as it is for me to wrap my mind around that fact I've already accepted it on so many levels. I don't need nor do I want sympathy from my family, but I deserve respect. I'm the only reason our lives are without financial worry. One day I will find my way to the peace I so rightfully deserve. So in the absence of peace like most men I need to find or create a distraction for myself... or maybe I just need to utilize an old, but steady distraction I already know well.

K.C. smiles to himself as he slips his smart phone out of his tight denim pocket. He scrolls to the name and clicks the phone icon. As soon as the phone starts ringing he can already smell and feel her sweet breath on his rock hard body. She really is the best lover K.C.'s sexual prowess has ever known.

She answers.

"Hello..." he growls sensually, "Did I catch you at a bad time? No, I understand, so tell him you don't feel well. Make him leave now! That's my girl... See you in thirty minutes Cidra."

Locked inside her bedroom Cam finally releases the intercom button near the door. She's heard enough already. She knew her husband was probably cheating on her, she just didn't think he was still dealing with Cidra Bell.

A week after they were married, she and K.C. stayed awake one night until 5 a.m. telling each other all their dirty little secrets. During that talk K.C. admitted to his dealings with Cidra Bell, Jaze's elementary school teacher. He said the fling with her was more than fun, but it would never be worth losing Cam's love again.

Cam lied and told him he had never lost her love, she belonged solely to him, and she would never again feel the touch of another man.

Standing there with a few tears streaming down her broken black face she slides down the wall to a sitting position on her lonely bedroom floor. She hears him step close to the door, probably trying to listen to see if she's awake.

Seconds later she can hear him bounding happily down their luxurious stairs in pursuit of his fair booty for the evening.

Cam wipes her painful face as reality's ugly truth plants itself firmly in the forefront of her tormented mind. Her gorgeous, wealthy husband is on his way half way across the city to have sex with a beautiful white woman who's absolutely obsessed with him. That pain is more than Cam's already wrecked mind cares to deal with tonight.

(Cam)

I could have stopped him. I could have cried, or pretended to be sick… or I could have just admitted to eavesdropping on his adulterous conversation with that nasty white bitch and then forced him to stay home with me tonight. But, I know full well with the double life I'm living with Whitney and her man Charlie Breeze, I have no room to place judgment on my restless husband. Knowing all the facts just never seems to make the pain hurt any less.

Unable to function any longer Cam's body surrenders to her cold bedroom floor as her mind gives way to the darkness.

As he drives, K.C. is actually trying to feel remorse for continuing to sleep with the woman his best friend is planning to marry. But he can't seem to find any sympathy for Jay. Cidra belonged to K.C. first, so in his mind she always will. The longer the superstar drives, the less he cares about the feelings of his clueless lifelong friend.

(Prom Night)

Jaze is in her mother's bathroom putting the imaginary finishing touches on her clearly flawless makeup and hair. Looking at her reflection she's sure she has finally surpassed her mother's shadow and beauty. She's sure they will always share a striking resemblance, but now her eyes and the fire behind them give Jaze her very own unique edge that sets her apart from her gorgeous mother once and for all.

Are you girls ready? Jaze thinks to herself as she pushes her growing breasts up higher in her bra and dress. **Tonight is the night when Jazemene Argelle Cole becomes a woman...**

"**Knock knock**... baby girl got a thug on her block..." the voice says from the other side of the door.

Jaze smiles hard. She quickly opens the door to find Bleek dressed to the nines in a white suit, and matching shoes, donning a red silk tie that matches Jaze's dress to perfection. His long dark dreads are freshly twisted and pulled up into a breath taking design on top of his head.

"Damn boy..." Jaze smiles even harder.

71

"You like it bae?" Bleek steps next to her in the mirror to check himself out.

"Yeah," Jaze steps in front of him to fix his tie, "but I thought you were just going to wear black pants and that polo I bought you baby…"

"Nah baby," Bleek shows his almost shiny bottom grill, "I don't do dances, but if I'ma do one you know I gotta go all out. I hooked up with the homie Charlle Breeze; he took me shopping the other day while you were out hoopin' at the gym. Its sposed to be a surprise for you boo."

"Well I love it." Jaze admits still unable to relax her tight smile.

"Where is my handsome *future* stepfather anyway…?" Jaze exits the bathroom to look for Charlie with her sinfully large grin still intact.

"Thank you Charlie!" Jaze rushes into the dread head's arms.

"Anything for you princess…" Charlie hugs her tightly as he smiles at her mother across the room.

"Preciate all your help, OG Charlie…" Bleek shakes Charlie's free hand as he continues to hold Jaze in his arms.

After hugging Charlie Jaze rushes to her mother.

"How do I look mommy?" she asks with all the seriousness left in the world.

"You both look great." Whit says standing up to straighten the back of her daughter's gorgeous red dress.

"Hell ya'll look like a kid version of us." Charlie laughs to himself.

"They really do..." Whit agrees with a laugh of her own.

The doorbell rings.

"I got it." Charlie opens the door.

"Mr. Breeze..." K.C. says.

"Mr. Cole..." Charlie replies.

"Daddy," Jaze wrinkles her brow, "I thought you weren't coming. After yesterday..."

"You'll always be my baby," K.C. interjects, "I told you no matter what we go through that will never change. I wasn't gonna miss this night for the world little girl. Your limo is waiting outside, now come here and take some pictures with your old man before you go."

After twenty minutes of various line ups and poses for pictures, Jaze and Bleek are finally ready to head to Prom.

"Bleek," K.C. says taking the boy's hand in his own gigantic hand, "take care of my baby tonight. I don't know much about you, but what I do know ain't good at all boy..."

Bleek doesn't respond. The intense real pain he feels from K.C.'s grasp won't allow him to.

"But," K.C. continues to stare through the boy while crushing his hand, "I've been instructed

73

not to judge you because my background ain't squeaky clean either. Have fun tonight boy."

"Yes sir..." Bleek manages to say without showing how much pain he's in, in front of his girl.

"Tonight is about my princess," K.C. reminds him, "I don't know what school you go to, or if anybody here has even taken time to check if you're in school or if you're some pervert posing as a teenager."

"*Daaad*..." Jaze whines taking Bleek's hand safely out of her father's deadly grip.

"I love you baby girl." K.C. promises as he bends down to kiss Jaze on her forehead and cheek.

As the two teens head out the three adults stand in the doorway and watch them.

As they approach the car, the limo driver hops out and rushes around to open the door for them. Once inside Bleek makes his way to the small bar and grabs a couple of beers out of the tiny fridge.

After sitting next to his girlfriend he hands her one of the cold beers.

"Bleek," Jaze smiles behind her hanging blonde bang as she hands the alcoholic beverage back to him, "You know I don't drink baby..."

"You do now," he opens both beers and hands Jaze's back to her, "drink up boo."

From the glare on his dark face she knows he's not kidding. His eyes always send chills through her body, not usually for the right reasons.

Over the years Jaze has become comfortable with the known fear she feels in the presence of her boyfriend. It's one of the only mainstays their relationship has.

Rather than start a battle she'll never win Jaze takes a fake sip of the beer and then sits it down near the window in one of the drink holding compartments.

After noticing the driver watching him closely through the rearview mirror, Bleek immediately lets the partition up to create the privacy he feels he deserves with the daughter of an over-protective, dangerous, billionaire.

With her back to Bleek Jaze stares out of the window up into the dark clouds and mystifying stars. Her gorgeous smile feels as if it will never fade again, and in this moment... even if only for a moment Josiah Bell is not the end and beginning of her existence.

"Bleek," Jaze says without turning around to look at him, "tonight is so beautiful. It feels like my wedding night. I can't wait to be somebody's wife one day... Do you think you'll ever get...?"

As Jaze turns around she finds Bleek removing his nice white pants.

"**Bleek, what the hell**..." Jaze's eye's double in size.

"I know you ain't think a nigga was going to prom foreal right?" he shows his bottom grill in the almost dark back seat of the private limo.

"*What do you mean Bleek*..." she asks with her entire face contorted in pure confusion.

"I put on a good show for your people all week boo," Bleek claims, "now lemme get what you promised... then you can have dude drop me off in the hood before you go to ya lil stupld ass dance."

"You *gotta* be kidding me," Jaze laughs, "This is a *joke* right? You are
not planning on letting me go to my *senior prom* by myself..."

"*Don't start acting lame Jaze*," Bleek removes his jacket, "*I told you*
I'm too real to go to some dance type shit you feel me?"

"*Hell no*," Jaze raises her voice, "I don't *feel you* at all *Bleek*! I am
not going to my senior prom *alone*! You'll get what I *promised*; just
wait till after the prom... *please*."

Bleek looks down at his pants around his ankles.

Jaze scoots close to him.

"Okay baby," she pleads, "we don't have to stay all night, I just wanna see who wins queen..."

Before she can finish her sentence Bleek
pushes her face with
unforgivable force.

"Get off me!" he growls angrily.

Jaze falls back deep in her seat staring at
Bleek through shaky hands.
Bleek fixes his clothes a bit and then leans forward
to get the
attention of the driver.

The partition opens.

"Aye drop me off up here on the left fool..." Bleek
instructs the driver.

"Bleek no," Jaze cries, **"Please... please don't leave
me Bleek!"**

Jaze is searching her eighteen-year-old mind
desperately for a solution. Something, anything she
can say, or do to make him stay.

(Jaze)

*I know what he wants, the same thing all
boys want... well except for Josiah Bell apparently.
My mind is made up; I'm going to sacrifice my
virginity to Bleek if he comes to the prom with me
for just an hour.
It's worth it. If I show up to prom alone I'm going
to be so
freakin' embarrassed. Come on Jaze you can do
this... speak, say something... anything.*

Jaze says nothing.

Moments later the limo pulls over to the side of the busy street.

"This is why I hate fucking with bougie hoes," Bleek opens the door, "I'm going back to the gutter where I belong. Bye rich bitch. Oh and tell OG I'm keeping the suit... never know when I might have a court appearance or some."

Jaze tries to speak but the pain in her heart and throat is too much
to overcome.

He's gone now.

Jaze is trying to catch her breath while squeezing her center tightly trying not to give way to her childhood habit of sudden urination.

The driver's heart is broken in two as he looks on through the partition.

"Should I call your dad or..." the driver breaks the screaming silence.

Jaze closes her eyes tightly. Then she opens them again as the oxygen seemingly returns to her personal airspace.

"It's no problem Ms. Cole, really I..." the driver stutters.

"No," Jaze interjects, "I'm eighteen years old. I'm an adult... I can handle this."

"Yes you are and yes you can," the driver smiles, "where to boss lady? Hell *you own* the limo."

"To the prom." she wipes more tears away.

"Yes ma'am," he tips his classy black hat, "if it's any

consolation... I think you look prettier without that dread headed clown beside you anyway. Every boy at the prom is gonna wanna leave the girl he's with for you."

"Thanks Bennie," Jaze finds her stunning smile, "do me a favor Bennie..."
"Anything Ms. Cole." he replies.
"Drive slow please, I have to fix my makeup."
"Sure thing Ms. Cole." Bennie pulls off slowly en route to the prom for the second time tonight.

Out of her small Michael Kors clutch purse Jaze pulls her makeup and a small hand held mirror.

In her mirror Jazemene finds several things she doesn't want to, and none of them involve her physical appearance.

She can see fear, doubt, and pure insecurity staring right back at her. She shakes her pretty little head several times trying to ward off the uncomfortable but familiar sensations swirling around her teenage mind. It doesn't work, she instead decides to just fix her makeup and walk into her senior prom pretending she knows she's the most gorgeous woman there.

"Pulling up now Ms. Cole..." Bennie alerts his young rich passenger.

After parking the limo right in front of the front door to enter the dance Bennie steps out and makes his way back to Jazemene.

He opens her door to find her makeup fully restored as well as her unforgettable smile.

"Are you ready Ms. Cole?" Bennie holds his hand out to her.

"Ready as I'm gonna be Mr. Bennie…" she admits.

As he helps her step out of her luxurious limousine she feels an absolute power come over her.

Out in front of the event center where the prom is being held kids are still lined up next to their dates waiting to get in. Jaze sees gay couples, lesbian couples, straight couples, and even solo prom goers like herself.

Looking passed them she leans to the side to see if she can see the end of the line as she pretends not to notice everyone watching her in all of her glorious perfection.

She may not feel perfect but every kid in line waiting to enter the prom knows she is tonight. Jaze heads towards the line.

"Right this way Ms. Cole…" a handsome young white man beckons her from the front door.

Jaze squints to see whether or not she recognizes the man.

She doesn't, but she heads towards him to find out what's going on anyway.

"May I help you?" Jaze asks the man trying not to notice his perfect teeth and lips.

"No ma'am Ms. Cole," he assures her, "You and your father have done so much already. You are not standing in any lines tonight, go on inside and enjoy something cold to drink."

"Thank you." Jaze smiles at him.

As she heads past the students at the front of the line; she's slightly holding the bottom of her dress up.

"Here alone *ice princess*?" an ugly white girl asks Jaze as she passes her.

"August Alsina didn't show up huh superstar…" her equally unattractive date adds.

"August didn't ask me *this time*," Jaze smiles at him, "But Chris wasn't able to get a security clearance in time to come so I'll just see him later tonight."

"*Chris Brown* was your date…" another girl asks.

"Not too loud," Jaze teases them all, "it's a secret."

The first hour of the prom Jaze drank enough punch to ruin her bladder forever. She danced a couple times, but not with anyone she particularly likes.

"Hey you…" the voice from behind her chills every fiber of her being.

Jaze smiles before ever turning around to look into his blue eyes.

"Jojo," she smiles as he hugs her, "you are getting so tall. And you look… wow."

"No," he contends, "Jazemene you look absolutely gorgeous. I didn't know you had this in you."

"Um, thanks *I think*..." she laughs.

"Nah, it's definitely a compliment girl," Jojo assures her, "I uh... I'm here with *Taylor Swift*."

"I know I've been watching you all night," Jaze admits, "No, wait I mean... Ugh this is *really*... awkward. What's her real name again, I know you're tired of me calling her Taylor Swift?"

"My name is Ashley..." Jojo's date startles Jaze from the rear.

"Oh hey Ashley," Jaze turns and holds out her hand, "I'm..."

"Jazemene Cole," Ashley interjects, "I know, *everybody* knows. Well it was nice meeting you. Josiah..."

"Cool," he smiles at her, "Um Jaze, I gotta..."

"Go... It's cool." Jaze grins and then hugs her childhood best friend again.

With her young heart still pounding loudly in her ears she watches him walk off in the distance with his beautiful date.

Long after the prom king and queen and their court have been announced the DJ puts his mouth close to the microphone and says he's about to play the last song.

Maxwell's song, "This Woman's Work" begins to waft in through the clear surround sound speakers. Jaze has always loved this song, but her kiss with her crush and best friend made the song even more important to her. That night and the feeling that night gave her could last a lifetime. Jaze looks around to see if just maybe Jojo might remember the song, and that night and come ask her to dance. After scanning the entire room Jaze soon realizes Jojo and his date are already gone.

Jaze opens her clutch to retrieve her cell phone. She texts her driver Bennie to let him know she's about to walk out. Once back safely in the limo the familiar tears rush her face.

With both feet on the seat tucked tightly in her chest Jazemene Cole attempts to hide her face from the whole world.

"Who am I hiding from?" she cries to herself. "Nobody's looking anyway," she wipes a few never-ending tears, "Not Bleek, not Jojo, nobody..."

"Where to now Ms. Cole..." Bennie asks pretending not to hear her private conversation with herself.

"I need some ice cream Bennie," she tries hard to stop crying, "And lots of it."

"I know just the place little lady," Bennie pulls off from the forgettable prom, "and after that how's about we head back to the mansion... I promised your dad you'd be home by 1 a.m."

"That's fine." She lies down across the large backseat to try to ease her pounding headache and bleeding heart.

With all the painful thoughts that are crowding her mind the most stressful one is the fact that Jaze knows full well what Jojo and little miss perfect, *Taylor Swift* did after they left the prom.

"It's all wrong," Jaze mumbles to herself, "it's supposed to me. I don't understand why he had to date a girl from *my* school or why that *stupid white boy* can't just see me and realize I'm *fine as hell*... and head over heels in *love* with him..."

"He will, Ms. Cole," Bennie assures her with a comforting tone, "In *his* time though... not yours."

Thirty minutes later Bennie pulls the limo in through the gates that surround the mansion. After thanking Bennie thoroughly for his kind words and service for the evening, Jaze uses her key to enter the mansion through the back door. Then she heads up to her room with a gallon of chocolate fudge swirl ice cream.

After climbing up into the middle of her bed Jaze gets semi comfortable, then she turns her flash on her phone's camera and snaps a good pic of her delicious ice cream.

With perfect slang and colorful emojis she creates a depressing Facebook status about how she's spending her after prom night. Seconds after posting the short emotional status she quickly panics and deletes it.

She then sends Josiah a goodnight text with the picture of her ice cream attached to the message.

With a few taps on her phone she turns on Maxwell's song, *This Woman's Work*, and eats another spoon full of her ice cream.

From the dark chair across the room Jaze can hear a delayed but distinct vibration.

She panics as she quickly reaches over to turn the lamp on next to her bed.

"I hope you brought two spoons fatty..." he smiles at her.

"*Really* Josiah..." Jaze pretends not to be excited.

He walks towards the bed.

"*Stalker much*..." Jaze says with a progressively dry throat.

"You should have locked your window back." He replies.

"Oh," Jaze laughs, "so because I didn't lock my window you think you can just..."

"Shut up and kiss me." Josiah tells her.

As he leans forward and covers her mouth with his he uses his feet to nudge both of his shoes off.

Jojo breaks the kiss. Then he stands back to take off his shirt.

85

Jaze's mouth and throat are suddenly no longer dry. As Jojo removes his pants, Jaze pulls her dress off over her head as best she can.

After his pants are on the floor Jojo helps Jaze finish removing her dress.

Left in nothing but her undergarments Jaze lays back and waits for her crush to make her a woman.

My God this boy's lips are my sunshine, his eyes are the windows to my own soul, and his heart is the most precious possession I could ever hope to obtain in life.

"Are you ready for me Jaze?" he whispers close to her ear.

Jaze hears him tear open his protection.

"Is that what you asked Taylor Swift...?" Jaze can't help but to ask.

"I didn't touch her," Jojo claims, "well maybe I touched her but nothing serious happened."

"Yeah right..." Jaze replies wanting to believe every beautiful word of his truth.

"I'm so serious," he contends as he finally gets his condom on correctly, "the crazy thing is Jazemene... I **think** I could be happy forever if you were the only girl I'd ever met."

"Wow Jojo..." she gushes in response to his statement and the sight of the size of him.

He smiles.

86

"Yeah," he continues, "With her it just wasn't right... I didn't feel... I don't know, but I do know it was supposed to be..."

"Me," Jaze interjects softly, "I already know Jojo... and I'm ready for you, baby."

Jaze closes her eyes gently as he positions himself just right.

"I love you Josiah Bell..." her temporarily still virgin lips whisper against his.

(The morning after)

Jazemene Argelle Cole wakes up with a smile that could cure anything in the world. Her body is sore and stiff but she welcomes the discomfort. She reaches over to check her cell phone. She has thirty-seven new text messages. Wow, thirty-seven new texts and not one from Josiah Bell. It's all fuckery from kids at the prom last night telling her how pretty she was, and thanking her for her dad funding their supercharged unforgettable prom to end all proms.

Jaze closes her eyes tightly as she relives the events of the night before. Her body begins to roll in her sheets as she licks her own sweet pink lips. In her mind she's still nestled perfectly in his arms. His arms that last night magically and delicately enveloped her tightly in their euphoric, seemingly never ending, serenity.

She opens her eyes smiling up at her ceiling fan spinning peacefully in lover's bliss. As she sits up, Jaze contemplates staying in bed forever as not to lose the beauty and the magnitude of the moments that transpired just hours ago right here in this very spot. She's sure that it goes without saying that Josiah Bell is now, finally, and forever her boyfriend.

Wait... what is... is that... yep that's blood! My blood!

Jaze suddenly feels all of her strength return to her body as she jumps out of bed and rushes to her bathroom to check her body. She can't understand for the life of her where the blood could have come from. It's on her inner thighs as well.

After googling a few things on her trusty smart phone Jaze understands perfectly. She quickly snatches her sheets off of her bed and balls them up by her bedroom door next to about fifty letters from colleges hoping she'll be playing basketball for them next season.

In the shower Jaze hums love songs softly as the passionate steam filled droplets rain down over her sore happy body.

This is the beginning of forever she thinks joyfully to herself.

(Days later)

A week went by after that morning and Jaze never heard from Josiah. He completely cut her off. He didn't respond by phone, email, or social media. A few more days pass and still no word from him.

It's been a long Friday and Jaze's mind has not taken a break all day. She's tired now, and it's the middle of the night but Jaze can't sleep at all.

There are only two things in this world she's ever been in love with, and that's basketball and Josiah Bell. She obviously can't have the latter so she rolls out of bed and grabs a pair of her old Jordan shoes and a pair of shorts to hoop in.

After she gets dressed she grabs one of her balls and quietly makes her way downstairs and grabs the keys to her bright blue BMW her dad just gave her for an early graduation present.

She could just shoot on her own goal but she knows full well she'll end up waking up the whole house.

So instead Jaze decides to head to the park. As she drives Jaze is hoping one day her heart can just fully recover from Josiah Bell. Her hope is there but she knows damn well he's always going to be right there... remaining a part of her like a pesky ghost or a tattoo on the back of her brain, forever reminding her just who she belongs to.

Hell that boy's life is tatted on every inch of her mind. A small part of her believes he might actually be thinking about her too.

Jaze pulls up to one of the twenty-four hour McDonald's restaurants. After buying a large Hi-C orange drink she heads to the outdoor court several streets over to shoot some hoops alone.

If the police attempt to bother her because she's there after hours, they'll leave her alone after they realize who she is.

"Damn It." Jaze says as she nears the court.

There's somebody already on the court.

"What an asshole," she grumbles to herself, "normal people should be sleep at this hour not in the park shooting a damn basketball."

Jaze parks the car, grabs her ball, and heads towards the court.

The closer she gets to the court Jaze's heart begins to sink deeper into her stomach.

"Stalker much..." he says.

"What the hell Josiah..." Jaze throws her ball at him hitting him directly on the top of his left shoulder.

Had he not flinched and jumped back the ball would have hit him in the face, her aim is exceptional.

"So you followed me just to **throw** shit at me?" he slings her ball back at her.

She catches it with no problem.

"What do you mean *follow* you...?" Jaze approaches him.

"I just got here not too long ago," he claims, "How else would you know to find me here?"

"First off asshole," Jaze steps closer, "I did not follow you, or come here looking for you. I came to shoot some hoops to clear my mind."

"Yeah I bet." He laughs.

"It's not funny Josiah," Jaze screams, "Where the hell have you been? And what the hell did I ever do to you?"

"Nothing." he says.

"So what was that..." she pushes him.

"What was what?" he holds a hand up to shield her from him.

"Really Jojo," she frowns hard, "Prom night..."

"Oh that," he smiles as he takes an awful shot at the goal, "It was fun... Thanks."

Jaze watches him as he retrieves his ball.

"Thanks," she glares through him, "You *do* realize I'm going to kill you right... like *literally* take your life?"

"I have a girlfriend Jaze," he reminds her, "You knew that before you let me smash."

"Is that what you did," she can't feel her face now, "you *smashed* me?"

"I mean yeah," he confirms, "It was cool though. No worries your shit is legit boo. And I didn't tell anybody I promise."

91

"Of course not, since you have *a girl*..." The chills running up and down Jaze's spine, and the shooting pain in the center of her brain are the only reasons she knows she's still alive.

"Yeah I do," he confirms again, "So is there a problem...?"

"A *problem*," Jaze steps nose to nose with his handsome young face, "Hell *yes* there is a problem. The things you said... that night, the way you held me... and what we did. *It meant... the world to me Josiah*..."

"Cool," he smiles after taking another bad shot, "that's wassup. We went hard on some *50 Shades* type ish right?"

"Don't flatter yourself fool." Jaze says as he chases down his ball yet again.

"Right." he says from near the goal.

"Well, there are plenty of goals out here so..." Jojo continues as he points to the other end of the court.

"Why are you with that *artificial* ass white bitch anyway Josiah?" Jaze openly ignore his obvious implication to go away.

"Why does it matter Jaze..." he starts.

"It matters Josiah," she cries, "It matters to me, because I know you don't love her."

"I do..." he claims.

"No, Jojo you really don't," she tells him, "You can't just fake the way you were with me that night. You ain't that smooth nigga. I'll play you for it…"

"Play me for what?" he asks.

"Your heart…" Jaze looks deep in Josiah's eyes.

"In what basketball?" he laughs.

"Yeah, what you scared white boy?" she taunts.

"Hell no," he claims, "but this ain't Love & Basketball Jaze, I suck… so if I play you for my heart… I might as well just get down on one knee and propose to you right now."

"I don't see you bending yet…" Jaze puts a hand on each hip.

"Not gonna happen Jazzy." He takes another terrible shot.

"Go to hell Josiah." Jaze spits.

"Not tonight," he continues, "Not tomorrow night… and not on any other *magical* night you *think* is just going to fall out of the damn sky."

"Damn Jojo…" Jaze wrinkles her brow.

"*Damn Jojo*," he mocks, "not gonna happen babe… but I am sorry."

"Sorry for what Josiah," she steps closer to him tears welling in her burning eyes, "Sorry for sneaking in my room, tricking me out of my virginity, and then ignoring me for nine days, twenty-three hours and forty-seven minutes? Or are you sorry that you're not man enough to admit how you really feel about me?"

"Tell me how I feel then Jaze," Jojo positions both arms behind his back, "Please by all means tell me how **the fuck** I feel…"

"I will…" She hesitates.

"Yeah… I'm waiting." He replies.

"You know what," Jaze shakes her head as the tears continue to fall, "Never mind. Point taken Josiah, I **don't** know. I honestly don't have a **fucking** clue **how** you feel. But I do know one thing; **everything** I've ever felt for you and wanted **with** you is some bullshit!"

She turns away from him with her ball clutched tightly to her stomach and begins running full speed towards her car.

"Jaze… Jaze wait!" he screams out.

She can't hear a word he's saying consumed by her seemingly permanent rage and fear.

The rage is embedded deep inside of her because of how stupid she was to fall in love with this fool as a little girl and never grow out of that childish love. The fear is at the forefront of her mind in this moment because she knows now life doesn't, and isn't going to turn out the way she planned.

Her life isn't like a movie. She isn't Monica Wright and she'll never have a soul mate as ruggedly perfect as Quincy McCall.

After kicking her car several times crying in powerful full force, Jaze opens the driver's side door. The door immediately slams back shut as she fills her entire body engulfed by his arms.

Jojo spins Jaze around towards him forcefully and then presses her back against her own car. With her head in his own hands he looks into the inner most parts of her being. Without a doubt that boy sees things in her eyes he's not willing to accept or admit.

"What Josiah..." Jaze cries.

"Shut up and kiss me..." he growls as he hungrily plunges his tongue between her submissive lips.

Josiah's mind is playing awful tricks on him. In a world where he could continue to grow and float through life on his good looks and charm alone... a world where he could be a successful bachelor for the next five to ten years of his life... his stupid heart is telling him to do quite the opposite.

If this kiss with Josiah could just last forever, Jaze could, and would die happily in his arms with his warm sweet breath and his powerful tongue inhabiting her welcoming mouth.

"Take it off..." He croons between sweet kisses.

Jaze reaches down and unties her large basketball shorts. After the knot is gone she allows them to fall down to her ankles.

Jojo immediately steps on her shorts with his right foot, and Jaze steps out of her shorts with her left foot only.

Jaze hopes this moment is exactly what forever feels like.

From his pocket Jojo pulls a red condom wrapper. He breaks the kiss for a second to bite the wrapper open. Once he has the rubber secure in his right hand he reignites the kiss.

Jojo pulls his own shorts down just far enough. Then with her left leg resting up on his right arm he takes her slowly.

"Josiah," she cries, "What if someone..."

"Let em watch," he smiles against her thirsty lips, "You belong to me."

"**Yes I do**..." she agrees with a tearful smile of her own.

With a sudden burst of strength Jojo lifts her up off the ground completely and allows her back to rest on her car.

Jaze wraps her ecstatic legs around him as he continues to rock up and down on his tip toes.

The pain is not quite as bad as it was the first time, but even if it was she wouldn't stop him. She would feel and endure the pain of their first time a million times over as long as she could feel it with him.

"Wait..." she whispers.

Jojo allows her feet to touch the ground again. Jaze reaches behind her and opens the back door of her car.

De'Lure

She pulls her shorts off of her right ankle and tosses them over the driver's seat into the front of the car. Then she climbs in the backseat of her car onto her back and awaits her crush.

Chapter 5
Graduation

After that night at the park with Josiah I didn't expect to hear from him. I knew full well I was just a booty call to him, but I guess part of me accepted that fact and just really didn't mind.

I got back with Bleek recently, and he's helped me make some major decisions. I start school next month at the U. The University of Miami has always been the school of my dreams even when I was a kid in Orlando. I'll be there for my education first and foremost but also to party my pretty little ass off...

As her classmates' names are being called and Jazemene Cole awaits her turn in line to receive her much deserved diploma she remembers the poem she was writing late last night when she couldn't go to sleep.

As I walk across that stage
I'll not give way to thoughts of rage
As my life turns to yet another page
Not a moment of my past I can change
So I power forward with the strength to forgive
I could end it all now and just kill or be killed
With the genes of my uncle I could prove duly skilled
Stepping into his shadow I know Lance would be thrilled
Josiah Bell's head and heart...

"*Jazemene Argelle Cole...*" The name rings out snapping her deadly thoughts.

Jaze walks confidently towards her principal Mr. Lamar A. Jones draped in a suit baring the school colors. He hands her the diploma as they pose for a picture, then he hugs her and it's all over.

After eighteen years of life, and twelve years of school all she gets is five seconds of recognition. As Jaze walks the rest of the length of the longish stage she looks out at all of the families and other members of her graduating class including the evil blue eyes of Josiah Bell. This moment feels like it should be a lot bigger, but she's slowly realizing the biggest part of it is already behind her.

(Hours Later)

At Jazemene's dad's house after graduation about forty members of her family and her dad's friends gathered to celebrate her big day.

Bleek is late but she's sure he'll show up at some point. Hell he wouldn't miss out on free steak and seafood.

"Jaze, baby," Whitney slurs standing near Charlie, "Mama, is so very proud of you baby girl."

"I think you've had enough hunny." Charlie takes Whit's drink away from her wandering left hand.

"Well," she snaps snatching her drink back, "*I think*... I'm grown as hell. Boy... do not play with me Charlie."

"This is Jazemene's graduation party," Charlie reminds Whitney as discretely as possible, "please don't make a scene. Your drinking has become a problem lately..."

"Jaze come here to mama baby..." Whitney beckons for her only daughter.

"Are you okay mama?" Jaze asks her mother.

"I'm fine girl," Whit slurs trying to keep her balance, "You are so pretty to me... Oh my goodness gracious girlie. Are you happy about today?"

"Yes mama." Jaze replies looking to Charlie for help.

"This is so weird," Whit laughs, "I'm standing here... looking at my daughter, my baby girl eye to eye. You used to be so little..."

"Yeah," Jaze agrees, "I'm eighteen now mama, I'm a grown woman. When people grow up they usually do just that literally as well..."

"Are you getting cute with me you little bitch...?" Whit snaps.

"Whitney give me that damn drink now!" Charlie reaches for it but misses.

"Yeah mama," Jaze looks from her to Charlie, "I uh think maybe you should give Charlie your drink I think you're embarrassing him..."

"Yeah mama," Whit mocks her daughter, "Your father ruined your little bougie ass, you're so weak. And you Charlie Breeze... are you embarrassed by me?"

"Are you serious," Jaze steps into her mother's face, "my father saved me, you are the one who almost ruined me by leaving me with no mother you sick bitch!"

"Oh shut up crying you little brat." Whit nudges Jaze backwards.

"Baby can you please just..." Charlie says reaching for the drink again stepping between Whit and Jaze.

"No," Whit raises her voice even more, "if you're embarrassed you... you little **crack dealer**, then you can just leave my rich, fine ass, baby daddy's mansion! You don't belong here anyway!"

"Fuck you Whitney." Charlie says pointing in her face.

Whit smacks his hand hard with her glass clearly injuring his right hand in the process.

Charlie rears back with his good hand.

"Hey man!" K.C. rushes over to snatch Whit out of the way of Charlie's impending slap.

"You like to hit women bruh," K.C. asks stepping in front of his woozy ex, "Hit me!"

"Are you serious dude," Charlie steps towards K.C., "my extremely intoxicated fiancé just pushed your daughter after cursing at her publicly... I stepped in between them and tried to take her drink for the fourth time, and you're running up on me?"

"Hit me!" K.C. exclaims.

"Hmm," Charlie grunts, "guess it's true; guess you are still in love with Whitney."

"Are you gonna swing or not asshole?" K.C. steps a bit closer.

"Nah I'm good bruh," Charlie throws his hands up in painful surrender, "she's a train wreck, you can have her."

After Charlie leaves, K.C. scoops Whit up and carries her into the house to lay her down.

Cameron notices the party has lost its flavor. She quickly grabs the microphone from the DJ.

"Hey everybody," Cam says into the loud microphone, "We are here to celebrate the graduation of my gorgeous and very gifted stepdaughter Jazemene Argelle, let's please focus on that. There's plenty more food and beverages in the kitchen if anybody needs anything."

(Upstairs in K.C. & Cam's bathroom)

In his gorgeous bathroom K.C. is kneeling over Whitney holding her hair back as she empties the contents of her drunken stomach into his once immaculate toilet. At this point she's only throwing up liquid and her throat and chest feel terrible.

K.C. leaves her side momentarily to fetch a cool wet towel to wipe her reddened face with.

Whit sits back on the floor in front of the toilet as her vomiting fit has come to an end at least for now.

"How did you get so drunk Suga Mama..." K.C. asks.

She shakes her head at him.

"I didn't even see you get that many glasses of anything since you got here." He recollects.

"I was drinking before I got here..." She admits.

"That explains that," K.C. sits down on the floor next to her, "but what's up with you and Charlie Boy... trouble in paradise?"

"I need to brush my teeth," Whit takes the wash cloth from K.C.'s hand, "I feel disgusting."

Whitney makes her way to her feet and then over to the sink.

"I'm guessing the toothbrush with the hearts on it is your wife's..." Whit asks.

"Uh yeah," K.C. replies standing to his own feet, "But I don't think you should..."

"Oh shut up Keldrick," she says putting toothpaste on the brush, "That girl and I have been through it all together this ain't the first time I've used her toothbrush."

"Oh right," K.C. steps closer, "On the island right?"

"Yep," Whit pulls the brush out of her mouth for a moment, "On the island. Why, are you jealous?"

"Maybe..." K.C. admits.

"Good." Whit looks deep in the mirror still trying to shake her terrible feeling.

"No, not good Whitney," K.C. steps closer to her, "You and Cam gave me so much shit about doing exactly what you both let that fucking Mexican do to you on that island!"

"First off," Whit turns to look at him, "Carlos is Puerto Rican, not Mexican. And I didn't know Cam was even on the island when I..."

"When you what Whitney," K.C. leans in, "When you ran away? When you said fuck me and our children and you abandoned me in the middle of planning our wedding that was damn near a decade in the making! Then after that I find out our son isn't even mine, and that little light skinned, green eyed mother fucker busts my balls every single day about that very shit!"

"I'm sorry Keldrick..." Whit looks down at the beautiful bathroom floor still very much drunk.

"You're sorry," he yells, "Hell no, Whitney hell no! That is not good enough. I don't really give a..."

K.C. stops his rant in midsentence as Whit reaches up and pulls her top down. Looking at her two perfect breasts K.C. can't help but reminisce on old times with his Suga Mama.

"Lemme make it up to you baby..." Whit says making it to her knees with ease.

K.C. doesn't try to stop her. He instead rests his back on the sink as Whit begins to take him slowly.

"I thought I heard yelling up here..." Cam pushes the door open to find her husband cheating on her.

"***Keldrick what the hell...***" Cam cries.

"Shut up and come help her out," he commands his wife, "hell you were doing it for Dr. Taco Meat."

Cameron Jiles Cole reluctantly obeys.

Chapter 6
A Wedding for Four

(Ty)

I'd much rather have my own private wedding ceremony, but I guess a wedding almost ten years in the making should be shared. Everybody thinks from the outside looking in my relationship with Osiana is just so perfect. It's not. Well maybe it is now, but it's been a very rocky road. I love that white girl to death, Lord knows I do but I'll die single before I let her dictate what our lives together can and cannot consist of. That's just not fair. She was so open years ago, and willing to trust me and let me be her man. But, now that I'm doing well for myself, and have been for quite some time, Osiana feels the need to flex her muscles and impose her will on my life and our relationship now more than ever. At first I thought it was just new and kind of cute, but then everything quickly went south and was completely out of hand. Osiana tried to take over my life and my company... hell the woman tried to be my man. I have to admit we should have been married about seven years ago, but every single time we set a date, life came around and slapped the shit out of us. One time my theme park was in a slump and the money wasn't quite right for the wedding Osi wanted. Another time she was angry at me and stressed because the doctor said my sperm count was too low to have kids. We both want children badly, but things happen. Anyway long story short, adding my best friend Jacody and his fiancé Cidra to the fold this go around will force me and my Osi to go through with everything no matter what. We have no intention on ruining their day with our eternal cold feet and excuses. Today is the day.

(Jacody)

Wedding bells huh? Man this is crazy. Everybody who knows me knows I love the ladies. I'm not supposed to be here right now. I'm not supposed to be wearing this suit, I'm not supposed to be considering having another child, and I'm not supposed to be standing here waiting on the most beautiful woman I know to walk down that aisle into my forever. No, this is exactly where I'm supposed to be. The number of particles in the entire universe is ten to the eightieth power, including all the galaxies there are one hundred octillion stars in the skies, and there are over seven billion people on our planet. The possibilities of the world around us are infinite, and out of all the scenarios that could have happened surrounding me and my wife to be... I'd be a damn fool not to admit at least to myself how eternally blessed I feel to have captured the heart, mind, body, and spirit of the one being God created just for me. Thank you Lord, I'll love, cherish, and respect my wife until you call me home into your precious Kingdom.

Both lost deep in their own separate minds, Ty and Jay are at the end of the aisle of Pastor White's glorious church sanctuary waiting for their brides.

K.C. is supposed to be outside in the lobby with the brides waiting to make his entrance.

"Are you sure this is what you wanna do," he whispers in Cidra's ear, "If you do this, you and I die today. It's over Cid."

"Are you serious right now," Cidra asks K.C. as quietly as possible, "Don't do this to me... Why can't you just let me be happy?"

"Come talk to me real quick..." K.C. heads towards a bathroom in the lobby, never even considering that Cidra wouldn't follow him.

Cidra Bell looks back at Osiana Blue, and then follows K.C.

Inside the bathroom Cidra awaits K.C. to speak.

He walks close to her.

"What the hell Keldrick," she fumes as quietly as possible, "Leave me alone, we both know damn well you're never going to marry me, so can you please just leave me..."

Before she can finish her statement he pulls her in his arms and begins to kiss her deeply and seemingly genuinely. Cuffing her round behind in his hands he forces Cidra to wrap her legs around him in her wedding dress as his massive arm lift her up.

K.C. spins around as gracefully as if he was back on an NFL football field dodging a tackler. Then he quickly pushes open the door to the closest stall. Once inside he sits Cidra on top of the back of the toilet.

He quickly unzips and unbuttons his pants and unleashes himself. Cidra has already pulled her dress up high enough for him.

K.C. positions himself perfectly, and then plunges in harder than ever before. He grabs hold of her mouth because he knows he's too much for her to handle all at once. He thrusts deeper and deeper.

The door opens.

"Cid," Osiana whispers, "We gotta go girl. Your business is your business, but I'm not going to let either one of ya'll ruin my day. Hurry up!"

"*Cooooooming*..." Cidra moans in painful bliss.

"*Oh, my, God... baby no*..." Cidra cries trying to keep her voice down.

K.C. looks behind him.

"Osiana," he smiles, "What the hell? Are you enjoying the show?"

"I am," she admits, "Just wanted to see what all the hype was about. Now can you please finish so me and *this one* can go become honest women... well at least *I'll* be an honest woman." Osiana smiles at Cidra through the crack in the stall door.

"Is that what you want Cid..." K.C. looks down into her eyes stroking as deep as he humanly can now.

"*What*..." Cidra cries.

"Are you going to marry Jacody?" K.C. asks.

"*Yes*..." she cries out.

"Cool." K.C. pulls out of her extremely wet center and grabs some tissue to wipe himself off.

Then he fixes his pants and belt as Cidra stares at him in silence.

"Welp," he smiles, "See you at the altar in ya white dress bitch."

After he's gone, Osiana rushes in the stall to catch Cidra as her body gives way.

"I got ya," Osiana says, "You're okay."

"Why are you helping me?" Cidra asks. "We barely ever hung out before the whole wedding thing." She continues.

"First off," Osiana says, "This is not a wedding thing, it's the beginning of the rest of our lives, and second we're both white girls who are in love with black men... so we gotta stick together. Now come on we are way past fashionably late."

(The Reception)

The wedding was exquisite and the reception is absolutely unforgettable. Tyrone refused to let K.C. pay for his and Jacody's wedding or any part of it. But they did both agree to let him pay for the reception, and boy did he pay for it.

Live statues and beautiful dancers are laced throughout the lively fenced in park. The reception theme is a winter wonderland, and even though it's the middle of the summer nobody at the gorgeous reception can tell. All thirty-six of the live statues and dancers are completely nude and masterfully painted from head to toe.

The men are all painted a strong shade of glistening ice blue, whereas the females are all painted to resemble pure white snowflakes. The beauty of them placed strategically throughout the park and interacting with each other is simply breath-taking.

Each statue has changed its pose every thirty minutes on the dot like clockwork. The beautiful blue and white bodies are all sculpted to perfection and they're definitely stealing the show.

The food of course is otherworldly as well. K.C. flew in three of the top chefs in the country and gave them all access to three separate top notch kitchens in Miami three days prior to the reception.

He paid for the hotel, transportation, and entertainment for their entire stay. With the three days each cook was given a specific style of food to cook.

They each had an ample staff and access to everything they would ever need to create a feast for the gods or a wedding reception for the best friends of Keldrick *"**Kool Hands**"* Cole.

The DJ for the reception needs no introduction and not even K.C. thought he could pull it off. He knows just how busy his wealthy friend of seven years now is. The one and only Dr. Dre showed up on time, in a magnificent mood, and looks to be on pace to spin live music all night long. Dre checks his watch, and then receives the nod from K.C. and lowers the music just a tad.

K.C. stands up with a wireless microphone in hand.

"Good evening," he says in that unmistakably deep voice, "Today I am… a **happy** man. I'm not perfect, and I never will be. I make mistakes, **terrible unforgivable** mistakes, just as we all have. But after I take time to think to myself I realize the error in my ways and I do everything in my power to make amends. Today my two best childhood friends joined me on this lifelong journey called marriage and I couldn't be happier for the two of them and their gorgeous wives. It's not every day a guy gets to be someone's best man, and today I get to be the best man twice at the same time. I love you both; you're my best friends… and my blood brothers."

"We love you too big bruh." Ty and Jay reply.

"To your wives," K.C. continues, "First Ms. Osiana Blue Carter… You are now my sister-in-law. I want to welcome you to the Carter and Cole extended family and know that if you or Ty ever need a thing I'm only a call or text away. **Please** call… I can't spend all this money in **three** lifetimes."

The crowd laughs feverishly.

K.C. looks over at Cidra Bell. Her heart stops at the sight of his mischievous smile. Cidra drops her head and awaits K.C. to out her and ruin the reception for everybody.

"Cidra Bell," he says into the microphone, "My old friend, and my daughter's elementary school teacher so many years ago… even though Jay doesn't share the same father as me and Ty, I still consider him my brother and you my sister-in-law. I know that you are everything any man could ever, **ever** dream of in a wife. Jacody is a very lucky man, and I pray nothing, **nothing** at all but blessings on

you and your marriage… may you satisfy him in all the ways you satisfied me… ***oops,*** damn. Wait I mean…"
The crowd gasps.
"Calm down everybody," K.C. laughs, "I didn't mean it like that. You see Cidra and I were very good friends even back before I signed my deal and moved here to Miami to play for the Dolphins. So, I just mean that the way she satisfied my need for a good friend, and a loyal confidant I know she'll be all that and more to my little brother Jacody."
Jay excuses himself from his seat and storms off. Ty kisses Osiana on the cheek and then follows Jacody outside of the park.
Ty finally catches up to Jacody.
"You good Jay…" Ty places a calming hand on his back as he leans on a bench on the outskirts of the park.
"Hell no I ain't good Ty!" Jay looks at his old friend.
"Let it go bruh," Ty tells him, "This is our day. That bullshit K.C.'s miserable ass is trying to pull in there man…"
"He fucked my wife at the wedding Ty!" Jay fumes.
"Blood of Jesus…" Ty covers his mouth with an unsure hand.
Jay shakes his head and looks off into the distance.
"So," Ty says, "When you say at the wedding… You mean like ***at the wedding***?"
"Nigga right there at our wedding!" Jay stresses.
"Wait, how is that shit even possible at a wedding?" Ty asks.
"Trust me it's possible." Jay assures him.
"How do you know it happened for sure fam?" Ty lowers his voice and steps closer to Jay noticing some of the live

statues near the edge of the park eavesdropping on their clearly private conversation.

"It doesn't matter how I know Ty," Jay cries, "I shouldn't have to know! ***There should be nothing to fucking know in the first damn place***!"

"Cidra," Ty says, "She told you? She might be lying bro... You know women like to make us jealous sometimes. A lie ain't nothing for a woman to tell, I don't care who she is."

"What about Osiana," Jay wipes new tears away, "Is she a liar too?"

"Oh nah," Ty replies quickly, "My wife doesn't lie period. We've been together way too long for all that bullshit."

"Okay." Jay replies.

"Wait my nigga," Ty turns Jay around to face him, "Are you telling me that K.C. hit both of our wives at the wedding on some freaky white girls gone wild threesome type shit?"

"What," Jay asks, "Hell no Ty. Osiana told me about Kel and Cid. She said she walked in on them doing it in the bathroom, right before they came down the aisle to marry us."

"Blood of Jesus..." Ty says.

"I know right..." Jay laughs awkwardly through his tears.

"Osiana is ***my*** wife though," Ty says, "Why the hell she ain't tell me what was going on?"

"I don't know Ty," Jay frowns, "But she didn't have to tell me shit. Did you notice how late they were coming down the aisle? My biggest clue was the smug satisfied look on Kel's face, and his zipper was only half way up. But the final straw was when my wife stood next to me before

God smelling like dick and balls and pure nasty bathroom sex!"

"What the hell Jacody," Ty steps close to him, "If you knew all this crap... why the **hell** did you go through with it?"

"Why did I go through with the wedding?" Jay asks.

"Yeah bro," Ty confirms, "we could have just..."

"No," Jacody interjects, "I'm a grown ass man Tyboonie. I was not going to ruin your day. A day you and Osi have been waiting on for **so** long. Hell no bro, this day was bigger than me."

"But you **had** to know K.C. and Cid had been messing around before today, I know you knew bro..." Ty says.

"I had no proof Ty," Jay explains, "I never had any real proof until today. But you know what..."

"What bro?" Ty shakes his head.

"The biggest reason I went through with the wedding is because I can't let that son of a bitch win," Jay claims, "Cid is my **wife** now, so **I** win and K.C. will **never** ever touch her again or set foot in my house. He will never be welcome in my home Ty. And if he ever does show up I'll shoot him dead and then call the police myself."

"Fellas..." K.C. smiles walking towards them from the park exit.

Jay turns to look at him with pure poison in his stare.

"Damn." K.C. steps back, "Was my speech that bad?"

"**Ahhh**!!!" Jacody rushes K.C. full speed tackling him to the ground.

Once they stop sliding across the rough ground Jacody sits up on K.C.'s broad chest and hit him several times in the mouth.

K.C. doesn't attempt to swing back or defend himself as he eats each punch.

"Don't stop now," K.C. demands, "destroy my ugly black ass face! You hate me don't you? Do us both a favor and kill me then!"

"You're sick." Jay says standing up.

"Don't be a pussy Jacody," K.C. taunts through a bloody bottom lip, "I fucked your wife right before she walked down the aisle and married you... I don't deserve to live... Kill me!"

"You know what Keldrick, you *don't* deserve to live you son of a bitch," Jay agrees, "But you don't deserve to die either. I want you to live every day with all the evil shit you've done screaming inside your sick mind! I won't be the one to do you the favor of taking your miserable ass life. But know this, we ain't friends, we ain't brothers... we ain't shit."

Jay straightens his suit and heads back inside his wedding reception.

Ty shakes his head at K.C. and then follows Jay back inside the park.

Chapter 7
College
(Jaze)

I'm twenty years old now and the last few years flew by way to fast. It was totally worth it though; college is extremely fun. And I honestly don't think fun is even an adequate word for me to describe this experience anymore. Unless of course fun has levels, because if fun has levels then this grossly surpasses whatever the top level of fundom is. I spend most of my time with a super cool gay guy named Cruz. Besides him, I have two girls I hang out with real heavy. I have three suitemates in my dorm, but only two of them have personalities that can coexist with mine for longer than a ten-minute span. The fourth girl doesn't want to be around me because she feels she won't get any attention from the guys on campus. I don't understand why she wouldn't, hell I'm not in the way. I don't want them; I mean I flirt at times but I belong to Bleek. He sleeps and lives in my room every single night. Well I guess that's an exaggeration he does get missin' sometimes. But after he gets tired of the streets he always finds his way back home to mama. It's cool, he has no worries. I'm the kind of woman that understands that men wander, that's just what they do. I never nag or complain I just stay, like a good woman should. I have my man's back and that will never change. I grew up in a similar situation so it's all too familiar to me. I don't remember everything because I was really young, but I do remember my mama crying while rocking back and forth in her bed at night holding me tightly. I understand now that my mother was holding me because she was missing my daddy. He had already been in prison for several years, and then he came out knowing my mother was waiting for him and still treated her like crap. So because of his disregard for my mother's heart she eventually became this super obsessed, violently angry, secret detective hell bent on forcing my dad to marry her or die. I blame them both. I blame my mom because she had plenty of opportunities to move on but she refused to. I blame my dad because his coward ass should have just left mom alone for good if he didn't want her, and just dealt with the child support situation he was dodging. I honestly don't think my mother would have ever actually put him on child support. She loved him way too much to actually ever hurt him, and low-key I think she still does. There's something really strange going on between my mom, my dad, and his wife Cameron. The night of my graduation I snuck up to my dad's room and through the crack of the bathroom door I saw him...

"*Jazemene* Cole," the voice startles her, "*hey boo*! Where have you been all my life?"

"Hey Cruz..." Jaze smiles at her flamboyant friend.

"Girl," he leans in close, "Were you over here day dreaming again?"

"I was," she admits, "I don't know... my mind just wanders all over the place every time I'm alone."

"I told you girl," Cruz pats her knee like an older auntie or cousin might, "You need a man..."

"Cruz," she starts, "I have a..."

"No ma'am," he interjects, "I mean a real man. You need one of these fine ass young steeds on this college campus, not your thrown away ass high school boyfriend who is a phone call away from being banned from this campus for living here and not **actually** attending our fine institution of higher learning... **The University** of **Miami. Go Canes**."

"Really boy," Jaze can't help but smile at his diction and energy, "All that though? And did you just call the men on campus young steeds? Aren't those like horses or something? And you better not call and tell a**nybody** about my Bleek living in my room."

"Whatever," Cruz rolls his neck, "If he brings me one of his thug ass homeboys that's down with the life... Then **maybe** I won't."

"Now you know that's never going to happen, Cruz," Jaze laughs loudly, "Nice try though."

"It was cute right..." he says with his mouth twisted tight to the left side.

"Very cute," Jaze agrees standing up from the table, "Just like this outfit boo. What are you wearing **today**?"

"Oh you like this," Cruz stands up to check himself out, "**Yes girl**, these are leather drop crotch pants... they were made by Fendi. **Very** exclusive boo. The shoes are Fendi as well. And what is this... piece that you're wearing **again** today Ms. Jazemene..."

Jaze looks down at her plain pants and shirt.

"I uh..." she hesitates to finish her statement.

"**Look** a mess," Cruz interjects, "You **do** realize you're rich right, and your **best** friend is gay **and** an aspiring fashion designer..."

"I know how to dress Cruz," Jaze reminds him, "I just..."

"Say no more," he interjects with a stiff hand to her face, "We've had this discussion **way** too many times before. Bleek says this and Bleek says that. I could fill an ocean with the bullshit your dumbass boyfriend says girl..."

"I don't understand, what's wrong with my man caring how I look in public..." Jaze grand stands as they leave the table to make their way into a nearby building.

"That was not a serious question." Cruz stops to look at his intelligent but socially clueless friend.

"It was a very serious question," Jaze assures him, "What the hell is wrong with my man being concerned about what I wear?"

"Well Jazemene," Cruz shakes his longish hair, "When that **man** of yours doesn't buy your clothes and you instead are the one who supports and takes care of his broke ass, he should never open his mouth to say a **mother fucking** thing about what you wear at all."

"Point taken..." Jaze says after processing what her friend said for a few quiet and awkward moments.

"Girl, **please**," Cruz replies, "I don't wanna hear that mess. Ya'll are all the same...?"

"What the hell does that mean Cruz," Jaze frowns, "All of who are the same?"

"Black women," Cruz contends, "Women in general who date men who don't give a damn about life. People who can see the chaos that is your life from the outside try their damndest to get you to see the foolishness that is your life. You don't listen and then even when you do, you're only pretending to listen just to placate whoever is failing to help you in that particular moment. It's sad really."

"I love you Cruz." Jaze has no idea what else to say.

"Whatever grrr, I love you too light bright," He hugs her tightly; "Now let's go eat something fat, I gotta put some meat on your poor bones **ASAP**."

(Whitney's House)

As Charlie takes her deeper now, Cam spreads her legs even farther apart as she lies on her strong back. She's never been much of a multi-tasker so it's hard for her to concentrate on keeping her lower body open and at the right angle for Charlie to strike with ease, while Whitney is riding her beautiful black face. Cam knows full well her primary job is to satisfy Whitney, so she's trying to just focus on that. With her dark masterful hands gripping her girlfriend's perfect yellow behind Cam sucks and eats Whitney's body into constant orgasmic convulsions.

As Whitney grinds and gently bounces on Cameron's beautiful face her hands clamped firmly on her headboard are becoming more numb by the second, but she doesn't care.

The best sex she and Charlie ever have is when their gorgeous little sex slave is over here with them. It's usually the best when the two love birds are angry with each other. For one they can make each other jealous by focusing all their attention on Cameron instead of each other, and they can and both do go hard on Cam most times taking their sexual frustrations and their usual state of secret unhappiness out on Cameron's body.

No worries though, Cameron loves every second of it. The best sex in her life now is also with them. Her husband, K.C. barely touches her anymore after almost ten years of marriage.

Cam is hurt by K.C.'s lack of interest in her sexually but she does understand that at forty years old Keldrick is trying to relive his glory days and he doesn't know how to just age gracefully and bow completely out of the fast life of NFL stardom.

So instead of nagging and complaining Cam just pretends to go workout three times a week and makes her way to Whitney and Charlie's house and blissfully obeys their every command from the moment she's inside their home.

Whit's sweet juices are dribbling down the sides of Cameron's mouth and chin now, but Cam can't free her tongue from her girlfriend's body enough to catch her precious love nectar before it runs all the way down her face to the expensive pillows she bought them recently. Cam smiles as she realizes how excited the female love of her life is, she's always wet, but never like this.

"**Cam**..." Whit cries out.

"**Mmmhm**..." Cam moans happily as Charlie continues to stroke between her now shaking legs.

"*I'm gonna turn around on your face*..." Whit tells her as she lets go of the stunning oak headboard.

Now facing Charlie, who's on his knees in the middle of the bed long stroking Cameron, Whit leans forward arching her back, with the bottom of her firm buttocks resting on the top of Cam's forehead.

With each of her yellow hands fastened tightly on Cam's surgically perfected breasts, Whit begins to bounce up and down on Cam's tongue and mouth gently to the beat of the slow jams playing through their new bedroom entertainment center. The entertainment center like most everything in the house is courtesy of Cameron, by way of one of Keldrick's massive bank accounts.

Charlie looks up at his girlfriend's face and closed eyes and realizes when he looks into her eyes while eating her himself, he never sees her look as happy and achingly close to ultimate satisfaction as she does now.

Hell she never closes her eyes period when Charlie eats her. Watching her moan while licking and biting her own firm pink lips, Charlie can feel himself about to burst at the seams.

After taking himself out of Cameron, amidst her disappointed groans Charlie climbs through her spread legs and opens Whitney's eyes to the most passionate kiss she's ever known.

Charlie's kiss alone elicits Whit's next few powerful orgasms. Whitney knows now in this moment again for sure that this man lives only to please her.

"You belong to me now and forever..." Charlie growls with his lips still pressed against hers.

"I know daddy..." Whitney moans still bouncing on Cameron's wet submissive mouth.

Charlie breaks the kiss as he stands up in front of Whit in the bed. He lets himself hang down and hit his woman in her beautiful face.

Whit grabs him gently and then quickly pulls the wet condom off the great length of him. No longer able to bounce with a new task at hand, Whit begins to simply grind on her girlfriend's face.

Charlie pushes Whit's head back so that she can look up at him.

"I want your tonsils..." he says.

"They belong to you bae..." she moans as she reaches forward to rub Cam's warm wet center in a perfect circular motion.

"Open your mouth..." Charlie growls, with a strong hand on each of his muscular hips.

Whit obeys with her longish tongue protruding from her mouth. Charlie stuffs himself in her mouth and then deeper into her throat. With each stroke Whit battle the sensation to gag on the girth and length of him.

She can handle it; she's done it so many times before it should come naturally to her now. She's old enough to know some things will never be easy though.

She chokes.

Charlie gently slaps her. Whit knows exactly what that love tap means. Anytime she gags on him Charlie slapping her means suck it up, and keep going. Charlie wants her to choke to the point she forgets Cameron is even in the room. He's even deeper now. Charlie reaches down to Whit's face to wipe the passionate tears from her eyes.

Whit pushes him out of her mouth.

"You love me baby..." she says looking in Charlie's eyes as she climbs off of Cameron's face.

"**Yes**." Cam moans.

"**She was talking to me you slut**..." Charlie growls at his slave.

Cam smiles at the obviously angry Charlie.

"**I know**." Cam admits.

"Play nice children..." Whit says grabbing one of the large nearby pillows. Whit lies on top of the length of the pillow facing her two gorgeous lovers.

"What you doin' babe," Charlie wrinkles his brows, "You done?"

"I am," she confirms, "but you're not."

"If you're done, I'm done..." Cam and Charlie say in unison.

"No you're not," Whit says, "neither one of you. Now, Charlie I want you to fuck Cameron silly. Give her everything you have. You don't stop fucking her until I cum from watching the two of you together."

"**Now**!" Whitney stares a hole through Cameron.

Cam looks down at Charlie and knows she'll have to do a little work before he'll be ready to follow his woman's orders adequately.

Up on her black knees the gorgeous Nubian goddess begins to lick the length of Charlie's almost soft member. After gently biting the head of him, she playfully flicks her tongue all over the tip of him.

Cam then takes the base of him in her left hand as she makes her way down to his love sack. After playfully fondling his scrotum Cam takes each one of them in her mouth. She can see him growing stronger now. Back up firmly on her knees Cam reaches around behind him just above his toned behind and pulls him forward into her hungry impatient mouth.

"Louder," Whit moans from her back now pleasuring herself, "I wanna hear you suck it..."

"What I tell you baby..." Charlie moans smiling at Whit.

"If you ain't making no noise you ain't sucking it right..." she replies spreading her precious lips apart with her already wet fingers.

Cameron begins to suck and slurp with new force and precision. Charlie is trying hard to make her choke so he can slap her. Nothing would satisfy him more than to smack the hell out of his future wife's preferred lover.

No matter how hard and deep he goes Cam takes him on with no problem. Charlie looks over at Whit with amazement at what their whore is able to do. The lusty glossed over look in Whit's eyes tell Charlie everything he needs to know.

"Turn around..." he growls pushing Cameron off of him.

Cam turns around but makes sure to turn her head towards Whitney. Charlie straps on another condom from the small nearby pile of sexual goodies and then takes Cameron hard from the back as Whit enjoys the view.

(Keep your eyes on the road)

"Have you given any thought to what kind of car you want yet son...?" K.C. asks K.J.

"First off," K.J. looks at K.C., "I'm not your..."

"You're not my son," K.C. interjects, "Okay I get it Keldrick! You think I wanna hear you say that every single time we have a conversation?"

"Apparently you do," K.J. frowns, "Since you keep calling me son."

"You are my son!" K.C. contends.

"I'm not!" K.J. replies strongly.

"So you have another dad right..." K.C. says.

"Yeah, **you know** I do!" K.J. confirms.

"Where the hell is he," K.C. asks, "What homework did he help you do, what project did he stay up all night helping you create just for you to lose it before you could turn it in... and what the hell bill is he paying to help keep you alive and well."

K.J. stops at a red light. His silence is deafening.

"I don't want to fight with you boy," K.C. tells him, "but although I'm an adult, I have feelings too. You pouting around my house denying that I'm your father and talking crazy to me... That is not cool at all Keldrick Jr."

The light turns green, K.J. resumes driving.

"Don't get quiet now boy," K.C. says, "You had so much to say just a second ago."

"Never mind..." K.J. mumbles.

"Nah hell no," K.C. raises his voice, "You and your sister got so much damn mouth, and ya'll ain't never wanted for shit. I made sure you both will be comfortable

127

for the rest of your lives but you're both spoiled and ungrateful. Now my question was... Have you given any thought to what kind of car you want?"

"I barely know how to drive I'm only fifteen," K.J. reminds him, "that's like picking out a book before you even know how to fucking read..."

"Tell you what you lil' smart mouth mother fucker you," K.C. fastens his seatbelt and sits back, "I'ma buy yo smartass a book instead of a car then. In fact, your stepmother has a whole collection of De'Lure books at home you can have one of those. Drive that, you ungrateful little bastard."

K.J. looks at K.C. with wide eyes.

"Don't look at me now," K.C. tells him, "keep your eyes on the road."

Chapter 8
Practice Makes Perfect

Jaze is hard at work on campus in the gym with her teammates, but she can't quite focus, as she lost deep inside her own thoughts trying to understand her life.

(Jaze)

I'm getting out of shape. I've never gotten tired this fast in my life. These girls are running circles around me. I don't train myself the way I used to, I'm getting lazy as hell, or maybe I'm just losing my love for the game. Probably a little bit of both, but when you imagine your whole life and spending it with one person for so long... it takes a major toll on you when you finally realize they don't and never will want the same thing you do.

"Okay ladies let's shoot some free throws." Coach yells out after blowing her whistle twice.

Jaze lines up near the baseline of the goal on the south end of the court to wait her turn. Coach is watching her closely.

Her teammate hits the first shot. They all clap twice.

She puts the second shot up a little too quickly and misses badly. The team claps once.

"Your turn Cole." The coach takes the ball and throws it to Jaze.

"No it's not coach its Brittney's turn." Jaze throws the ball back to the coach.

"Brittney, go switch places with Cole." Coach instructs the tall Caucasian center.

Brittney obeys.

"Now it's your turn Cole." Coach says tossing Jaze the ball again.

Jaze catches the ball a second time and now walks to the free throw line with a smug look on her face.

"Oh you have an attitude," Coach asks, "Everybody on the line now! Every time you miss a free throw Jazemene Cole, the whole team is gonna run."

"Coach I'm not in the mood for this." Jaze bounces the ball hard against the floor.

"Shoot the ball Cole." the coach blows her whistle again as the team lines up on the baseline.

The gym door opens.

"You almost done bae," Bleek asks from across the gym, "I'm tired as hell."

"You're tired," Coach takes a strong step towards the thuggish young man approaching her court, "what is it that you're tired of sir, because you look to me like you don't do anything."

"Shut up talking to me *dike*," Bleek says, "I'm in the car Jaze; I'm dippin' in five minutes *wit* or *witout* you."

"Get the hell out of my gym *asshole*," Coach points to the door, "And Cole you go with him I can see why your attitude is so poor lately."

Jaze kicks the ball down to the far end of the court and then storms out after her angry boyfriend.

(Mama's Girl)

130

After a long trying week Jazemene decided to stay the weekend at her mother's house. The weekend was much needed. Jaze endured her mother as much as possible, and though she'd never admit it she enjoyed their time together Friday and Saturday.

It's Sunday evening now, and the plan is for Jaze to go back to her dorm tonight. This way she'll be there on campus for class in the morning.

Jaze is trying to rid herself of all the negative and draining thoughts in her mind. Nothing she's tried has worked.

(Jaze)

My mother's an A.K.A. And everybody knows my mother's an A.K.A. How does everybody know that? Because she'll never let any of us forget it. Whether it's the constant unnecessary meetings she has, or the excuses to fly across the country for a pearl counting convention, or the fact that literally everything the woman owns is either pink or freakin' green. Don't misunderstand me I love my mother and the sorority. I also love the fact that because of my gorgeous mother being a member of Alpha Kappa Alpha Sorority Incorporated I'm considered legacy. So, if I so choose to answer her challenge and pledge I'm a shoe in to cross with flying colors. But I think I want to follow in my stepmom Cam's footsteps and become a Delta instead. The Greek fraternities and sororities that African Americans founded so long ago have grown so much over the years and are recognized and respected globally. Each one is laced with its own rich traditions and history that anybody who is connected to them should feel immensely proud of. I want to pledge something, for the simple fact that I know my affiliation with a sorority will open doors for me in the business world in the future. Yes, I am very wealthy but I refuse to spend any more of my father's money once I graduate. I'm going to build my own life and fortune independent of his success.

"Ready to go baby girl…" Whit sticks her head in Jaze's designated room at her house.

"Guess so," Jaze sighs trying to ignore her mother's pink and green shirt, "mom, do you own any other clothes?"

"What's the matter with you," Whit sits next to Jaze on her neat bed, "Where did that come from?"

"I'm sorry." Jaze shakes her head and then lies on her mother's ample bosom.

"I just don't know what to do." Jaze admits.

"About pledging?" Whit asks to be sure.

"I just feel so much pressure coming from so many different directions…" Jaze explains.

"What different directions," Whit asks, "Is Cam pushing you to pledge Delta?"

"What," Jaze looks up at her mother, "no, she's…"

"Because damn it I play about *a lot* of things," Whit stands up from the bed, "but you are *my legacy.* There is *no* pressure and there is only *one* direction. You were born into this *and I*…"

"*I, I, I,*" Jaze screams, "Damn it mama do you *hear* yourself? Are you really gonna sit up here and continue to act like one of those *crazy obsessed white dance moms*?"

"I'm not acting like them…" Whit steps close to Jaze.

"Yes you are," Jaze screams, "Damn it…"

"Do not use that language in *my* house," Whit points at Jaze, "You may be twenty but you are still a child in *this* house."

"*Your house*," Jaze laughs, "really lady? This ain't your house; show me a bill you pay. Please, I'll sit here and wait. Please, please show me where you paid anything since you've been here for the past *ten damn years*!"

"This is my house," Whit tries to stifle her building emotions, "*I* live here, and this is *my* house. I *deserve*…"

"You deserve what Whitney," Jaze laughs again, "Because my father is rich and successful, you think you deserve to live free? You got life fucked up!"

"Jazemene Argelle Cole…" Whit can't believe her ears or eyes.

"Right," Jaze grand stands, "Now I'm the asshole right? *Get a life*. The only reason you have this house is because of me. I *would* say because of my brother and I… *But* we both know your *whoring* around created the puzzle that is my baby brother's paternal situation. Good job mom, *really* awesome."

Three warm tears are visible on Whitney's reddening face.

"And *another* thing," Jaze steps close to her mother, "I'm angry for good damn reason so you can copy, paste, and delete those crocodile tears. I asked you *five* times to *not* email me the A.K.A. newsletter every day, I never asked for you to send me the magazines, or

133

anything else you keep forcing on me... You make me hate that I ever tried to reconnect with you. **Yes,** there is pressure, and the majority of it is from you!"

"Okay," Whit steps back wiping her tears away, "Okay, I um... I don't blame you for your words or your anger. I'm **not** your enemy Jazemene. I love you, and I am so **very** proud of you... I want you to be a part of my organization because it will help..."

"It will help **you,**" Jaze screams, "not me mother! It will help **you** sleep at night; you spend every waking second trying to find ways to live for and through me. **It's sick! Stop it, now!**"

"We need counseling Jazemene," Whit tries to stroke her daughter's hair, "I think you're still dealing with unresolved issues that I had hoped we buried years ago..."

"You **think...** I'm dealing with **unresolved issues,**" Jaze pushes her mother away from her, "**You, my mother** abandoned me to run off to a magical island to be a **sex slave**. Hoeing here in the states wasn't enough for you anymore; nope you had to take your act global. I hate you, as much as I damn tried to love you and everything about you... mama I can't and I don't think I'll ever truly love or forgive you. I can't. I'm way too smart to listen and continue to pretend to fall for all of your incredibly stupid and selfish excuses. If you didn't want to be with my father... and you were planning on running away, why did I never... Why didn't taking me with you ever cross your **fucking** mind mom?"

"I'll be in the car," Whitney cries, "It's getting late and I need to get you back to your dorm."

"**_Fuck_** that dorm mom," Jaze cries, "And **_fuck_** you for coppin' out! Why is it that so many women, especially my black women play the victim role so damn much? You don't win today **_lady_**; you are **wrong**... You've **been** wrong!"

"**_Damn it Jazemene_**," Whit exclaims, "Shut the hell up and get out of my house!"

"This isn't your house you **_slut_**!" Jaze fumes.

WHAP!!!

Whit slaps Jaze so hard she falls back across her once perfectly made bed.

"It's true," Jaze cries, "I'm not stupid mom! When dad bought you this house ten years ago... he said after you got stable, **_you_** and Charlie would foot your own bills! You aren't rich Whitney, you don't work, and neither does your man!"

"Shut up!" Whit screams boiling with rage.

"So I thought about it long and hard," Jaze climbs back out of her bed, "And decided to do a little financial research on my dad's accounts. I saw where Cam has been taking care of your sorry ass for all these years! I also went through her phone and saw all your disgusting pictures and messages back and forth!"

"No..." Whit cries taking an uneasy seat on her daughter's now disheveled bed.

"Yeah Whitney," Jaze stands over her mom, "I know all about your secrets."

"Leave me alone Jazemene..." her mother cries.

"Hell no," Jaze replies hitting her mother hard across the face, "That's for every careless and inconsiderate fucking thing you ever did to me, my brother, and my father!"

Whitney doesn't move or respond.

"Stop being weak and get up Whitney!" Jaze nudges her mom's limp leg.

"*Mama*..." Jaze cries out.

(Ty and Osiana)

"Ty please get off the phone..." his wife asks from the hotel bathroom.

"One second baby," he says, "There's a problem at the park."

"There's always a problem at the park," she steps out of the bathroom, "We are on vacation. You sir are supposed to be unavailable for three more days."

"Roger," Ty says into the phone, "That is **not** how we do business. No, I don't... look I don't care if the fat lady is wrong, she's a customer so she's always right. Now **refund** her and let her enjoy the park for free..."

"Baby..." Osiana whines standing in front of her new husband in nothing but a thong and heels.

"Listen Roger," Ty ignores his wife, "it's okay. Her fat ass is gonna buy enough food while at the park to recoup the lost cash from the three refunded ticket sales. She's not beating me; I own the park, so I'll always win in the end."

"I know how to get you off that damn phone..." the ex-detective smiles kneeling down in front of his chair.

"You do it," Ty says into the phone, "to let her think she's winning Rog... **oh, baby... damn**. I gotta go Roger." Ty throws his phone on the bed and then gently grabs the back of his wife's beautiful blond head to guide her to success.

Chapter 9
Drop Out

(The Real MVP)
(Jaze)

This is the longest walk in my life. Five more steps and all of my childhood dreams die and in turn my unavoidable impending decisions will give birth to my new reality. I realize that I, like most young women in my generation have more relationship goals than career goals. I can't have and raise kids, and be there for my future family while juggling my life as a professional basketball player. There are so many obvious obstacles that I don't want to face, so I won't.

Jaze knocks on her coach's door.

"Come in..." the coach says.

As Jaze steps inside the office she's sat in so many times before, she can't hide the anxiety on her open reddening face. This time much like the very first time Jaze ever sat in this office, Jaze is consumed with nerves she doesn't understand how to control.

Coach is dressed from head to toe in team clothing as always. Her dark brown hair is pulled back into a ponytail that allows you to focus on the serene nature of her unforced beauty. Coach knows something is terribly wrong with her star player, she can sense it.

"Are you pregnant Cole?" Coach asks.

"No ma'am." Jaze frowns.

"There's something wrong," the coach stands up behind her desk, "Is somebody bothering you Cole, because for you I'll kick their asses off the team effective immediately. Just say the word... who is it Kaley, Lindsay... no I bet it's that bitch Stephanie isn't it?"

"No," Jaze laughs lightly, "Calm down please. I'm not pregnant, and nobody's bullying me, but I do appreciate the fact you would go that far for me coach."

"Well," the coach smiles, "legally I can't. But I could make them run laps until they quit. But hell yes honey I'd go the extra mile for you... you're the best player I've ever coached. It's very rare that a player as skilled as you, and naturally athletic as you are, with a high basketball I.Q. is as coachable as you are. You are every coach's dream Jazemene." sadly

"I know you keep telling me that," Jaze smiles down at her own feet, "which is why this is so hard for me to do what I have to do..."

"And what is that Cole?" the coach asks.

"I quit coach." Jaze tells her.

"You gotta be pregnant," the coach yells, "Just tell me Jazemene!"

"I swear to God I'm not pregnant coach." Jaze claims.

"Then why are you quitting my team Jazemene Cole?" she asks.

"I don't wanna be a career tomboy," Jaze says, "The WNBA will never pay me what I know I'm worth coach. So, my boyfriend and I believe..."

"Boyfriend," Coach says, "That idiot who interrupted my practice the other day? Jazemene why are you with that asshole? You can do…"

"So much better," Jaze interjects, "I know, I know coach. I've heard it all before, and if Prince Charming is going to swoop in and magically sweep me off my feet he sure is taking his sweet damn time."

Coach shakes her head.

"There's just not enough money in the sport to obligate my entire life to it coach…" Jaze claims.

"But you're already rich girl!" the coach exclaims.

"No, **my father** is rich." Jaze explains

"Save it Cole," the coach says, "I know the whole spiel about not wanting to live off your rich father's money, and you wanna get it on your own. I also understand how professional sports, is a man's world, and it's not lucrative enough for females in many cases. Well you know what, that doesn't apply to you little girl. You are the most transcendent player I've ever coached or seen in my life, and I've been in this game a long time Jazemene. Yes, women don't make the money men do in pro sports, and yes it can get hard once you have kids and a family, but you are the type of rare talent that is good enough to change the sports world forever."

"Maybe so Coach Miller," Jaze stands up to leave, "But I won't be changing the sports world in this lifetime."

De'Lure

(Jaze and Bleek)

As they ride along the almost busy streets of Miami Jaze is lost in her thoughts yet again. She doesn't have to concentrate on anything because Bleek's always driving. He always controls her steering wheel and not just in the literal sense. She does whatever Bleek says or wants.

Jaze has cornered herself with a real fear of loneliness. Her fear of being alone coupled with her fear of the break up backlash she'll undoubtedly receive, from her Facebook friends, as well as her Instagram and Twitter followers after posting countless pictures and statuses with and about her perfect boyfriend who's anything but.

Bleek turns the music down and taps Jaze on the top of her head.

"Where you at boo?" he asks.

"Damn, you been so spaced out lately." He tells her.

"Oh nah," she fakes a smile, "I'm fine baby."

"You sure," he asks, "cuz we almost at your dad's crib."

"Yeah I'm straight," she lies, "everything is just happening so fast you know... but I'm ready to come clean with my dad about everything."

"Cool," Bleek smiles flashing his new bottom grill, "I'ma come in with you though boo. I don't want nothing to go wrong."

"I can handle it baby." Jaze tells him.

"Trick, what I say?" Bleek glares down at her.

"Okay King Bleek." She mumbles.

141

(At the mansion)

(Jaze)

As I step inside my father's cold mansion I can't help but succumb to an old awkward feeling. From the doorway I stare at the very spot where I stood urinating on myself at my birthday party so many years ago. I remember rushing up to my room strongly considering suicide. I tore off and threw my expensive new dress and shoes out of my upstairs window down onto the front lawn. After deciding jumping out of my window head first would prove way too painful if I was unlucky enough to survive the fall, I instead jumped in the shower to wash the foul piss smell off of my panic ridden body. My arms and whole body were wound so tightly because of the mental strain my insecurities placed on me. With all my strength I could barely reach up to the top of the shower rack to fetch my towel to bathe myself with. Not long after my shower while I lie there sulking painfully in my bed, a voice came to me from the other side of my bedroom door. It was the only voice I wanted to hear, the only voice that could possibly comfort and save me. Josiah Bell had shown up late to my tragic birthday party to fix as much damage as he could. He spent the rest of the day with me singlehandedly creating one of my sweetest memories to date. The only one sweeter was when he came though that same window I contemplated diving through to take my own life, and he waited for me after prom... Then he kissed me and took me with him on a sensual journey to my unforgettable physical awakening. Now I stand here on the base floor of my father's castle hand in hand with a boy, a man who is nothing close to Josiah Bell. Life isn't perfect and it doesn't play out or end like romance novels do, but you can't pout or even spend a second stressing about what could have or should have been... you just settle and play the cards you're dealt, especially if you don't have a strong hand to begin with.

"Dad, where are you..." Jaze yells from the front door.

"I'm up here baby, come on up." K.C. replies.

"Stay down here Bleek," Jaze lets his hand go for the first time since getting out of her car, "I'll be back in a minute."

As she takes each step Jaze's smile is fading more by the second. She knows full well her father is not going to agree with or accept her new decision. And why should he? No father who claims to love his daughter would agree to the news she's about to tell hers.

"You look like you're in a good mood today princess." K.C. wrinkles his left brow.

"Hey daddy..." Jaze hugs her father tightly.

"Mmmhm," he smiles down into her awkward eyes, "I guess you saw what I put in your account last night huh?"

"I did; you don't think $20,000 was a bit much though dad..." she puts a hand on each hip.

"Well, you're **twenty** years old," he takes a seat on his enormous bed, "By the way how did you spend the last money I put in there so fast?"

"Bleek is building a studio in our apartment..." Jaze explains.

"**Right,** you did move out of the dorm," K.C. recollects, "Your mother told me that. Am I paying for your apartment too?"

"It's funny you say **too,**" Jaze laughs, "I'm not the only person whose housing you're paying for."

"What does that mean?" K.C. stands up.

"Nothing dad," Jaze looks away, "I came here to talk to you about something else."

"No," her father yells, "What the hell are you talking about Jazemene?"

"Daddy, please don't put me in the middle of anything..." Jaze begs.

"Tell me know Jazemene Argelle!" He demands.

"Okay." She sighs.

"Okay what," K.C. replies, "I'm waiting. Start talking!"

"Cameron," Jaze starts, "has been paying for Whitney and Charlie's house and everything else for that matter since you told her to stop." Jaze awaits her father's reaction.

"You liar." Her father laughs.

"It's the truth dad," she claims, "Are you serious right now? Why would I lie about that?"

"Why the hell would my wife still be spending *my* money to pay for my ex's house," he screams, "that she lives in with her boyfriend?"

"Maybe because Cam is in love with Whitney dad..." Jaze explains.

"She barely even likes Whitney." K.C. laughs.

"Oh no she *loves* Whitney," Jaze laughs herself, "Whitney is the maternal figure she never had, and the lover you never could be. I know more about them both than you ever will dad, because you can't see anything past your own reflection in your million dollar mirrors."

"This is what you came to do Jazemene," he asks, "break my heart..."

"You asked," she reminds him void of emotion, "I came to tell you I'm dropping out of college."

"No you're not!" K.C. reaches around her to slam his bedroom door shut.

"You already quit the basketball team," he continues, "I closed that door because I know damn well that lil' thug is downstairs listening and waiting for you. I was young before Jaze; I wasn't born with these couple strands of gray hair."

"It's more than a couple." She says.

"This shit is not funny Jazemene," K.C. takes hold of both of her shoulders, "That fool put a key in your back and he's the only thing driving you."

"This was our decision *together*," she claims, "We are a real couple, not like this fake, unhappy, slave and master relationship you and Cam have."

"Jazemene get the hell out of my house..." K.C. shakes his head.

"Leave and once that twenty thousand is gone you're cut off." he continues opening his bedroom door.

"That's the main reason I came to see you to tell you I don't want your money," Jaze claims, "you can take the twenty back."

"Get out!" her father bellows.

"I am *father*," she frowns, "You sit in here cooped up in this dead ass mansion like your King Midas or somethin', you really act like every fucking thing you do or touch is gold. You ain't perfect dad, but you are too damn blind to see that all your women cheat on you just as much as you cheat on them. Everybody seems to be on the same page except you."

"When you are no longer welcome at either one of your parents' homes, your life has become very ugly Jazemene Cole," K.C. tells his only daughter, "It's a terrible thing to go through your adult life at odds with your parents."

"Well," Jaze smiles, "In that respect I'm just like my mother and father huh?"

"What the hell does that mean?" her father asks.

"Mom doesn't get along with grandma and grandpa," Jaze reminds her father, "And well, both your parents are dead now, but they *never* did love you dad, *did* they?"

"Watch your fucking mouth Jazemene," K.C. warns, "You will not talk to me like you do your mother!"

"Oh boo hoo dad," she screams back, "Fuck that let's talk about it, get it all out in the open! Your father was a **pedophile** and a **faggot**, who never loved you enough to even **molest** you. And Mama Cole used you **and us**, your kids to make money until the night she died."

"That is not true Jazemene and you know it!" K.C. steps back trying to defend himself, from the powerful emotional blows his daughter is slowly killing him with.

"Oh its true dad," she confirms, "every single word of it is true. The night she died, the night your baby brother killed your mother I was awake... I stood right there and watched him beat her to death! You were next dad. Uncle Love had already opened this very bedroom door, he had his hand on his gun and was ready to waltz in here and blow you and Cameron away forever. But K.J. and his pretty ass eyes saved you both. God, his eyes are gorgeous. I wish Uncle Love was my father too so I could have gotten the good genes."

"This is my last time saying this you **evil little spiteful bitch**," K.C. steps into her face, "Leave my house and never speak of my name again! Take your disrespectful little bastard brother with you, and if you ever hit your mother again, **I'll make sure you never hit anybody else in your life!** Yeah, don't look surprised, your mother called and told me exactly what happened."

"And you believed her," Jaze says, "whatever I'm gone."

K.C. watches his only living biological child storm away from him filled with so much anger.

Take My Breath Away 3

(Cam)

The beach is calmer than usual today. The cool comforting breeze feels as if it's washing over my body cleansing me from all the sins and lies I live out daily. The waves are gently crashing in, almost in slow motion like some creative montage in a movie about a rare exotic island. There are children, dogs, and full families all around enjoying themselves, but as I walk my ears can't hear a thing but my haunting thoughts. Will this eternally be the only life I know? Every day I'm unhappy and so alone living inside a concrete and glass castle fit for a queen. I'm married to one of the most successful black men in history. Although he's in his forties now he still has a very young soul and is just as gorgeous as he was the day I met him. I do not deserve the luxuries he's so blessed me with, but I refuse to renounce them. I also belong to another man and his future wife, but my husband has no clue. I cater to them like a real modern day slave, and the worst part is I don't just enjoy it... I fantasize about it whenever I'm not there with them. I don't have sex with my husband often, but not for my lack of effort or willingness, he simply just prefers not to utilize me for that particular wifely duty on a regular basis. My husband is unfaithful. That is the worst feeling for any wife to know, but I'm unfaithful, dishonest, and disloyal myself so I've no room to talk. I often wonder how much if any would our strange distant marriage change if I told him all of my secrets. If I bared my naked soul to him in true light would he accept my words of truth and love me for my honest, selfless, admission... or would he scold and then destroy me leaving me financially, emotionally, and physically naked forever? As we walk along this beach hand in hand I can't help but to daydream about so many things I may never have the nerve to incite or admit in respect to my marriage. He loves me, of that I'm so very sure but I do wish my marriage could be a little more like the ones little girls dream about. Maybe truth is the first step. Maybe being open and honest can be as good as they say. I'm ready. I'm going to tell him everything now.

"Cameron..." K.C. wakes his wife from her silent daydream.

"Yes my love." She replies with a well-played seemingly confident smile.

"How long have you been sleeping with Charlie and Whitney, and how much of my money have you spent on them over the past ten years?"

Cam's entire body goes cold and then numb.

(Jaze's Apartment)

Jazemene's boyfriend Bleek is milling over his deep thoughts as he smokes a few blunts back to back to back.

(Bleek)

Bitches are made to be broken. You gotta break a bitch down before you can rebuild em. A pretty bitch is the easiest bitch to break down. They got the lowest self-esteem outta all women. My girl bad, she probably the baddest chick in the city. But I don't let her know that shit. Hell no, I down play that bitch every chance I get.

"Baby…" Jaze opens the front door to her apartment.

"Wassup…" Bleek looks up at her through a dark cloud of marijuana smoke.

"Are you hungry, I'm cooking some noodles?" she tells him.

"What yo rich ass know about some noodles?" he laughs.

"I wasn't born rich Bleek…" she leans down to kiss his dark lips.

"Nah I'm straight on the noodles bae; just make me a couple hot dogs." Bleek tells Jaze.

"Ok baby." Jaze smiles down at him.

"Oh and make some Kool-Aid too." he instructs her.

Jaze twists happily back into the house in her short shorts after Bleek smacks her bottom.

"I wouldn't cook his ass nothing." Cruz frowns from the couch leaning way back with his dramatic left arm draped over the top of his head dangling down to the other side of it.

"Yes you would Cruz shut up," Jaze laughs, "If you had a man like that you would do whatever it took to keep him."

"Child, please," Cruz changes the channel on the television, "I've had plenty of *little boys* like Bleek… because that's exactly what he is a little boy. I don't care if he is like twenty-six now, he still a kid mentally."

"He's twenty-four Cruz," Jaze twists her pink lips to the side of her pretty face, "I'm twenty-one... and you sir are a hater."

"Whatever." Cruz rolls his eyes as he stands up and makes his way to the kitchen.

"If he was my man," Cruz says looking down in the pot of hot dogs, "I would show your clueless ass exactly how to handle..."

The door opens.

"**Heeey** King Bleek," Cruz smiles, "We made you some hot dogs, do you want any mustard on your weenie?"

"Nah I don't eat weenies bruh." Bleek says as he falls flat on the sofa in front of the couch.

"Yeah I **bet** you don't **hmm**..." Cruz looks at Jaze who's staring at him shaking her head.

"What girl..." he gasps dramatically.

"Leave my man alone please," Jaze laughs, "and please go sit down I'll bring you a **weenie** when they're done."

"Okay boo," Cruz makes sure to walk right in front of Bleek's face, "don't bring me a little one now, you know I like my meat long and strong."

"Sit yo ass down bruh!" Bleek barks at Cruz.

"You're not my father Bleek," Cruz stands his ground, "So, you can direct that tone to somebody who gives a fuck about you."

"Jaze, you betta get this fag before I smash his lil gay ass!" Bleek rises up from the television.

151

"You wanna smash *my lil gay ass*," Cruz laughs tauntingly, "*gay*. I know you gay, I'm just waiting on Jaze to see through ya clear rainbow façade."

"The food is ready Bleek," Jaze ignores the confrontation, "How many do you want?"

"Fuck that food!" Bleek slaps Cruz hard across the face.

As soon as he hits the floor Cruz pulls a blade out of his back pocket.

Bleek's eyes triple in size instantly. Cruz pounces back up and chases Bleek around the back of the sofa.

"Cruz what the hell are you doing," Jaze screams, "please put that damn knife down."

As fast as her athletic legs will carry her Jaze runs and bounds up on the sofa in between her boyfriend and friend.

"Get that fag outta here!" Bleek exclaims.

"Don't call him that!" Jaze tells him.

"Nah don't worry bout it Jaze," Cruz continues to try to reach around her, "I'm bout to nip and tuck his ass, we gon see who's the fag then."

"*No*, Cruz just leave... please!" Jaze begs her angry friend.

"Fuck him," Cruz screams, "he shoulda never put his funky dick beatin' ass hands on my pretty face!"

"Pretty," Bleek laughs, "Nigga you look like a ninja turtle."

"Bitch please," Cruz rolls his neck, "You wasn't saying that a few nights ago. The night Jaze got too drunk and passed out..."

"Nigga my girl don't believe yo **lonely** bitch ass," Bleek laughs, "you funny as hell tryina insinuate I'm gay though my nigga."

"Insinuate," Cruz claps several times in mock awe, "that's a big word for such a tiny brain. Tiny like your little..."

"Cruz, get out of my house now!" Jaze fumes.

"Fine," he smiles, "I'm gone, but boy I promise you, somebody gone put a bullet in yo stupid ass one day."

"It's all good," Bleek's taunts as Cruz exits the apartment, "I'm King Bleek bitch I'm bullet proof!"

(Ride With Me Adventures)

As Ty walks through his crowded theme park, he thinks back to all the times this entire reality was only a pipe dream. His brother made everything happen almost eleven years ago and it looks better now than he ever imagined it could. Long gone are the days of Tyrone Carter lazing around on his mama's couch before he ever got a job, and even the days he slaved away at Six Flags over Georgia.

Ty is now and will forever be his own boss. The business at hand today, is something he's more proud of than almost everything else he's accomplished over the years.

"Roger," Ty says approaching one of his highest ranking assistants near the center of the enormous park, "you know my wife Osiana…"

They shake hands.

"We've never been properly introduced;" Roger smiles after kissing her hand, "Very nice to meet you Mrs. Carter. And may I add you are a very lucky woman your husband is a creative genius."

"Yes I know." she returns his fake smile.

"Thank you Roger," Ty says, "before I make the announcement I wanted to tell you first, that Osiana is going to be taking over the management of our human resources department."

"**Wow**," Roger chokes a bit, "**Wow**… um that's really great sir, but you already promised that position to **someone else** six months ago."

"Really," Ty asks, "Who?"

"Me Mr. Carter…" Roger reminds him.

"You're absolutely right Roger," Ty looks at his wife and then back at his employee, "I'll tell you what Rog, you can move up and become my head supervisor over the entire park. How's that sound?"

"Well," Roger tries not to smile, "It does pay more, its more responsibility, plus paid vacations four times a year… Oh who am I kidding, hell yes Mr. Carter I'll do it!"

"Awesome." Ty takes his wife by the hand as they follow Roger to the Human Resource building near the rear of the park.

(Back at Jaze's apartment)

The apartment is empty for once as sixteen-year-old K.J. is all alone deep inside his videogame bliss.

He knows he could go live and travel with his father when he's not lost in depression, or at least get a lump sum of cash from his legal father K.C. But he knows his sister needs him right now, and he also knows she wouldn't approve of him taking a handout from her father in turn admitting they couldn't survive without his money.

K.J. pauses his video game to finish his second bowl of Frosted Flakes cereal. As he walks his almost empty bowl into the kitchen he contemplates what his life would be like if he had never left his biological father's side to move back home to finish school.

He could have easily continued to travel and see the world with his father Love, and maybe even study abroad. There are so many things K.J. knows he and his father could have done, before he became depressed again and started slipping back into painful insanity.

What happens when a clearly genius, raw serial killer loses his mind? He disappears and nobody wants to be the first one to find him.

After sitting back on the couch and un-pausing his game K.J. hears keys in the door.

Bleek walks in with Roland, Obie, and two girls Angel, and Scooter.

"What up lil bro..." Bleek says in his raspy voice through a sneaky smile.

"I ain't your lil bro *Dewey*..." K.J. replies.

As both girls burst into laughter, K.J. continues to play his game never looking up for a second.

"Bitch I told you bout calling me that!!" Bleek pounces on K.J. before he can attempt to defend himself. As Bleek chokes him, Ro and Obie both begin punching him in his sides and head. They continue to beat him until his screams become inaudible.

"Back off!" King Bleek commands.

As Obie and Ro back up, Bleek stares down into the bloody eyes of K.J.

"Get the fuck out lil nigga..." Bleek growls with pure venom in his dark glare.

"I pay rent here..." K.J. says through two busted lips.

WHAP!!!

Bleek slaps K.J. with everything in him and then quickly snatches him off of the couch and puts him over his shoulder.

"Scooter get yo ass in the back and take them pants off!" Bleek barks as he opens the door.

With one hard thrust he tosses K.J. to the ground and then sends him rolling down the stairs with a swift kick. Before K.J.'s bruised body hits the bottom Bleek slams and locks the door.

(Late that Night)

"Aye Jaze..." Bleek says in the darkness from the barely open bedroom door.

"Yeah bae..." she mumbles as her head sinks deeper in her pillow as it spins round and round.

"Get up boo," Bleek says, "my homeboy bout to come holla at you bout that rent money."

"Okay," Jaze mumbles trying to get to her feet, "I'm up bae."

"Aight now," Bleek replies over the music from the front room, "he paid me bae. He gave me half the rent so you be a *good* girl aight?"

The dark clouds in Jazemene's head are trying hard to fade away, but they're slowly just being replaced by bright stinging lights that leave her head feeling like it's about to explode.

"You *ready* bae," Bleek laughs a low guttural laugh, "*Yeah* you ready bae..."

"Bleek," Jaze moans, "What did you do to..."

The bedroom door slams shut.

The slam startles Jaze; she barely catches her balance by grabbing hold of the raggedy dresser near the bed before she falls. She knows if she falls down or lays back down she'll never get back up.

The bedroom door opens.

"*Light bright damn near white*..." the familiar voice says after closing the bedroom door behind him to drown out the music in the front room.

"*Roland*," Jaze squints trying to make out his round face, "what are you doing in my room?"

"The *king* sent me..." Ro smiles in the darkness as he slowly pulls off his huge sweaty black T-shirt.

As he walks around the bed in her direction Jaze can see his robust belly glowing, as the sneaky moonlight shining in through the windows rudely illuminates it.

Jaze covers her face and stomach as Ro steps face to face with her. Once the urge to vomit passes she allows her hands to slowly melt back down to her sides.

"Hell yeah," he growls reaching behind her to creepily rub her lower back, "I been wantin' you for a minute light bright."

"What," Jaze smiles trying to gain some composure, "what are you talking about Ro, and where the hell is my Bleek?"

"King Bleek up front countin' that money I just blessed y'all broke asses with." Ro explains proudly.

"Wait," Jaze holds up both hands, "Why did you give Bleek money Roland?"

158

"Because," he growls as he rubs her flat stomach, "Y'all bout to get evicted cause the rent three months behind fool..."

"No it's not," Jaze tries to step back but finds herself pinned against the dresser, "I give Bleek the rent money in cash every first of the month..."

"Yep," Ro leans in to kiss her neck, "And that nigga smokes it up and buys Jordan's every time."

Jaze's dangerous drunken stupor is starting to subside.

"Roland get the hell out of my room please," Jaze tries to push the much bigger man away from her but fails, "**Now** Ro, and tell king Bleek to get his black ass in here now!"

"**Hell no**," Ro unbuckles his belt, "Not until you get me straight first boo..."

"What you mean get you straight," Jaze can hear him unzipping his dingy jeans in the darkness, "I don't know what you think this is Ro... But I'm not touching your nasty fat ass."

"Might be **all** that," Ro laughs dropping his pants to his ankles, "But right now you belong to me bitch."

As the five letter word, continues to ring in her head Jaze can feel something inside her breaking down.

"Let's go hoe." Ro growls grabbing Jaze by the back of her almost sober neck forcing her down to her shaky knees.

Jaze looks up at Roland in the darkness with more hatred in her glare than this world has ever known.

She puts her right hand on his left thigh, as she uses her left hand to carefully and quietly open the bottom dresser drawer.

"There you go," Ro moans leaning back on the bed, "I'm waiting on *you* light bright."

"Ok..." Jaze says as she wades through the clothes in the drawer. She's reaching deeper and deeper inside the drawers but it's not there.

"Stop teasing me light bright," Ro growls, "Let's go."

Jaze leans in and opens her mouth as the tears start to fall.

She reaches inside the drawer one last time just a little bit further.

Got it! Cold hard steal.

Jaze swiftly grabs the gun while simultaneously punching Ro in his genitals. Then she quickly falls back aiming the gun at him.

"Just stay on the bed Ro!" Jaze demands.

"You little bitch!!!" Ro growls as he swings at her as best he can.

BANG BANG!!!

Roland's limp body falls on top of Jaze. She quickly wiggles from underneath him covered in his

160

dark pungent blood. Jaze can smell his body relieving itself already.

She jumps up and rushes towards the door full of rage, and embarrassment, but most of all hate.

Jaze pulls the bedroom door open, gun still in hand. Her vision is almost clear now but she wishes it wasn't.

She could have lived a thousand more years and been fine if she never saw what she sees right now.

"Scooter, are you **serious**..." Jaze frowns painfully.

"Hey girl..." Scooter says obviously drugged out her mind as she continues to bounce on Bleek.

"Bleek, what hell!!!" Jaze screams out.

"What you doing with my strap Jaze?" Bleek's dazed red eyes widen a bit as he stops Scooter from bouncing on him.

"Shut the hell up Bleek!" She screams out crazily.

"Nahh man," Bleek mumbles through the haze of all the drugs in his system, "I knew I heard some... you were in there fuckin' wit shit. I knew I heard yo lil **dumbass** in there shootin' my strap girl..."

"Jaze!!!" a voice yells bursting in through the front door.

Jaze raises the gun as quick as she can, three shots ring out and everything goes black.

Chapter 10
Lovely

(Love)

I said I would never return to this city ever... I could have gone any single place I wanted to on the planet. I could be anywhere in the world right now but I'm right here where I died... and that, this thing was born. I can hear my heart bursting through my chest; I've been unstable for some time now. I want to be... I can be better; I have to be better for my future. I can't succumb to the voices and extra personalities any longer I have to be strong, and be there for my boy. The real pain I feel mentally... constantly is a pounding darkness I wouldn't want to curse my worst enemy with. I've done things, so many things that I shouldn't be proud of, but I am. I'm so very proud of the destruction I brought to all of the sick and innocent bastard's souls who crossed my path or wronged me in my lifetime. People, a lot of people looked up to us, to me... the Florida Finisher. I still get fan mail everyday posted on several web pages and social networking profiles my people have created in my honor. I've been close many times to responding to them but I know if I relinquish my identity I'll end up back in that cage. I can't handle, the world can't handle what I'll become if they ever force me back into that cage again. The summer is fast approaching, I know my son, my only

child K.J. will want to come travel with me as he does every summer. My mind isn't right now though...

Love can feel his face vibrating. He finally opens his darkening green eyes for the first time in two days. The vibration is constant. As his eyes begin to be able to focus he can see bright lights flashing all around him. He can't move his arms, or feel his legs. The only thing he can almost control is his head. The darkness is too powerful, the stench of the rotting things around his soiled body are more than intoxicating. Love sneezes hard twice.

"How did they find us..." he whispers to the almost dark room.

"We finished the job Osiana wanted us too," he whispers again as the lights stop flashing, "We are **supposed** to be free forever..."

Love can feel his arms, and now his hands. He reaches up to his face but he can't find his nose. In its place is something hard and warm.

The violent vibration begins again. Someone has obviously snuck in his room and planted a tracking device in his skull.

Love turns his head to the left on the smelly old drool stained pillow his head has been resting on for the better part of 48 hours. The tracking device falls out of his face but the lights continue to flash.

Next to his bed he can see something plugged into the wall.

It's a charger, a cell phone charger.

Love rolls over out of his bed to find his overcharged cell phone vibrating, and emitting the bright lights that alarmed him.

It's a phone call.

"Hello," he answers, "Jaze... Yeah I'm here baby. No Uncle Love is fine. How are you? What? Are you serious? And you're sure they're both **dead**? **Damn it**! Are the police on the way? Okay. Text me the address now, and I'm on the way."

Love listens to his niece.

"Oh okay," he says into the phone, "yeah gunshots aren't that rare at all in that complex, I know it well. The police aren't coming anytime soon, just sit tight, and do not let that girl leave. I know Jaze, I know... no worries princess I haven't spoken to your father in a while. I'm not going to tell him a thing. Okay I'm coming from Orlando so it'll take me a minute but I'll be there as soon as I can."

Love jumps in the shower and turns the water on full blast. With only his hands and a bar of soap he scrubs his body fiercely for the better part of ten minutes. After drying off he puts on all black, snatches his charger out of the wall, quickly packs only the things he actually needs and rushes out of the door to drive full speed to Miami.

(Hours later at Jaze's Apartment)

Jaze, K.J., Josiah, Scooter, and Bleek's dead body are all sitting in the front room of the dark apartment.

"Jaze I can't believe you fucking killed them," Scooter screams, "and now your stupid lame ass is holding me hostage! The charges just piling up on yo dumbass."

"Scooter please shut the hell!" Jaze points the gun at her.

"I ain't got no worries," Scooter claims, "You only shoot when yo bitch ass is scared."

"Oh really," Jaze steps closer to her disloyal friend, "you wanna test that theory bitch?"

Scooter doesn't respond.

"How long were you fucking my man Scooter?" Jaze asks still aiming the gun at her skull.

"He was never your man Jaze," Scooter laughs in her face, "You was just his duck bitch. I was his girl. We used to fuck in yo bed all the time while you was at work. Ask your brother lil gay ass..."

"Bitch I ain't gay I just didn't wanna hit yo trash ass." K.J. throws the television remote at her head.

"Is it true K.J.?" Jaze asks.

"Hell no I ain't gay sis!" K.J. frowns.

"Not that fool," she says, "Did Bleek fuck her in my bed?"

"Yeah," K.J. confirms, "I wanted to tell you sis."

"So why didn't you K.J. damn?" Jaze cries.

Jaze stalks over to Bleek's limp body and kicks him hard in between his legs.

"I wanted to tell you," K.J. explains, "But I didn't wanna lose you sis. You had a habit of putting that idiot before everybody else."

"That's not true," Jaze cries, "And he wasn't that bad..."

"Look at my face Jaze," K.J. exclaims, "Who do you think did this to me?"

There's a light knock on the door.

"That's gotta be dad." K.J. rushes to the door and opens it.

K.J. looks up at his dad through still swollen eyes.

"Who the fuck did this to you?" Love asks gently holding his son's face in his hands.

"Jaze needs you, dad I'm fine." K.J. claims.

Love shakes his head as he walks in dressed in all black with his long dreads neatly tucked under large skull cap.

"Who the hell are you?" Scooter asks.

"Your worst nightmare," Love admits, "Now shut the hell up your time will come. Son what the hell happened to your face I'm not gonna ask you again? I'll kill whoever did this to..."

"Don't worry about it dad I heal fast," K.J. says, "But you should stick around more. I need you."

"You're right son," Love agrees, "I'm here now."

Love looks at his niece who's still holding the murder weapon.

"What's up Jaze?" he asks.

"There..." Jaze points to the sofa.

"Yeah I saw that one when I walked in." Love says walking over to assess the damage closely.

"Jaze," Love smiles at her, "you are way too calm baby girl... I think you got more of me in you than I thought."

"This was an accident," Jaze admits, "But both of these bastards deserved it."

"I'm sure," Love smiles, "Now you said there were two, right? Where's the other one?"

"Bedroom..." Jaze replies.

Love heads to the back to check it out.

"Jaze," K.J. says looking down at a black smart phone, "Did you ever go through this idiot's phone?"

"No," she walks towards him, "He always had it locked. Why?"

"I'm just reading his texts..." K.J. says.

"Gay ass," Scooter says, "you a snitch ass nigga too K.J.!"

"Ignore her," Jaze tells her baby brother, "How did you unlock it K.J.?"

K.J. laughs.

"That dumbass nigga's code was 1, 2, 3, 4," K.J. explains, "here read some of this shit..."

K.J. hands Jaze the phone.

"Are you fucking kidding me," Jaze covers her mouth with one of her shaky hands, "I don't believe this shit."

After observing Roland's fat dead body Love reemerges into the front room.

"What now?" Love asks.

"That asshole Bleek," she starts, "and his friends were planning on killing me or at least leaving me for dead after they killed my dad."

"Wait," Love says, "that's not making sense Jaze why would they kill your dad?"

"Bleek knew my dad changed his life insurance policy and his will," Jaze explains, "Since K.J. proclaimed he wasn't dad's son and wanted nothing to do with him, dad left everything to me, and the insurance policy now has me and Cam as the only two beneficiaries."

"How could Bleek know all that though Jaze?" Love walks closer.

"He said," Jaze cries, "He wanted to **marry me**, and **be a family**... I believed him, I really thought he..."

"Loved you..." Love interjects, "No time for tears now baby girl, at least now you don't have to feel bad about killing the bastard since he was planning on doing you in anyway."

"Damn right." Josiah agrees.

"So," Love says, "He was going to marry you, and then have his boys knock my brother off, and then take all the money from you..."

K.J. nods his head up and down in confirmation, as Jaze walks a few feet away into the kitchen area.

"Okay don't worry about it," Love says sitting down next to Bleek's limp body as if he's still alive, "first things first, you need some help Jaze."

"I thought you were her help Love." Josiah says.

"I am," Love confirms, "But she may need more than me."

"Meaning what Uncle Love..." she asks.

"To beat the police you gotta be the police," Love explains, "or be a criminal genius. None of you kids have enough of me in you to claim to be a criminal or a genius so let's not even visit that thought."

Love looks over at his son. "Well not yet anyway..."

"***Be*** the police though dad," K.J. stands up, "What does that even mean?"

"If you listen son," Love raises a calming hand, "and give me time I can explain."

"And I am everything you are Pop," K.J. claims, "I can do everything you've ever done and more."

"Don't talk like that son." Love tells his only child.

"Why not dad I..." K.J. starts.

"Because I said so," Love interjects, "I am not proud of the fact that you know a lot of the things I've done and I'm paying for those sins every day. I was... I am very sick mentally. It works for me because I was hurt by a lot of people throughout my life, and unlike most people I was capable and willing to destroy every one of my attackers."

"Exactly dad..." K.J. says.

"But I don't want that for you," Love interjects again, "You are young and smart. The world is at your fingertips. You should want more than the painful past your father lives with every single day."

"Love, I don't mean to interrupt but what were you saying about being the police...?" Jojo asks.

"Right," Love refocuses his thoughts, "so I don't mean to actually be the police of course... but you will need them on your side."

"Right so how do we do that Uncle Love?" Jaze asks anxiously.

"You need a detective," Love says, "One of the best the state of Florida has ever seen..."

"**Auntie Osiana**..." K.J. says.

"Bingo." Love smiles that handsome chilling smile.

"But isn't she busy running the human resource department at the park now," Jaze wrinkles her brow, "She's never gonna come on the run with me..."

"What do you mean *me*," Jojo frowns, "I'm not letting you out of my sight."

Jaze blushes.

"No I don't mean like..." Jojo starts.

"Now that is too cute..." Love says.

"We know *exactly* what you mean Jojo," K.J. teases him, "don't worry Jaze is obsessed with you too. Anyway, so dad... how do we ask Osiana to come help *us*?"

"Who said anything about asking her?" Love smiles again.

"So let me get this straight," Jaze tries to stop blushing so she can pay attention to her uncle's instruction, "You want me..."

Jojo clears his throat.

"You want *us*," Jaze corrects herself, "to kidnap an ex police detective?"

"Now you're thinking like a criminal genius." Love stands up.

"Are you serious dad?" K.J. asks standing up as well.

"Very." his dad replies.

"But we don't have a clue how to kidnap anybody Uncle Love..." Jaze whines.

"You didn't have a clue how to kill a man either until today right," Love smiles at his young niece, "No worries, I'll kidnap Detective Blue, you three just have to convince her to help you."

"So what now," Jaze asks, "What do we do with Scooter and the bodies?"

"I'll handle that," Love assures them, "Here give me your keys, and take mine. Drive my car back to Orlando, and head straight to the Extended Stay hotel on Universal Boulevard. The key to room 129 is in my cup holder in my car. Stay there until I bring Osiana to you."

"Thanks Uncle Love," Jaze rushes into his arms, "I'll owe you for life."

"Don't mention it princess," he smiles down at her, "I already owe you for life. The kidnapping, Mama Cole, the gunshot..."

"Yeah you're right," she smiles, "Let's go guys."

"No." K.J. looks into his father's eyes.

"What do you mean no son?" Love asks fervently.

"Jaze you and Jojo go ahead," K.J. tells them, "I'm staying here with you, dad. I didn't shoot anybody. I have no reason to run. Dad you and I can handle Scooter, the bodies, and Osiana... **together**. You owe **me** a lot **too**."

"Fine," Love agrees," looking from K.J. to Jaze, "Jaze is this girl your friend or..."

"Hell no." Jaze replies.

"Gotcha," Love smiles, "Go ahead princess; your brother and I will meet you in the O by tomorrow morning."

"Okay Unc." She replies opening the door.

"And take care of my niece Josiah Bell." Love calls out behind them.

"No worries Uncle Love." Josiah replies.

The two of them rush downstairs to the fire engine red Camaro parked next to Jaze's BMW and speed off in it quickly.

Chapter 11
Like Father...

(Hours later)

As they trek back in from the woods without the bodies, Love and K.J. both need a bath badly. No time for that now though, their day's mission has only just begun.

After getting back into the blue BMW Love checks all the mirrors to see if anyone is watching them.

The coast is clear.

"Where's your phone son?" Love asks without looking at K.J.

"Right here..." K.J. pulls out his iPhone 6.

"It's Friday," his father says cranking the car, "The theme park should be booming all day. Call your Uncle Ty and ask him about a job."

"I already have a job dad." K.J. contends.

"Listen to me son," Love says as he pulls off from their secluded location, "Don't think right now just listen and follow my specific instructions."

"Okay dad." K.J. listens to each instruction his father gives him and then obeys perfectly.

(Tyrone's House)

As they pull up to the house Love can't believe his eyes.

"Wait, wait, wait," Love laughs, "Ty owns a theme park now and this is the biggest house he could afford?"

"Nope," K.J. says, "He and Osiana have a house by us too, this is just their summer house."

"So that idiot has a summer house in the same city as his primary home?" Love asks.

"Yep." K.J. confirms.

"Why?" his dad looks at him.

"Beats me," K.J. replies, "now are we gonna kidnap Auntie Osiana or just sit out here until she sees us? I'm sure all that training she got as a detective is still deeply embedded in her."

"Very astute son," Love smiles proudly, "So because of that fact we have to be extra careful and perfectly precise. Here take this rope and let's go son."

K.J. obeys and then follows his dad.

As they approach the side of the house in route to the back door they can hear loud music inside the home.

The windows of Osiana's new all black Audi parked in their driveway are all down, with colorful floral arrangements strewn all across the backseat.

The back of the house is lined with empty boxes about six feet high. The air smells of cooling apple pies and rain.

Before trying the back door, Love reaches down and puts his hand on his son's chest.

"You feel that?" Love whispers.

K.J. nods his head with wide eyes.

"And you hear the beat in your ears?" his father asks.

K.J. nods again.

"No matter how many times you commit a crime," Love whispers, "if you're actually a good person at heart that feeling will never go away. Don't ever lose that beat son; it'll save you, like **you** saved me. You gave my beat back to me."

K.J. nods again.

"Here put these on." Love hands his son a pair of black gloves.

K.J. clutches the rope to his chest with his arm and quickly slides each glove on ignoring his rapid heart.

Then he watches his dad successfully pick the lock on the back door. No alarm sounds.

They're both inside now.

"Stay low..." Love whispers.

K.J. nods while keeping eye contact with his murderous father.

"You watch my back," Love whispers, "And I'll watch both of our backs."

"Yes sir." K.J. whispers back.

They inch closer to the first room.

It's empty so they keep moving. After checking two more rooms Love stops cold in his tracks.

"Listen..." he whispers with a finger to his full pink lips.

K.J. closes his bright green eyes tightly.

"She's upstairs in the shower..." he whispers to his dad eyes still completely closed.

"Bingo." Love whispers.

They take the beautiful well-polished wooden stairs slowly just one at a time. Once they reach the top floor they swiftly make their way to the master bedroom.

(K.J.)

This is so fucking cool. I'm kidnapping an ex detective with my dad who's a real life serial killer. I'm trying hard not to miss a thing; I want to learn everything he's willing to teach me. Okay we're inside the bedroom. He's no longer crouching down at all. He hasn't since we were downstairs. I get it, we don't have to be as cautious now because we know she's here alone because Ty is at the park, and we also know exactly where she is and what she's doing. As we near the bathroom door we can hear Osiana singing happily. It's some old ass song that probably was hot and then got wack before I was ever even born. Dad just shushed me. What the hell? Can he hear my thoughts? He's crazy as hell, but I don't think Pops is that crazy. Okay now he's approaching her bed. He just grabbed something, I have no clue what he's doing, but I'm staying put. Or not? He's motioning for me. Okay, let's get it. Damn! We just snuck passed the open bathroom door. The entire shower is glass just like my... well Jaze's dad's shower at the mansion. I just caught a glimpse of Aunt Osiana's butt, and damn that is one fine white lady. Lord, please forgive me, but damn my godmother is fine! Dad's holding up his hand. Either we're about to go in, or he's telling me to wait here. Or he's saying something totally different than either of

176

those things and I'm lost as shit. Damn it! I really hope Auntie Osiana doesn't try to put up a fight. Dad said that he doesn't want to hurt her, but he said in his mind self-preservation, helping Jaze, and my wellbeing trump all else. The shower just went off. Oh shit. Oh shit. Oh shit! It's about to get real. Boom, she's stepping out. We can see her from this angle, but she can't see us. She's drying off rather quickly, she must have had plans. Hope not, cause it's over with for that shit. Note to self, self... next time you hug Auntie Osi, make sure you accidentally grab her butt. Check. Ok she's dry. Here we go, panties on, shorts on, bra on... and now the shirt. She grabs her towel again, and the look in Dad's eyes' just completely changed. God, please don't let my Dad turn into Lance right now and do some psycho shit. She just put the towel completely over her head to dry her hair. Damn. As soon as she put it over her head dad rushed her like an angry starved animal finally released from its constricting cage. Yep, we got her. Best day ever!

"Hand me that rope son." Love says.

"Love is that you?" Osiana asks.

K.J. hands his father the rope.

"Son," Osiana says with her towel wrapped tightly around her face, "K.J.? Hunny are you here too? Talk to Auntie K.J. what's going on?"

After her hands are tied securely, just as her towel is over her face Love leads her out of her bathroom and then out of the bedroom towards the stairs.

"Love," she screams, "Love, please talk to me! Say something Love! Why are you doing this? Don't do this Love, please... please don't..."

"Will you be quiet detective?" Love asks calmly. "We're about to walk outside." He tells her.

"Why are you doing this," she cries, "Ty needs me, please don't kill me..."

"It's okay Auntie," K.J. says opening the backdoor, "we're not going to hurt you. We need your help."

"With what," she tries to calm her racing heart, "And why not just ask?"

"Because we couldn't take no for an answer." Love explains.

"Son, go around front and make sure the coast is clear." Love instructs his eager to impress son.

"Yes sir." K.J. obeys.

Seconds later he peeks back around the corner with his thumb up.

"Where are you taking me Love?" Osiana asks finally able to breathe again.

"To the car," he says approaching the blue BMW, "duck your head." he says.

After carefully putting Osiana in the backseat and removing the towel from her head, Love and K.J. jump in the front.

As Love drives off Osiana watches him closely as he takes her phone that he found on her bed out of his pants pocket.

"What are you doing with my phone Lance?" Osiana huffs in pure rage.

"Now, now," Love smiles in the rearview mirror, "You know much better than to call me by *his* name. It's not safe to say things like that Detective Blue."

"Ex- detective," she corrects him, "*My phone*... what the hell are you doing with it?"

"I'm texting Ty," Love explains, "I'm telling him you got a call to come do a special assignment back in Orlando. They're offering you too much cash to refuse."

"He's never going to believe that." Osiana scoffs as her hands are becoming progressively numb still tied tightly behind her back.

"Oh, he will," Love smiles sliding her phone in his pocket, "I sent your secret signature with the text, so Ty has no reason not to believe a word of the text."

"What secret signature," Osiana wrinkles her brow, "How could you possibly know about..."

"You're an ex-detective," Love laughs, "You've seen a lot of sick crazy things, so of course you and your husband have text codes. I went through your sent messages to Ty, and all the ones that seem outlandish you wrote #Starbucks. If I'm not mistaken that's where you and Ty originally met. Right?"

"You are sick," Osiana smiles, "Pure genius, but very freakin' sick my brotha."

"Thanks," Love looks at her through the mirror, "But don't start that lame cool white girl shit please."

"Point taken," she says, "So where are we going, and why are my hands tied? If you wanted me dead, I would have been done by now..."

179

"I am not going to kill you, detective." Love reiterates.

"Jaze needs your help Auntie." K.J. explains.

"What's wrong with Jaze," Osiana asks, "is she in any danger?"

"You'll know soon enough Ms. Blue." Love turns the music up a bit.

"***Mrs. Carter***." Osiana corrects him.

(Jojo and Jaze)

"Jaze we've been drivin' for two and a half hours I gotta eat something." Josiah says after turning the volume down on the radio.

"Yeah I'm hungry too," she admits, "but I just wanna get safely inside the Orlando city limits."

"We should be close now right?" he asks.

"Less than fifty miles," she checks the GPS on her phone, "nah, on second thought I'm about to die. Let's get off on the next exit and grab something really quick."

"I can wait but if you're ready to stop that's cool too." Jojo says letting his window down.

"Yeah there's a McDonald's off the next exit," she points at the sign up ahead, "we're only like thirty to forty minutes away from Orlando."

"Cool," he replies, "After we eat I'll drive the last little bit to the O."

"Wow thanks," Jaze says hitting Josiah on his shoulder as she takes the exit, "You could have offered to drive an hour ago sir."

"Nah you were still really amped up before we left," he explains, "you needed to drive to calm down."

"I wasn't that amped," Jaze claims, "I was just, I don't know..."

"Jaze," Jojo looks at her, "trust me you were freakin' amped, and now you seem to be back closer to normal."

"Maybe you're right." Jaze says pulling into a handicap parking space near the front of the restaurant.

"You **know** I'm right," Josiah says, "what do you want, I'ma run in and get it."

"You sure you don't want me to..." Jaze starts.

"No, I told you I got it, there's no need for both of us to go in." Jojo tells her.

"Wow," she laughs awkwardly, "Are you embarrassed to be seen with me? Am I **that** ugly?"

"Are you serious right now?" he asks.

"This really isn't that deep Jazemene," he continues, "Are you hungry or no?"

"Just lost my appetite." She turns her head towards the driver's side window.

"You have the worst fucking attitude I've ever seen!" Jojo claims.

"I'm not hungry Josiah," she says, "just go get what you want and don't worry about me."

"Fine..." Jojo hops out the car and slams the door behind him.

(Jaze)

I don't know why I fight it, but I don't have a choice. I do have a choice but I can only feel close to

181

happy with one of them. I can try to move on from this man again, and live the rest of my life comparing every man I meet to him knowing they'll never mean to me what he does. Or I can stay as close to him as he'll allow me to, and deal with whatever emotional bruises come with the territory. I have no idea what his motive is, but he's here for a reason. I love him, he knows that. Maybe he just loves the fact that I love him so much, or maybe... just maybe he's scared to admit that he actually loves me back.

Jaze pretends she doesn't notice Josiah leaving out of the restaurant headed to the car. She cranks the car up and waits for him to get situated.

"Here," he says handing her a wrapped sandwich, "I got you two McChicken's, ketchup, mustard, and extra pickles."

Jaze tries her hardest to fight it, but somehow her beautiful smile cracks the surface of her angry façade anyway.

"How do you know me so well?" she says still looking down at one of her warm sandwiches.

"Just a lucky guess," he lies eating several fries at once, "now drive please."

Chapter 12
Extended Stay

As she pulls up to the hotel where her Uncle's room is Jaze can't help but fall prey to her screaming private thoughts. In her mind Jaze is on her honeymoon, with her new husband, the handsome Josiah Bell.

She looks over at him as she puts the car in park. He's currently lost in his phone probably texting some random chick. He has no idea how much love for him lies tattooed deep inside the gaze on him at this very moment. Jaze knows full well she could and would die for this young man without an inkling of hesitation.

"We're here…" Jaze breaks the silence.

"Cool." He says grabbing the room key out of the cup holder.

Without making eye contact with anyone at or near the front desk Jaze and Jojo walk inside the hotel lobby and take an immediate right to head towards some of the rooms.

They have no idea where Love's room is, but knew much better than to cause suspicion by stopping by the front desk to ask. Luckily the initial hall they turned on is the one Love's hotel room is on.

"129." Jojo says pointing at the door on their right.

He puts the key in, awaits the green light and then pushes the door open. Josiah lets Jaze walk in first as he helps himself to a calculated gaze at the wiggle in her walk.

"This is really nice." Jaze says of the recently cleaned room, equipped with fresh linen and soaps.

Jaze smiles brightly as she makes her way to the window straight ahead. She thrusts open the curtains allowing what's left of the day's sunlight to wash in through the window over her tired body.

"Yeah it's not bad at all." Jojo agrees.

Jaze pulls her hair back into a cute ponytail and then dives across one of the beds in the room.

"How are you feeling Jaze...?" Josiah asks making his way into the nearby bathroom.

Jaze rolls over to look at him. She blushes instantly when she sees him pulling himself out to use the restroom.

"Um I'm fine," she rolls over in the opposite direction, "the bathroom has a door for a reason Jojo."

"It's not like you've never seen me before." he smiles that devilishly handsome grin as he zips himself up.

"Yeah." Jaze covers her face with one of the many pillows on the bed as he climbs in the bed next to her.

"Just *yeah*..." Jojo replies looking down at the pillow on top of his friend's head.

"So what happened," she asks, "like how did you and my little brother end up together today?"

"Well actually," he smiles again, "Me and little Keldrick always stayed in contact even when you and I weren't so tight."

"Why..." Jaze removes the pillow on her head just enough to see his pretty blue eyes.

184

"Uh, I don't know Jazemene," he says, "I just wanted to make sure he was okay. You know... you guys moved out of the castle and into your own place. Love wasn't around... so you know the kid needed a father figure."

"Right," Jaze laughs, "That's your story and you're sticking to it huh?"

"Yep." Jojo leans back on the wall mounted headboard and closes his eyes.

"Yeah I don't think you're being honest with me Josiah Bell." Jaze reaches up and gently hits him with a pillow.

"First off," she continues, "You're only twenty-one; K.J.'s almost seventeen... so how much of a father figure could you be?"

"I don't know you'll have to ask your brother." Jojo closes his eyes again after repositioning his hair from the pillow blow to the head.

"You see who he came running to get after your asshole boyfriend beat him up and kicked him down the stairs." Jojo explains.

"Wait," Jaze sits up next to him, "Bleek did what?"

"Seriously," Jojo replies, "Did you not see your brother's face, neck, and back? Bleek and his punk ass homeboys jumped little Keldrick. Then after they got through, Bleek carried him outside like trash or something and kicked him down the freakin' stairs."

"I'm becoming happier and happier that I shot that mother fucker." Jaze admits.

"Question…" Josiah crosses his arms and looks over at his childhood bestie.

"Answer…" she says with her longish tongue pointed at him.

"Cute," he smiles, "no but seriously though Jaze, why were you dating that idiot?"

Jaze lies back down, turning her head and body in the opposite direction of Josiah.

"What is that the cold shoulder?" he asks sliding down horizontally to snuggle up behind her.

She doesn't respond, but she can't pretend being close to him doesn't feel nice. Jaze gently pushes herself back on him in a wiggling motion trying to find the most comfortable position.

"Answer the question **Big Head**," Jojo delicately rubs her tight soft ponytail, "Why were you with him?"

Jaze quickly rolls over to face him. Face to face and body to body, he stares deep into her soul, as his captivates her.

"Because Jojo…" she finally speaks.

"That's not good enough…" he starts.

"It doesn't even…" Jaze starts to say.

"It matters Jaze." Jojo interjects.

"No, it doesn't," Jaze contends, "None of it does actually; and you proved just that *less* than an hour ago in McDonald's parking lot."

"What the hell," Jojo wrinkles his brow, "and just how the hell did I do that?"

"Leave it alone Josiah." Jaze tells him.

"Hell no," he replies, "I'm not leaving shit alone, and you still never answered my question."

"What was the question Josiah?" Jaze groans.

"Don't call me Josiah," he tells her, "and you know what my question was."

"No I don't know," Jaze claims, "so either ask it again or drop it."

"Why were you with that asshole Bleek?" he asks again.

"Because I couldn't have you!" she finally admits trying to hide her awkward embarrassment.

"So you were with him to make me jealous," he asks, "that doesn't make sense because I never really ever saw you two together. Try again..."

"Not to make you jealous," she explains, "just to fill as many of the gaping holes I had in my life created by your absence."

Josiah smiles leaning down close to her face.

"Wow," Jojo whispers close to her lips, "That shit was deep Jazzy..."

"Whatever." she blushes as he blesses her with three of the sweetest kiss her lips will ever know.

"And you know I hate that name..." she reminds him.

"So." Jojo replies gently running his hand along her fair cheek allowing the blueness of his eyes to delve deeper into her smooth chocolate soul.

"Don't call me Jazzy..." she frowns in jest.

"I'll call you whatever I **want**," he growls with his ample lips pressed lightly against her left ear.

Jaze closes her eyes as she giggles in full submission to the tickling sensation of his vibrating lips on her ear.

He pulls back now. There go those eyes again.

"Sir," she smiles, "what womanly torture did my God have in mind when he decided to create you?"

"Jazemene," Josiah closes his eyes briefly, "Your words are so real. But I don't know how to react I'm just not as good with words as you are. I'm supposed to be sweet talking you, not you..."

"Nope," she interjects with two smallish fingers pressed against his lips, "Don't ever sweet talk a lady Josiah... if you ***don't*** really mean it, ***don't*** say it."

"Who says I wouldn't mean it?" he hits her with a pillow twice and then quickly jumps up standing on the bed with it clutched tightly in his hands.

Jaze stands up as well, wearing a gorgeous smile clutching a pillow of her own.

"Aren't we too old to pillow fight?" she asks with a crooked grin.

"Nope." He smacks her twice knocking her back down on the bed.

(Buffalo Wild Wings)

When Whitney asked K.C. to meet her at Buffalo Wild Wings, he knew something was wrong or something had changed.

188

(K.C.)

Whitney's always been stubborn, and so am I. Neither one of us would ever go out of our way, this late in the game to get to each other's attention. But she did last night. She texted me and asked me to meet her here today at 1p.m. And of course I'm early and she's late. I swear men waste at least thirty-five percent of their lives waiting on women. From mama, to girlfriends, from wives to baby mamas, all we do is wait for years and years on damn women!

"Hello handsome." Whit says finally approaching the table from behind him.

K.C. stands up and helps Whitney to her seat.

"Thank you." She says.

"Very welcome," he replies, "how are you?"

"*Well*," she sighs, "I've been better."

"I'm sure." K.C. replies looking down at the menu.

"Don't worry about that menu hun," she says, "I already told the girl at the front to just bring us thirty wings."

"Yeah," Whit confirms, "They're only like sixty cents each today."

"Whitney I can assure you I'm not worried about the price of the wings." K.C. laughs.

"Oh I know," she laughs with him, "I only mentioned the price because *I'm* paying for our meal."

"Oh…" K.C. pretends to be impressed.

"Yeah," she smiles, "it's the least I can do. You've done so much for our chil… I mean our daughter. And I want you to know I do appreciate you."

189

"Well thanks for the wings then I guess." K.C. locks his large hands together calmly and then leans in to really look at his ex.

"What's wrong?" Whit asks meeting his stare.

"Oh nothing," K.C. lies, "Tell me though because I am curious... the wings you're buying with *your* money, how did you *make* that money Whitney?"

She doesn't reply.

"I mean you *don't* have a job do you," he asks, "You told me you had an online business doing floral arrangements for funerals... but that was just another lie wasn't it? And the obituaries on your Facebook page I'm sure you stole them *or* just created them yourself."

Whit still can't find her voice as she tries to find some weakness in the strong eyes of the man she knows better than she knows herself.

"Keldrick honestly..." she starts.

"No, do not use that word *ever*," he interjects, "There was no *online* funeral floral arrangement business, no *real* funerals, and the only thing that's dead is the tiny shred of trust I had in you and my wife."

"That's not my fault," Whit says, "Cameron is holding up her end of a deal that you know nothing about, without it you wouldn't be married to her in the first damn place."

"Please explain." K.C. leans back in his seat as the delicious smelling wings are delivered to their table.

"May I get you both drinks?" the server asks.

"No ma'am," K.C. waves the server off, "she's about to give me all the tea I need."

190

"You were marrying **Megan** Keldrick," Whit explains, "Cam and I couldn't let that happen so..."

"So you killed the woman?" K.C. asks with real fear in his eyes.

"No, we didn't kill anybody" Whit claims, "well not technically. We kinda made a deal with Love..."

"You paid my brother to kill my wife," Kel starts, "Because, Megan and I **were** already married... You paid him to kill my wife just so that my ex, my wife's twin sister could take her place at the altar with me?"

"We didn't pay him," Whit says, "All he wanted was a relationship with his son. So, I hesitated but then eventually agreed. I'm sorry."

"You're sorry?" K.C. laughs standing up from his seat, "Enjoy your wings Whitney, I seem to have lost my appetite."

"Don't leave me again Keldrick," Whit says with no emotion, "it's getting really old."

"I learned from the best," K.C. says, "at least when I leave you still know how to find me."

"I didn't come here to talk about that." Whit says.

"Of course not," K.C. walks back again, "if it was left up to you and my lying cheating wife this little secret would have gone to the grave buried in the crack of both of your filthy deceitful assess."

"Really," Whit says, "boy you must have lost what little mind you had. You cheat on that girl every chance you get; you even fucked your best friend's fiancé right before she walked down the aisle..."

"Damn," K.C. says sitting back down, "Is that shit on Facebook or something, how does everybody know that?"

"I came here Keldrick," Whit tries to calm her tone, "to talk to you about our relationship with our out of control daughter or the lack there of. And, I also think somebody I care a lot about may have cancer."

(Back at Extended Stay Hotel)

(Jaze)

The jets in this Jacuzzi are simply heaven. I could sit in this thing all night I swear… no but then when I get out my body would be all wrinkled or whatever. And look at him. He's seducing me with his eyes again. I hate that I love that boy the way I do. He has a power over me that he will never understand. Even when I was Bleek's, I always belonged to Josiah Bell. Oh God he's coming over here. Ugh I hate him. He's walking slowly through the center of the hot tub towards me. Damn it here I go blushing again, God I am so stupid and weird. Wait, he's smiling bigger now, I guess my stupid awkwardness is cute. I don't know. God why won't he just say something… Nope, never mind he doesn't need to say a word, this kiss is definitely better. I love the way he massages my lower back when he kisses me as I run my fingernails along the length of his. He's coming closer my legs are inviting him into my precious center. I am not having sex in these people's Jacuzzi though. No, why did he just do that? He knows I can't resist his damn touch. He's close enough now that I can feel all of him on my stomach and in between my legs. As he stands up in front of me I think I know what he wants, but I hope he knows he's not getting it. At least not here.

"**No**..." he asks with a lustful grin.

"I don't do that sir," Jaze returns his smile, "especially not out here."

"Oh really," he positions himself between her legs again, "So you don't get down in public... **anymore**?"

"No sir." Jaze shakes her pretty head.

"Not even with me?" he asks.

"I hate you, you know that right?" she twists her pouty pink lips.

"I think..." Jojo pulls his boxers down a bit below the water.

"You think what sir..." Jaze says close to his neck opening her legs wider for him.

"I think," he kisses her softly, "That you'll do exactly what I say..."

Josiah grabs hold of himself with one hand as he kisses her, and with his other hand he pulls her bikini bottoms to the side at their center. Jaze closes her eyes briefly.

"You know what **no**," Jaze says gently pushing him back, "I can't do this."

"I'm sorry you feel that way Jazzy." Jojo pulls his boxers up and stands up in the Jacuzzi with his stiff member protruding in plain sight.

"Don't leave Jojo," she pleads, "talk to me."

193

"No," he pulls away from her, "I don't wanna talk!"

"Why not?" she cries.

"Because damn it," he steps out of the water completely, "haven't you noticed it's always the same conversation between us...?"

Jaze opens her mouth to speak.

"Don't talk," he leaves her words forever stuck inside of her throat, "I know you were about to say not every convo we have ends up like this, and In essence that would be a true statement. But fuck true statements and conversational content, I'm looking at the bigger picture here... and Jaze in the grand scheme of things, everything between you and I always come back to **this** point. It's a sick and sad cycle."

"**Sick... and sad**?" she cries.

Jojo shakes his head as he dries off with the large white towel.

"When did my emotions and I become sick and sad to you Josiah?" Jaze asks tasting her own warm salty tears.

"You honestly wanna know..." he asks finally looking at her.

"I have to know..." Jaze cries looking way up into the evil starry night sky.

"The moment you read that report in my mom's class back in fifth grade," he admits, "when you told everybody including my mom's jungle fever ass that you were going to marry me."

"This is still about color Josiah," Jaze stands up from her seat inside the Jacuzzi, "Are you fuckin' kidding me?"

"You don't get it Jaze!" he stresses throwing his towel down on the ground near the pool.

"Oh I think I do…" Jaze wades through the water close to where he's standing.

"No you don't," he fumes, "you don't understand shit!"

"Wow," Jaze smiles through her burning tears, "so now I'm dumb too right? The nappy headed little black girl's too dumb to comprehend your complex thoughts right Josiah?"

"Don't say my name like that." He points at her.

"Or what *Josiah*…" Jaze repeats the word she was forewarned about.

"Don't fucking say it again!" he demands.

"And if I do," Jaze steps out of the water dripping everywhere, "what are you gonna do Jojo, beat me like your dad used to do your mom?"

"Fuck you bitch." Josiah walks away.

"Oooooh," Jaze laughs wiping more of her pointless tears away, "You're a real big man Josiah. You just called me a bitch… You're weak as hell Josiah Bell!"

He stops cold in his tracks and turns around to look at her.

"You know what?" he says walking back towards her armed with a menacing scowl on his face.

"Nope," she crosses her arms, "do tell…"

"You wanna talk about my mom," he says, "but you're just an evil spiteful bitch just like *your* mom!"

"You're a racist idiot," Jaze whimpers, "and I hope I never see you again in my life."

She walks past him making sure not to make any contact with his body.

Josiah reaches out and grabs her arm.

He snatches her close to him to look in her eyes clearly.

"I'm not racist Jazemene." He claims.

"You just called your mom a *jungle fever ass*," she reminds him."

"Jazemene..." he looks at her sternly.

"Josiah..." she returns his serious stare.

"I'm going to marry a white girl." He assures her.

"Whoop Dee fuckin' doo," she screams, "what the hell are you telling me for? Go find one to marry; I'll meet my tall dark king one day."

"Would you please shut the hell up," he raises his voice again, "You ain't marrying anybody Jazemene!"

"Damn," Jaze laughs awkwardly through her tears, "Am I that damn bad sir? You think no one would ever marry my black ass?"

"Your black ass belongs to me!" he pulls her close.

Jaze quickly pushes him off of her.

"So let me get this straight," she laughs again wiping away more tears, "You can marry a girl as long as she's *white*... but I can't marry *anybody*, *ever* because my *black ass* belongs to you?"

He doesn't respond.

"You really are weak as fuck Josiah Bell," she looks him up and down with the left side of her mouth curled up, "You must think this stupid shit is funny?"

196

"You're right," he mumbles with his blonde head down, "I am weak. I'm not *that* guy."

"What guy," Jaze steps closer to him, "Who Bleek? **Fuck** Bleek!"

"No," Jojo looks at her, "I'm not talking about that idiot. I'm not the kind of guy that can live an entire lifetime being stared at and talked about. Having a black wife will warp and hinder my social, spiritual, and career life."

"You are so weak." she reiterates.

"So with that said," he steps back from her as tears fill his own eyes, "Yes, I am weak. I'm too weak to live a life that is subject to judgment every single day, too weak to ever tell my dad I ever thought about marrying a black girl, and most of all I'm just so damn weak... *for you*."

"What..." Jaze wrinkles her brow and tilts her head.

"Do you have any idea," he cries, "how much it **hurts** and how **hard** it is to stay away from you for even **one** second? Of course you don't."

"Jojo..." Jaze reaches up to touch his perfect face.

"Jazemene I have loved you since the very first time I *ever* laid eyes on you." Jojo admits.

"Yes, baby..." Jaze cries.

"I even told a friend of mine back in elementary school," Jojo claims, "I told him I had a huge crush on you. He was the first person to ever tell me I couldn't like you because you were different. I know now he was just a kid repeating some dumb shit he probably heard his dumbass parents say at home... but that conversation stayed with me Jaze. That boy, that little pale faced kid looked at me with real disgust in his eyes when I vowed my childish

197

feelings for you. I am glad he never told anybody, but I never wanna feel what his stare and his words made me feel that day again."

"He was an idiot Jojo." Jaze says.

"He was," Jojo agrees, "and so was I for listening."

"You were nine Josiah." Jaze reminds him.

"No excuses," he says, "And to be honest Jaze, I don't know if I'll ever be man enough to marry you... but I promise you this... if you're down I'll be your best friend and lover forever, and I'll never **ever** leave your side as long as you promise to never leave mine."

"Damn," she cries, "Boy, I've waited my entire life to hear you say... **well, most** of that."

As they fall into their first honest embrace with each other the real kisses that follow send identical tingling sensations down both of their young backs.

Chapter 13
Blue's Clues

(In the hotel room)

Jaze is in the shower singing her life away and Josiah is watching some movie on the T.V. that he's seen before but not in a while. Well he thinks he's seen it but he's not really sure, so now he's just waiting to see a scene that can really jog his memory.

As deeply as he's mentally processing the movie, he's still smart enough to know that his brain is just trying to escape from the reality of the conversation he just had with Jazemene.

There's a knock at the door. Jojo rushes towards the bathroom as his heart begins to pound louder and louder in his chest and ears.

He taps on the bathroom door.

"Jaze..." he whispers.

She's still singing and can't hear a word of what he's saying.

"Jazemene..." he taps harder as the knocking on the door starts again.

The water turns off. Jaze cracks the door.

"Somebody's at the door..." Jojo tells her.

"It's probably just my Uncle Love." She replies.

"Or," Jojo says, "It's probably the police. How the hell are we supposed to know?"

"How would the police even know I'm here Josiah?" Jaze tries not to panic, but it's hard not to with the way Josiah's blue eyes are bulging out of their sockets.

"They're knocking again." Jojo says looking behind him.

"Open the door Jojo," Jaze instructs him, "the only person who would notice Bleek, or Roland are missing is Bleek's mom and she won't come looking for him until at least next week.

"Okay." Jojo says making his way to the hotel door.

Jojo peeps through the peep hole in the door.

He immediately opens the door.

"What took you so long?" Love asks walking in with Osiana in front of him and K.J. behind.

"Where's Jaze..." K.J. asks.

"In here." She calls out from the bathroom.

K.J. looks Josiah up and down with an amused grin.

"Jojo," K.J. laughs, "what the hell do you have on?"

"Wait till you see your sister," Jojo laughs lightly at himself, "We didn't have any clothes bro, so we had to go get something to wear from a gift shop on International Drive."

The bathroom door opens and Jazemene emerges wearing and I love Orlando tank top, and Minnie Mouse leggings.

"Well aren't you too just the cutest couple?" Osiana looks from Jojo to Jazemene.

"Auntie Osiana," Jaze pouts walking towards her, "I need your help."

"I know baby," Osiana opens her arms to receive her niece, "but somebody has got to tell me what's wrong. I can't help if I don't know what the problem is."

"How about this," Love walks towards the door, "Jaze you come with me so we can talk, and K.J. you fill your Auntie in about what's going on."

"Ok dad." K.J. agrees.

"Sure Unc," Jaze walks towards the sofa to fetch her Jordan shoes.

"Don't try anything cute Detective Blue," Love taps his left pocket, "You're here to help, just do that and make it back home to your husband safely."

As they head out of the door K.J. begins to explain the situation to his ex-detective Aunt by marriage.

(Outside near the pool)

"Jaze..." Love sighs taking a seat in one of the hotel chairs outside the gated pool area.

"Uncle Love," she says, "What's wrong?"

"I don't know," he sighs, "You tell me Jaze."

"Wait what," she frowns, "what the hell is that supposed to mean? You're looking at me like I'm lying about something or..."

"Or what?" he interjects.

"I don't know what that look is Love," she claims, "but it's very creepy."

"As you should already know sweet niece of mine," Love stands up and walks towards her chair, "I read people abnormally well..."

"And you're telling me this why?" she looks up into the deadly greenness of his gorgeous haunting eyes.

"Well," he says walking around behind her chair to bend down and whisper in her left ear, "I'm the living dead Jazemene as well as the only genius you'll probably ever know. Secrets don't exist around me, I see through you and everybody else I choose to. I know the truth..."

"About what Love," Jaze frowns as her heart rate increases, "what the hell are you talking about?"

"Never yell at me Jazemene," he warns her, "I'm not your mother or your father, I'm something **much** darker."

"Unc you're really starting to scare me..." Jaze admits.

"Ding, ding, ding, ding," Love startles Jaze with his sudden, loud, energetic burst, "Bob, I think we have a winner!!! I am the scariest mother fucker you will ever meet beautiful niece of mine, but as long as you've known me you've never admitted that you fear me. You watched me **end** your Mama Cole that night, and said nothing... that's the real reason I brought you out here."

"What," Jaze turns to look at her Uncle, "This is about my Mama Cole?"

"No," Love tells her, "This is about the fact that you never forgave me for killing her."

"So you brought me out here," Jaze stands up and turns around to face him with crossed arms, "to scare the living shit out of me just so you could get some petty ass closure about killing your mother?"

"Well when you say it like that it sounds kinda sick..." Love smiles.

"Oh it is sick," Jaze assures him, "and I'm not smiling Uncle Love. I forgive you."

Without looking back Jaze storms back inside the hotel towards the room.

Love sits down in the chair Jaze was just sitting in as he listens for the door to the lobby to close loudly behind her.

With his dreaded head down, eyes closed, and his long locks falling all around his face he readies himself to submit to the voices.

The door to the lobby flies back open violently. Love's eyes are still closed tightly.

"Hell no," Jaze says rushing back towards him, "that conversation does not end like that! You know what Uncle Love I'm a killer too now, just like you. I know exactly how it feels to spill another human's blood and end their existence."

"I know Jazemene..." Love says.

"***Do not*** cut me off," she commands, "I also know just as much about reading people as you do if not more."

"Is that so?" Love looks up at his niece standing over him.

"Yeah it is," she confirms, "this little talk and the whole scare tactic situation was never about me it's all about you..."

"Jaze you don't know..." Love starts.

"Shut up while I'm talking Uncle Love," Jaze interjects, "I saw you that night, no I saw through you that night. When you came to our house that night you didn't really believe you could carry out the horrible things you

203

had planned to do. You sat in prison for five years fantasizing about destroying all the people you blamed for destroying you. You hated everybody so much you tried to forget about how much you hated your damn self. But you never really did, and you never forgave yourself for all the fucked up things you've done. You cried that night Uncle Love... I saw you crying holding Mama Cole's dead body in your arms rocking from side to side. I'll never forget it; it still plays in my head some nights like a sick old horror movie. And honestly the only time I still piss on myself like I did when I was a kid, is when I have that nightmare... *Your* nightmare. You gave birth to a new monster the night you murdered your mother Uncle Love, but that monster wasn't you... it was me."

Jaze leaves her Uncle alone to think for the second time this evening. Love closes his eyes and waits for the door to slam again.

(Whitney's House)

"So now what?" Charlie asks looking at Whitney.

"He didn't say he was going to stop paying the bills baby," Whit explains, "I'm just letting *you* know, that *K.C.* knows."

"This shit is embarrassing as hell." Charlie assures her.

She doesn't respond, she doesn't know how to.

"He must think I'm some lazy punk bitch," Charlie begins to pace, "I'm getting a job tomorrow."

"Babe..." Whit whines.

"That's not up for discussion Whitney." He says.

204

"What happened to the money you had saved up?" she asks.

"What eleven years ago?" he asks.

"Has it been that long?" she frowns.

Charlie nods his head.

"Damn I'm old..." Whitney sighs.

"No you're not baby," he approaches her with sincere eyes, "You are like fine wine..."

"I know; I know I get better with time." Whit waves her hand back and forth unimpressed with the sentiment.

"Hell nawl girl..." Charlie gets down on his knees in front of her on the sofa.

"Then tell me Charlie, how am I like wine?" Whit crosses her arms and tilts her head slightly.

"You're always wet." He says reaching beneath her long dress to pull her cute lace panties off.

"What are you doing boy..." her scowl fades into a faint smile.

"Oh shut up..." he pushes her back against the sofa and then allows his tongue to take flight and then dive deep inside her precious fruit. Her moans give him the power to go stronger and longer. Whit pulls her dress up higher and then locks her legs around Charlie's active head. Grabbing the crown oh his dreads Whitney pulls his hungry mouth closer to her wetness. Charlie's tongue can't quite keep up with the rapid winding and grinding of Whit's lower body, but lord knows she appreciates his effort. Charlie pulls her even closer now. Whit leans forward over the top of his head as he sucks and devours her remarkable body. With perfect balance Charlie stands

205

up with Whit's legs now dangling over his muscular shoulders. His face is smothered in her creamy juices as his mouth is slowly beginning to fatigue. He lays her back down on the sofa. After kicking off both of his Polo boots, Charlie takes his pants and underwear off as well. Whitney is lying back with her legs spread wide enjoying the show. Charlie is the only man Whit has ever been with who's blessed with a body that can almost compete with Keldrick's. From her view Charlie's chest and stomach look like a chocolate paradise that she could lie on for eternity. Stroking himself in a downward motion Charlie bypasses Whitney's open legs and makes his way to her head. He lays himself on her forehead momentarily as he moans with pure ecstasy, and then he taps himself on her puckered lips several times. Whit slowly slips her tongue out through her perfect pink lips. He tastes like caramel and he smells like strong slow roasted cherries. Looking up into the dark abyss of his gorgeous dark dreads Whit can't help but to smile as her heart rate doubles instantly. With his left hand Charlie throws his strong dreads back over his head to see his woman with a clearer view. Charlie steps back just a bit as Whit turns on her side to face him. With both hands she takes hold of him as best she can and begins to take him on as only she can. After wetting him thoroughly she's ready to feel her man inside of her. Charlie picks her up again and carries her into their bedroom to give her all that she can take.

(Do you still love me...?)

De'Lure

As Keldrick sits in his car at the edge of his driveway his aging mind is stuck. He remembers vividly being a poor kid in Orlando. He never had the best clothes as a kid, but his daughter almost landed a deal to launch her own clothing line at fourteen. When he got old enough to drive, his mother couldn't afford to buy him a car; Jaze owned her first vehicle again at fourteen. His success in the NFL has afforded him things he honestly never dreamed of, but now his affluence is beginning to drain him. He no longer has dreams, because he has everything any human being could ever want. Well everything except peace. He takes his foot off the brake and reluctantly inches closer to his usual parking space behind the house.

After turning the car off, he closes his eyes and lies back on his comfortable leather seats. He hears the back door to the house open. He hopes it's not his wife. As he lay there with his eyes still closed he knows full well who's approaching his car. No one lives at the mansion anymore but he and Cameron. No it could always be his brother Love, maybe he broke in, murdered Cam and now is coming to take him out. As K.C. opens his eyes, Cam is standing at his window staring down at him. She smiles, he closes his eyes again. Cam opens his door.

"Do you still love me Keldrick?" she asks without a shred of confidence in her voice.

"Straight to it huh…" he replies with no emotion.

"I need to know Keldrick," she kneels down before him, "I need to know."

"What's for dinner," he asks smugly, "did you actually cook or am I paying for some full course delivery meal again?"

"Damn it K.C.!" Cam slaps him hard across the side of his face.

He laughs heartily.

"You really don't care do you?" Cam steps back with her arms crossed the tears are near now for sure.

K.C. steps out of his car and begins striding towards his house as if his wife is not standing behind him falling completely apart from the inside out.

"I should have kept shooting!" She screams.

K.C. stops cold and turns to look at her.

"What did you say girl..." K.C. walks towards her.

"I wish you died when I shot you fifteen years ago!" she cries.

"So you want more bodies on your record huh Cameron?" K.C. raises his left brow.

"What is that supposed to mean!" she cries.

"You know exactly what it means," K.C. glares at her, "you will kill anything that doesn't fit or changes your perfect *fucking* fantasy world!"

"I'm not a killer!" Cam cries.

"Oh yes you are Cameron Jiles," K.C. steps closer still, "you are responsible for two despicable murders that I know of."

"That's a lie," she screams out, "Keldrick don't do this please!"

"Don't do it," he asks, "Don't do what? I'm not killing anybody am I?"

"Neither am I..." she cries.

"Of course not," Kel jumps at her in anger, "You ain't got nobody left to kill! You tried to kill me when you found out about Whitney, then you killed or had your twin sister Megan killed at our wedding and took her place at the altar with me. I'm more than sure you've tried to take Whitney out before, and you told me how your sick ass used to stalk Dr. Carlos Sanchez."

"Keldrick..." she cries.

"I'm not finished," he fumes, "you said you didn't wash your ass for days. You lived in your car and stalked that poor taco eating son of a bitch from home, to work, and then back home again. And the only reason you didn't kill him and his lady at the time, was because you got the text message from Tyrone to meet him at the mall for my surprise proposal that you turned down and embarrassed me for life."

"Baby we are so far passed all that." Cam reaches for his hand.

"I'm not done," he growls snatching away from her, "all you've ever done is embarrass the men in your life. You left Sanchez in the mall for me when I had amnesia, then you left me after I proposed to you in front of the whole world for Tyrone. Then you left him after you found out we were half-brothers."

"I'm sorry baby." Cam wipes more tears away.

"Tell me Cam," K.C. crosses his arms, "I know you slept with Ty, did you sleep with Lance too."

She doesn't respond.

"You did, didn't you," he asks, "you bitch! What about Charlie and Jay?"

"No," she screams, "Jay never touched me!"

"But Charlie did?" K.C. laughs awkwardly.

"I don't wanna lie to you Keldrick," she sobs, "you're my husband."

"Am I," he replies, "Did you just figure that out this very second, because you've been doing a damn good job lying to me so far damn it!"

"I'm sorry baby..." she cries out.

"No you're **not** sorry Cameron," he pushes her away from him, "and I'm not your baby! Fuck it let's do it... two years ago when our son that we **never** talk about died in that pool, it was because of you."

"No!" she cries out at the top of her lungs.

"Yes he did," K.C. screams, "Kelmeron was only six years old and felt like the woman who gave birth to him would always protect him! But you couldn't do that could you?"

"I never meant to..." Cam can barely stand on her weak feet now.

"Oh you meant it bitch," he says with confidence, "your actions were absolutely premeditated. After Mama Cole's murder I had security cameras installed all around the mansion... even overlooking the pool."

Cam's heart drops as her painful watery eyes double in size.

"I can explain... Keldrick, baby I can..." she cries.

"Oh now yo ass can explain," he yells, "you waited until everybody was gone from the house, you took my only biological son outside to swim. Or hell I'm sure he thought he was just going to swim with his fuckin' mommy. You brushed his hair upstairs in his room after you gave him a bath. You put him on a pair of the swimming trunks I bought him in Atlanta that same year. You even kissed him goodbye sitting on the edge of his bed before taking him downstairs, outside to the pool. I watched that tape over a thousand times Cameron. The way you walked and acted, it was as if you were escorting him to his execution."

"It wasn't supposed to happen..." she cries.

"Apparently it was," K.C. says wiping his own tears away, "you carried my baby boy, my **only** son near the middle of that pool, and you threw him out in the middle and watched him tire himself out struggling to stay above water. I watched you stand there with your arms crossed waiting for him to die. He cried and screamed for you to save him! Oh he cried over and damn over again for you! *Mama, mama* please help me *mama*! I can still hear his voice from the video."

"I'm sorry..." she whimpers.

"No Cameron, fuck that," he screams, "don't apologize you didn't even really cry at the funeral. The only thing psychopaths like you are actually sorry about is getting caught. But I'm proud of my boy; I realize that you hated him because he wasn't the perfect son you always dreamed of. He was autistic I get it, but damn it he was ours Cameron!"

"You're right," she screams out, "you're absolutely right! I had to live day in and day out in this mansion with

Jazemene and K.J.'s perfect little yellow assess, knowing full well my little ugly, black ass son was retarded!"

"No he was not," Kel slaps her across her jaw, "he was different but he was learning and progressing daily. And my boy fought so hard that day, I'm still proud of him. You stood there, and waited, and waited for him to die but he was too strong just like his daddy. He refused to die. So then you took off your shirt and dove in the pool and held him below the surface just long enough to end his innocent life. You *sick* fuck, and the only reason I never turned you in or told a soul is because of the insane love I had for you and the chance I stood at losing everything I had because of the family brand we built together for the past ten years."

"I do not deserve this Keldrick..." She cries.

"Yes you do," he yells, "Damn it I forbid Jaze and K.J. to ever even talk about Kelmeron again because I didn't want people asking too many questions. America fell in love with us all over again with our sad story about how our poor autistic son wondered out to the pool and tragically drowned to death. I let my greed and public perception; stop me from sending you to prison where your sick ass belongs!"

Cam shakes her heavy head.

"This is why I *cheat* on you and treat you like *shit* now," he cries, "I knew what you did to our son Cameron... I *always* knew. And then... and then you had the *nerve* to *continue* to cheat on me too. Like the shit was okay."

"And you know what else," Kel continues, stepping close to her, "to be honest... at our wedding, standing at that altar with you all those years ago I prayed to God you were Megan. I honestly didn't love you anymore even back then Cameron. I wanted a second chance, and only Megan was capable of giving me that."

"No," Cam screams, "you do **not** mean that! Don't say **that**! Please don't say that…"

"It's true Cameron," K.C. crosses his arm enjoying her pain, "I was just so tired of everything and everyone that once I figured out I was with you and not your twin I just didn't care anymore."

"Why would you say that," Cam covers her trembling tear stained face, "Why would you tell me this **now**! I wasted **so** many years loving you, a man who doesn't care if I live or die…"

He walks face to face with her.

He leans down close to her left ear.

"Every single time we ever had sex as man and wife, I imagined you were her…" he whispers.

Looking down into her watery eyes he swears he can see her heart and soul breaking simultaneously. K.C. turns to leave again. As he walks away the power Keldrick Cole feels is indescribably wonderful.

"You…" Cameron reaches out to him but her arm falls short.

The sharp pain shooting through the right side of her body has forced her brain to stop functioning and her heart to stop beating. As the pure blackness consumes her she falls to the concrete as her mind, body, and spirit no longer have a desire or purpose to live.

K.C. turns around just in time to see her left cheek and then the left corner of her forehead smack against the ground as hard as he's ever seen anybody's head hit concrete. The immediate blood flow was expected.

(K.C.)

Cameron once told me, that Dr. Carlos Sanchez explained to her that... we control nothing. He said we think we're in control, but that thought is really just a false idea that's been imprinted on our brains since birth. We are now, and will always be controlled by our fears, and the things we love. The man was crazy as hell, but a genius all the same. Mortality as well, is something we are never in control of; we're here today and could be gone tomorrow. What we can control is what we do with the time we are allotted on this precious earth. We search throughout childhood, up through adolescence, and into adulthood for our purpose. Even if we find our purpose it can't fully complete us. A man can gain the whole world but without a person, the right person to spend his life with he will never be fully happy or know the true feeling of completion. When people die, we have no choice but to move on, and it's better that we do. The longer we hold on to our dead the closer we get to them. Now while that sounds like a good thing it's anything but. It's terrible when people die, and it's one of the worst things we as humans ever go through, but trying to keep

people here once they're gone is not good for us or them.
We must fully accept their passing, grieve accordingly,
cope, and then we must heal and move on with our
empty lives.

"I WAS YOUR FIRST
THAT FACT REMAINS THE SAME
I DON'T EVEN KNOW HOW WE FIRST BROKE UP
THAT SEEMS STRANGE
FLOWERS FELL FROM THE CEILING
WHEN I DEFLOWERED YOU
I FELT LIKE I EMPOWERED YOU
TO TOWER OVER THE COWARDLY DUDES
WHO TRIED TO DEVALUE YOU
SEE GIRL I TREASURED YOU
FAR BEYOND ANY MENTAL ESCAPADE
TO WANNA PLEASURE YOU
I WANT TO EMOTIONALLY MEASURE YOU
WHEN I LOOK INTO YOUR EYES
AND FIND YOUR SOUL
I FIND MY HEAVEN'S DEW
YOU'RE EVERY BIT AS HEAVENLY
AS EVERY ANGEL IN THE SKY
AND EVERY MAN ON EARTH'S FANTASY
FROM YOUR HIPS TO YOUR LIPS TO YOUR EYES
BUT YOUR MIND FLIES
FAR BEYOND ALL THE BEAUTIFUL BLUE
BUTTERFLIES
MY EYES SPY IN DISTANT SUMMER SET SKIES
SOMMERSAULTS

MY HEART FLIPS
EVERYTIME IT DIPS INTO THE POOLS OF YOUR EYES
IT SKIPS
THEN MY HEART DRIPS
HONEY DOWN THE SMALL OF YOUR BACK
AND IN BETWEEN YOUR LIPS
JUST A FANTASY NOW
OUR LOVE HAS LONG PAST AWAY
BUT FACTS REMAIN FACTS
I'LL BE YOUR FIRST TILL MY DYING DAY"

(K.C.)

I wrote that poem for Cameron two years after she went missing. I used my best possible handwriting and wrote it down on scented pink paper with a red pen. I signed it with my heart and sealed with a kiss as I rolled the poem up just right to fit inside a small empty bottle of Passion Absolute 1985. James Radicon the founder and supposed creator of Passion Absolute wine was touched by God himself. The man's wines are more than divine they can set the mood for any possible occasion. And so... to send a poem, a letter that special there's no other bottle I would have ever placed it in than a perfect pink bottle of Passions 85'. I ultimately sealed the letter with the bottle's cork and sent it off from the edge of the beautiful beach near my house. The waves took hold of the bottle immediately as if they had been commissioned for this job to deliver my precise words, my soul binding vow to my Cameron Candice Jiles. I never knew if she ever got the bottle or my poem, and I'm intelligent enough to know that it was impossible that she ever would. But that moment I lived in was absolutely euphoric... from the very instance the inspiration to write hit me, to the second I put pen to paper, and until the moment that pink bottle of Passion left my hand.

Chapter 14
The Plan

(In Orlando at the hotel)

"Okay Jaze," Osiana takes a deep breath, "you have a few options you can consider. Now before I lay out your choices, please understand that I did not put you in this situation, and I cannot control what happens once your choice is made. Everything is ultimately in the hands of the authorities, if you choose go that route."

"I'm listening Auntie and I understand." Jaze assures her.

"Okay, good." Osiana inhales deeply and then exhales watching Love out of the corner of her eye.

"So you can go back to Miami," Osiana starts, "go to the police, and turn yourself in..."

"**Hell no**," Love interjects, "Next option."

"You didn't even let me finish..." Osiana says eyeing the gun on Love's lap.

"Finish Auntie." Jaze says.

"If you turn yourself in to the police in Miami," Osiana explains, "that will show good faith. You can claim that Bleek and his friend attempted to rape you, you grabbed the gun and in self-defense you shot them both. You may still do time, but it won't be nearly as long as it will if you force the police to find you."

"Option **number two** please..." Love says.

"That's really her safest option Love." Osiana assures him.

"Forget safe," Love sits forward, "I want the best option for her to walk away like this never happened."

"She can try to make it across the border through Texas to Mexico." Osiana says.

"Bingo," Love says, "So Mexico is the best place or is there somewhere else she can go?"

"I don't have any money Uncle Love." Jaze turns to face him.

"I have a few hundred on my debit card." Jojo says.

"I'm broke," K.J. says, "I was supposed to pick up my Domino's delivery check today back in Miami."

"**Hell no**," Love says, "Look... Josiah, are you going with my niece?"

"Wherever she goes, I'm not leavin' her side." He replies.

"Fine," Love pulls his phone out, "I'll wire a couple hundred thousand to your bank account Jaze. Just write down your account and routing number."

"Unc you don't have to do that," Jaze says, "And I don't want to go to Mexico."

"Why don't you just turn yourself in Jaze?" Osiana pleads with her.

"Let me just put this out in the open," Love stands up, "No one on God's green earth is ever going to find the victim's bodies. Plus, I mutilated them a bit, so if she turns herself in and can't explain what happened to the bodies that won't go over well with the white pigs in blue."

"What did you do with the bodies Lance...? I mean Love?" Osiana asks.

"Jaze you have to leave the country baby," Love tells his niece, "Not forever but at least until everything blows over. Besides with a couple hundred grand in Mexico you'll be set hunny."

"I know Unc," Jaze walks into his arms, "and I'm sorry about what I said outside, I'm just stressed and tired... and scared Uncle Love."

"I know baby," he hugs her tightly, "and what you said outside needed to be said, don't you take a word of it back. Okay?"

"Okay." She replies.

"Look at me," Love says looking into his niece's eyes, "You were right, you pegged me right on the head, so I don't want you to ever feel bad about being smart enough to see through anybody, especially me."

"Whose alcohol is that in the corner?" Osiana points at several bottles near the sofa.

"Well it's my room so..." Love heads to the bathroom.

"I need a drink," Osiana says, "May I..."

"Knock yourself out," Love calls out from the bathroom, "pour me a shot too, the glasses are in the kitchen."

"Perfect." Osiana says taking a tall bottle of white alcohol with her into the kitchen.

"Hey Josiah," Osiana says, "Why don't you kids head on over to International Drive and get some fresh air?"

"I'm down." K.J. says.

Jaze looks at her little brother with tight eyes.

"Oh, I mean you two should go," K.J. sits back down, "I wanna chill with dad anyway."

"Nah it's cool little bro," Jojo says, "We can all go. Let's leave Love and Ms. Osiana alone to figure out what we should do."

The toilet flushes.

"That's a great idea," Osiana says, "Now you kids run along now, before Love has something to say."

They leave.

Love emerges from the bathroom and washes his hands. After he dries them he makes his way to the kitchen area where he finds Osiana with one of his bottles of alcohol, two shot glasses and a bottle of Dasani water from the fridge. She hands him a shot. He throws it back quickly. She takes hers, and then pours him another. Love throws the second shot back as well.

"Where did the kids go?" he asks.

"Oh, they're just outside by the pool." She tells him.

"If I didn't know any better," Love smiles, "I'd say I think you wanted to be alone with me."

"I'm nowhere near drunk enough to admit something like that sir..." Osiana laughs.

"I bet." Love smiles as he turns the television on and takes a seat on the sofa. Osiana brings him another shot, with the bottle clutched in her other hand.

(Magical Midway)

"Man this is so crazy," Jaze says walking towards the table where K.J. and Jojo are seated with a slice of pepperoni pizza, "This is the same table I sat at with my dad when I was a kid. Then I went inside the game room and Uncle Love…"

"My dad was sick Jaze." K.J. interjects.

"Was," Jaze replies, "he never changed K.J."

"That's not true Jaze." K.J. takes a bite of his pizza.

"Don't get it twisted," Jaze says, "I love your dad. He's my favorite Uncle, and I think the fact that he's criminally insane and genius is cool as hell, but I don't like you looking up to him the way you do."

"Why not?" K.J. asks.

"It's dangerous Keldrick." Jaze reminds him.

"Don't call me that," K.J. demands, "maybe I should start killing people until everybody starts calling me L.J."

"See," Jaze points at him, "saying shit like that is **not** okay K.J."

"You know what though…" K.J. says with a full mouth.

"Don't talk with your mouth full." Jaze says.

"Sorry," K.J. says, "but nah on the way here to Orlando my dad said that you're a lot like him. He said you scare him because you're the only person who he can't sense fear in."

Jaze looks at Jojo.

"Jojo can I borrow a twenty," K.J. asks, "I wanna go check out the go karts."

"Sure bro." Jojo grabs a crisp twenty-dollar bill out of his pocket and hands it to K.J.

After he's gone, Jaze still doesn't know what to say.

"Jazzy…" Jojo touches her left arm.

"Do you think it's true?" she asks.

"What that you're like your uncle," he asks, "hell no baby. That shit couldn't be further from the truth."

"I'm not so sure Josiah," Jaze wrinkles her brow, "I killed two people, I shot and killed two human beings, and if I can be completely honest it felt good to destroy them both."

"So," Jojo replies, "they were hurting you."

"My life wasn't threatened," Jaze says, "at least not by Bleek. He was on the sofa... naked, and Scooter was riding him and I don't know I just blacked out. When you guys came rushing through the door I panicked and shot."

"It was a crime of passion," Jojo assures her, "you weren't in your right mind."

"It was perfect." She says.

"Yeah okay," Jojo replies, "I'm just glad you didn't accidentally shoot me and little Keldrick."

"I never felt more alive in my life than when I was holding that beautiful gun." She claims.

"Don't say that baby," Jojo says, "You weren't stable. You put what five or six years into that asshole Bleek, just to catch him screwing your friend in the front room. You snapped, and it's understandable... maybe not in the court of law, but I get it."

"That's not the only thing," Jaze tells him, "when my uncle pulled me outside when they first got here, he basically told me that he's scared of me because I don't fear him. *That* part of what my brother said is very true. I killed two people Josiah; don't you find it the least bit weird that I'm not even nervous?"

"Are you done with your pizza?" Jojo asks folding his empty paper plate in half.

"Yeah, don't have much of an appetite anymore." She hands him her plate and he walks them both to the nearby trashcan.

"Come on," he grabs her hand, "let's take a walk."

"What about my little brother?" she asks.

"He's a big boy Jaze, besides we're not going far anyway." He assures her.

As they walk hand in hand; to Jaze the stars up above have never shined so bright and the air has never smelled so sweet. There's real unmistakable beauty in the rare moments in life when we are exactly where we're meant to be, and with the person we're meant to be with. Jaze would die now happily in this moment with him, if he would agree to pass away with her. She wouldn't dare say as much, because she's fully aware of how creepy the sentiment would sound spoken aloud. So, instead she just smiles enjoying the lively tourist atmosphere.

"Come on." Jojo pulls her with him towards a mostly closed, two story business complex across the street from the C.S.I. tourist attraction building on International Drive.

"I'm coming," she grabs hold of his left hand with both of hers, "but where are we going?"

"Behind this building to have sex..." He tells her looking up at the ***Old Stars 52 Barbershop*** on the second floor of the business complex.

"Yeah, that's what we're ***not*** going to do," she laughs, "what else would you like to do..."

"My dad used to bring me to that barbershop upstairs." Jojo points straight up at the red and white sign above the shop.

"Really?" Jaze asks holding his hands tightly.

"Yeah," Jojo confirms, "A guy named Angel owns the shop, he used to cut me and my dad's hair. I used to get my hair cut... exactly like my dad every single time."

"Jojo..." Jaze turns to look up into his eyes.

He looks away from her and starts back walking. Jaze refuses to help open old wounds inside the man she loves, so she remains silent.

As they walk through the breezeway to the back of the building Josiah is sure she'll submit to him. And he wants her right now more than he would ever verbalize.

As they round the corner to the back area of the building Jojo looks around to make sure they're alone.

He looks down at her with clear lustful intent. She tilts her head and flashes a goofy smile.

"Jojo, I am not having sex with you behind this..." Before she can finish her statement her back is pressed plush against the back wall and his tongue is fighting with hers for an unknown goal.

Reaching behind her inside her leggings Josiah squeezes her firm bottom instantly heightening his own arousal. His moan sends chills down Jaze's spine.

(Jaze)

I know I'll never tell this man no again in life. As he kisses and moans grow deeper I can actually feel all of my nerves melting away. Why should I be nervous anyway, I'll be twenty-two years old in six months. I'm grown as hell, and if my man... this man that I love wants me here and now, then that's all the incentive I need to take this risk.

She wiggles side to side as Jojo holds their kiss steady while trying to pull her pants down.

"One foot out..." he moans in her mouth.

Jaze uses her left foot to pull her right shoe off, and then lifts her right leg to take her leggings completely off of her right leg.

Jojo reaches in his back pocket and grabs his wallet. Jaze open her eyes as she continues to accept his wet hungry kisses. Jojo pulls a condom out from one of the small compartments in his wallet.

After returning his wallet to his back pocket, he holds the condom in one hand and massages Jaze's bright orange panties right where it matters most.

As she readies herself to submit fully to the powerful sexual urge possessing her body Jaze can barely stand still.

His hand is progressively aggressive; he's rubbing her wetness harder than necessary but she would never stop him for a second. She wants nothing more than to be, and fulfill his every desire.

As he raises the condom and readies his other hand to rip it open, Jaze gently grabs the condom from his hand and slides it back in his pocket. He opens his eyes, to find hers fixed on him.

She undoes his pants and pulls them down far enough. He smiles as she jumps into his arms with her beautifully athletic and willing legs wrap around him.

Jaze leans back against the wall to help him support her as he tries to fit in. With her bright orange panties pulled to the side Josiah enters her body naked for the first time.

He can feel everything. As her body grips his, he tries to steady himself so that the best feeling his young body has ever known can last at least a little while longer.

She's so warm and wet it's becoming too much for him to handle. She continues to bounce on him until he holds her body still in his hands by grabbing hold of her firm behind.

She understands.

She begins to grind instead of bounce now, and go slow instead of fast. The sounds of her passion filled moans are forcing the adrenaline in Jojo's body to deceive his mind.

He leans forward and begins to pump faster; her toned ass is still perfectly molded in his strong hands.

Too much, he slows down again and moves his hands from her behind to her lower back.

Just the thought of her butt could finish him off now.

Jaze climbs down and Jojo takes a step back awaiting her next move. She steps towards him and with one shoe on and one shoe off she stands on her tip toes to kiss Josiah gently.

Then she turns towards the wall and bends down grabbing both of her ankles.

Jojo steps closer and smacks her round bottom twice sending his arousal into hyper drive. The motion in her butt when he slaps it sends chills down his spine creating a feeling he can see himself becoming very addicted to.

He slaps her twice more.

Now close behind her he enters her tight body again. She's no longer making noise, so Jojo pushes deeper now.

"I love you…" she moans.

"What?" he replies slowly increasing the speed of his strokes.

"I said… *I love you…*" she moans from somewhere deep inside her pounding chest.

"I know you do." Jojo grabs both of her hips and begins to jump as deep inside of her as he possibly can.

WHOOP WHOOP!!!!

Two Orlando Police cars pull up behind the building quickly. Both officers' park, and then jump out of their cars and begin running towards Jojo and the still half naked Jaze.

"*Oh shit.*" Josiah says.

Jaze pulls her pants back on as fast as she can, grabs her shoe, and then runs close behind Josiah back through the breezeway towards International Drive.

It's obvious the two aging officers will never catch the two young adults on foot. The officers give up quickly and run back to their cars; and drive back around to the front to cut the Jojo and Jaze off at the pass.

By the time the officer's pull back onto the front street there's no sign of either Jaze or Josiah.

Kneeling down behind the C.S.I. tourist attraction building, Jaze and Josiah laugh heartily as they try desperately to catch their breath.

Jaze puts her other shoe on and then tries to stand up straight.

"Come here you." Jojo pushes her against the wall and kisses her twice.

"You know what?" she says staring into his large blue eyes.

"What…" he replies turning his head to look off into the distance.

"I recant my earlier statement about that gun," she smiles with her mouth pressed to his right cheek, "I've never felt more alive than I do **right** now."

(Love & Osiana)

Ten shots later Love is exactly where he wants to be. Osiana is watching him closely with an almost satisfied grin on her face. As she runs her fingers through her full blonde hair she contemplates her next move.

"You know Love," she whispers in his ear, "Tyrone is the only black man I've ever been with…"

Love smiles.

"So you've never been with a light skinned brother before huh…" he asks.

She shakes her head no.

"And as much as I hate to admit it, you are the most attractive black man I've ever seen in real life." She claims.

"What does that mean…?" Love laughs as he lies back on the sofa with his gun still on his stomach.

"You know," Osiana smiles, "there's always these **unbelievably** beautiful black men on television, but I've never met one as gorgeous as you in person."

"Then get over here and test the beautiful waters girl…" he mumbles.

Osiana walks between the twin hotel beds and makes her way to the radio on the table. She turns it on and finds the right music to set the mood.

She doesn't know what station the radio is on but Brian McKnight is willing her to sin happily with his wonderfully melodious voice.

She closes her eyes and enjoys the filthy thoughts of Love running ramped through her mind. As she turns around she catches Love checking out her ample behind.

She smiles as she tries not to blush. She walks back towards the sofa slowly, but with seemingly clear intent. Standing beside him now as he lies on the couch, Osiana looks down into the magnificent green orbs God gave this man to see with.

Love reaches out and puts a hand on her thigh. Osiana pulls her shirt off over her head. After removing her shoes and her shorts as well, she stands there waiting for him to control her.

Love licks his full pink lips.

Osiana can feel his tongue touching his own lips at the very core of her being as her passion box begins to secrete love juices. Love begins to fidget with his belt.

Osiana reaches behind her and caresses her own firm buttocks.

Her soft and perfectly smooth skin is heightening her own arousal as well as Love's. She removes her bra and throws it to the floor.

Love looks up at her as she begins to fondle her own breast. He can no longer hide his attraction to the blonde beauty. He opens his pants and releases himself as Osiana's eyes triple in delighted size.

She falls to her knees before him like a loyal subject before her king. She grabs him with one hand and turns her head to the side to see it at a better angle.

"This **never** leaves this room Lance Orlandis Vinson..." she says.

"What happens in the hotel **stays** in the hotel..." Love says pushing his gun off of his chest onto the sofa.

With her head still tilted Osiana kisses him from the base to the peak. Then with her tongue flicking about recklessly she tries to touch every inch of him.

She looks up at him; the lust and dazed happiness in his eyes are the only appreciation she needs, to know she doing her job to perfection.

She pushes it back and makes her way down to his balls. As she sucks and caresses them Love's legs begin to flex involuntarily.

He moans, and then she follows suit as the passionate attraction between them is so purely mutual.

Still sucking and rubbing his sensitive sack, she strokes him with her free hand.

"Get your ass up here..." Love moans.

Take My Breath Away 3

Sitting back up straight on her knees Osiana smiles up into his lazy green eyes again as she takes him on as deep as she can. Her throat is filled to capacity but she continues to let him stroke inside of her mouth from his back.

Love reaches down to hold her head in place as he has sex with her warm wet mouth. Osiana's hands are both on Love's right thigh as she's still taking him from the side of his body. She's holding on for dear life as he digs deeper in her skull for a point he may never reach.

She pulls away as her reflexes give way to a short gagging fit. After she regains her composure she readies herself to submit to his hands again.

The saliva from the corners of her mouth is seeping out perfectly as his entire penis is now covered in it. Love moans again as he notices the tiny spit bubbles forming in the corner of mouth as he watches her mouth from the side as she takes him on.

Her throat seems to be growing deeper by the second. Love wants to stop and have vaginal sex with her, but her mouth feels every bit as good as any vagina he's ever experienced.

She moves his hand and leans forward with a vengeance. Down, down, down she continues to throw her mouth down on his strong throbbing member.

The sound of her masterful performance is sending new shock waves through Love's tensing body. She stops just before he reaches his climax.

Love knows she wants to feel him inside of her. He reaches in his pocket and retrieves a magnum condom. He hands it to her and then pushes his pants down a bit more. His gun resting beside him isn't allowing him to get completely comfortable.

After giving it some careful thought, Love grabs his gun and points it at Osiana. She sits there staring down the barrel of the gun holding tight to the golden packet.

Love turns the gun around and hands it to her, he trusts her now.

He knows that his body now has complete control over this woman. Osiana takes the gun and sits it on the floor next to the sofa. Then she opens the large condom and rolls it down the length of him with her mouth.

"Damn..." he growls lustfully.

"White girls do it better..." Osiana winks at him and then smiles as she stands to her feet.

She turns around to show him her round ass again.

As he reaches out to touch it, she strategically bends over to give it an even fuller appearance. Love's body is aching for her as he looks on at the sight of her ass appearing to grow before his very eyes.

He realizes his drunken eyes are definitely playing tricks on him but he wouldn't change a moment of this experience if he could.

With her pretty blonde head near her dainty pale ankles Osiana reaches up to remove her underwear.

Love turns his body on the sofa towards her as he sits up on the edge of it. With her legs open Osiana grabs hold of him and then impales herself with his large penis as she sits back on him.

With his hands gripping her slim firm waist Love guides her up and down on his rock hard body.

"Ohhhh!" she screams out leaning forward as her body is already giving way to multiple orgasmic ruptures.

With her hands on his knees to keep her balance Osiana steadies herself for the harsh pounding she knows will soon follow.

(Whitney & Charlie)

"That was so good daddy." Whit rolls over to lie on his broad chocolate chest."

"Yeah it was Suga Mama..." Charlie agrees.

"Never call me that again," Whit smacks his ripped stomach hard, "Are you stupid? Why would you do that?"

"What," Charlie smiles awkwardly, "It was a joke Whitney **calm** down."

"**Bad** joke Charlie." She rolls over to the far side of the bed.

"Damn." He groans.

"Damn is right fool," she throws a pillow at him; "every man I've ever dealt with has known damn well they were in a never ending competition with my first. It wasn't fair to them then, and it ain't fair to you now, but its reality."

"Why does that have to be reality?" Charlie asks rolling over to face her.

"Because it just is Charlie!" she exclaims.

"It's all in your mind baby," he tells her, "you can overcome those thoughts. If you say that's not the case, then it no longer is."

"That's bullshit Charlie," Whit tells him, "mind games and tricks have no effect on real love."

"Damn." He replies.

"What now Charlie..." Whit turns towards him.

"Real love huh," he says, "So you're still in love with him?"

"What are we talking about here?" Whitney laughs.

"Hell yes I am," she admits, "Whitney Michelle Powell is now and will ***forever*** be ***in love*** with Keldrick Jermaine Cole."

"So what the hell is my purpose?" Charlie asks.

"Oh baby," Whit rolls over close to him, "your purpose is to ***stay*** Charlie. Just stay. You're gorgeous, street savvy, loving, and loveable but..."

"But you're not in love with me..." he says.

Whitney's phone begins playing Maxwell's song "Lifetime".

"Hello," she answers, "Kel. Wait, she what? Damn it! Are you serious? Where is she? You're there now? I'm on my way now."

Whitney jumps out of bed and rushes to her drawer to find clothes.

"What's wrong," Charlie sits up in bed, "What happened to Jaze?"

"I haven't talked to or about Jaze for days," Whit tells him, "I have no idea where that lost child of mine is."

"Wasn't that her dad on the phone?" Charlie asks.

"Yeah," Whit says pulling on tight pink sweat pants, "Cam had a stroke."

Whitney makes her way into the bathroom fully dressed where she turns the water on in the sink and puts toothpaste on her toothbrush.

Charlie heads to the closet to find pants.

"Is it bad?" he calls out from deep inside the closet.

"Won't know the details until I get there." She says rushing back out of the bathroom.

"Give me a minute," Charlie says stumbling out of the closet and into his pants, "and I'll..."

"You're not going Charlie," Whit tells him, "I told you, you stay."

"What?" he replies.

"I'll call you later." Whit grabs her keys and heads for the front door.

"I'm a man Whit," he yells, "Not a dog!"

(Double Cross)

"***Dad***..." the voice is trying to break through the darkness.

"Dad..." the voice speaks again.

It's hard to discern the good voices from the bad ones now.

"Dad, wake up please..." K.J. reaches down into the tub to shake his father's half naked body.

Love opens his eyes, but can't seem to focus them on his frantic son.

From his sore back Love presses his finger to his lips.

"Shhh," he says, "We don't wanna wake up the black beast."

236

"What?" K.J. wrinkles his left brow closing the bathroom door behind him to be alone with his father.

"Is Whitney still sleeping?" Love asks.

"Dad, are you okay," K.J. asks, "And my mom is in Miami."

"Dad," Love squints, "I don't have any kids. What's going on here?"

"Dad it's me K.J.," he pleads, "please don't go crazy again daddy I need you."

"Is K.C. here?" Love asks.

"No dad..." K.J. cries riddled with pain and panic.

"So he already went outside," Love raises up, "I have to get downstairs before Cameron shoots him... it's my job to kill my brother not hers. I'll just kill that bitch so she won't get in my way again."

Love barely makes it out of the hotel tub on his two wobbly legs. K.J. fixes his pants and belt for him, and then stands aside as his dad reaches for the door. Standing there in the now open doorway are Jaze and Josiah.

"I heard everything Uncle Love," Jaze's calm eyes are focused on her Uncle, "now I need you to calm down."

"Uncle Love," he laughs, "Whitney what are you talking about baby? I don't... I don't have any nieces."

"Unc you're having a flashback from like sixteen freakin' years ago..." Jaze reaches for his shaky hand.

"Whitney, please stop playing with me," he snatches away from her, "I have a pounding headache. Where is K.C.?"

237

"I'm not Whitney Uncle Love," Jaze screams, "I'm her daughter Jazemene! And my father is safe; he's back home in Miami."

Love laughs again making his way past her and Josiah towards the window on the far wall.

"Dad," K.J. steps out of the bathroom cautiously, "Where is Auntie Osiana? When we left she was here with you two hours ago."

K.J. looks into his sister's eyes, she can sense and see his fear but he can't find an inkling of hers.

Josiah stands behind Whit and K.J. behind him as they all watch Love stare aimlessly out of the hotel window.

"Whitney," Love says turning to look at Jaze, "What's going on here? Your apartment was on the second floor when I fell asleep... now we're on the first floor. And who are these dudes?"

"I'm your niece Jazemene," she growls, "Now snap out of this and focus! Where the hell did Osiana go?"

Love sits down on the bed near the window facing the three of them.

"Okay," he laughs, "I see what this is. Okay, okay Whit you win. I admit it, K.C. is my big brother, and your daughter Jazemene is my niece. Where is the baby anyway?"

"I'm right here Uncle Love," Jaze yells, "and you need to wake the fuck up now!"

"But my Jazemene is only five years old..." Love squints at her.

"Not anymore Uncle Love," she pulls up her Facebook page on her phone, "Look."

Love takes the phone in his hands.

"That's you, me, and my parents at our mansion in Miami." Jaze explains.

Love throws her phone down on the floor and immediately starts beating himself in the head.

"No, no, no!" he screams out.

"Lance, get the fuck out of my head!" he continues to rant.

K.J. rushes past Josiah to his father and wraps his arms around him.

Love breaks the embrace, to hold the teen back far enough to look at him. K.J. stares back at his father covered in tears.

"**The child will save you**..." Love whispers pulling his son back close to his sore body.

"**I'm so sorry**," Love cries, "Jaze... hey, Josiah all of you I'm so sorry. I sometimes have these spells..."

"It's okay Uncle Love," Jaze walks closer to them, "but right now I need to know what happened to Auntie, did you hurt her in anyway, please tell me you didn't kill her."

"I... I honestly don't know Jaze," Love claims, "we were drinking, and then she started stripping..."

"And what happened?" Josiah asks stepping forward.

"I blacked out guys," Love tells them, "I really don't know."

Jaze's phone vibrates. She quickly checks it.

239

"Oh shit," Jaze says, "It's a text from Auntie... she says, "I'm sorry Jazzy; please turn yourself in." She must have called the police."

"We have to leave now!" Josiah grabs Jaze's hand.

"Wait," K.J. says, "we're right by International Drive."

"What's your point K.J.?" Jaze asks.
"There are always cops and sheriffs in this area," he reminds them, "Plus auntie Osi used to work for Orlando P.D."

"Right," Jojo agrees, "so if Osiana wanted Jazemene to get caught the police would've already been here by now."

Love smiles.

"Why are you smiling dad?" K.J. frowns.

"I get it," he says, "she called the police but she didn't tell them exactly where we are because she wants us to escape."

"But why would she call the police if she wants us to escape Uncle Love?" Jaze asks. "That makes no sense at all." She continues.

"She's a fan." Love says.

"Of who..." Jojo asks stepping forward.

"Me," Love explains, "Didn't ya'll ever wonder why I never went down for the crimes I committed?"

"So," Jaze starts, "Osiana didn't turn you in or the evidence she obviously had against you because she was a fan of your crimes?"

"Bingo," Love says, "Now I think she's a fan of yours as well baby girl. Now I need everybody to get what you came with and let's get the hell out of here now."

(The hospital)

As Whitney sits in the hospital parking lot she's more than conflicted. She has no idea what to expect when she gets inside.

(Whit)

On the one hand Cam is my girl and I don't want anything bad to happen to her, but in the back of my mind I know full well she's the only thing standing in between my own inevitable marriage to K.C. So if by some tragedy or stroke of luck she passes away Keldrick will fall helplessly into Suga Mama's open loving arms. I have my insurance policy in my back pocket just in case things don't go my way smoothly.

Whitney burst in through the front of the hospital with her heart drumming louder and louder in her ears. Her nerves are causing her to repeat Cam's hospital room number over and over again.

On the elevator she says a short precise prayer. As the elevator doors open seconds later she knows the next several moments could reshape the rest of her life.

She knocks and then opens the hospital room door. Inside she finds Keldrick at Cam's bedside, crying holding her left hand close to his lips.

"Oh baby…" Whit breaks down immediately at the sight of her big strong high school sweetheart overcome by real emotion.

She rushes to him wrapping her comforting arms around him.

"How bad is it?" Whit cries in a barely audible tone.

"They don't know." K.C. buries his face in his hands.

"They say they don't know," he continues, "she just wanted me to take back what I said. All she wanted me to do was tell the truth… she just wanted me to say I loved her. And I do Suga Mama, Lord knows I love her."

Whit leans back a bit.

K.C. looks up into her eyes that don't seem to be producing tears anymore.

"Do you love her more than you ever loved me?" Whit asks.

"Damn it Whitney," K.C. cries, "She's my wife!"

"Answer my question Keldrick." Whit demands drying her old tears away.

"I wanna know," she continues, "if she doesn't wake up, or if she's not going to be okay are you going to finally be *my* husband?"

"Are you really doing this now," K.C. asks, "here?"

The door swings open, as police officers rush in.

"What the hell is this?" K.C. asks holding his hands out to keep the cops away from him.

"You're under arrest." The first officer says.

"Have you lost your damn mind," K.C. replies, "Under arrest for what?"

"Domestic Violence and attempted murder." The second officer says pulling his handcuffs from behind his back.

"Don't resist them Mr. Cole." The doctor says entering the room.

"What the hell is this?" K.C. asks looking into the face of the doctor.

"It's out of our control Mr. Cole." the doctor claims.

"What's out of your control?" K.C. asks pulling his phone out of his pocket pressing several buttons.

"Well Mr. Cole nobody here is stupid," the doctor says, "now we all believe you love your wife but..."

"But what!" K.C. screams putting his phone back in his pocket. "You don't think I hurt her... do you?" he asks.

"The thing is," the doctor walks past him towards Cameron, "the blunt trauma that your wife suffered to her head, there's almost no way it could have happened the way you said it happened."

"Almost," he screams, "almost, you're telling me that you're having me locked up because you don't think the small possibility that my truth is the actual truth is actually possible? That's the dumbest shit I've ever heard!"

"If you didn't do it," the first officer says, "Why the hell are you so defensive?"

"I'm not trying to be defensive," K.C. says with calming hands, "I want us all to get to the truth."

"Then put your arms behind your back before I hit you with resisting arrest!" the officer says.

K.C. obeys submitting to the officer's cuffs.

"Mr. Cole," the doctor says, "Your story just doesn't add up, plus you were also in here hugged up with your highly publicized ex, the mother of your children Whitney Powell, while your wife lies there in a coma that **you** caused."

"What the hell does hugging Whitney have to do with the possibility of me hurting my wife?" K.C. wrinkles his brow tightly.

"Mr. Cole," the doctor says, "If you really didn't do anything wrong you'll be fine."

"Oh yeah," K.C. replies, "How many times have you been a black man in handcuffs, jail, or court?"

K.C. looks from the doctor into Whitney's eyes.

"Suga Mama," he cries, "Suga Mama, tell them I wouldn't hurt my baby... Tell them I would **never** hurt her!"

"You're wasting your time Mr. Cole," the doctor laughs, "we know the truth, Ms. Powell is the one who let us know that your relationship with your wife has a long history of abuse. She's the one who called the cops not us."

"Answer my question Keldrick." Whit says.

K.C. can't believe what's happening.

"This woman is crazy!" K.C. screams. "Don't you see what's going on here?" he continues. "She can't have me so she wants to destroy me!" K.C. screams out.

Whitney looks at the cops and then back at Keldrick.

"I guess I got my answer fellas," Whit smiles, "take him away officers."

"Are you serious?" K.C. exclaims. "You evil conniving bitch," K.C. continues, "I'm not going down for this, but every one of you mother fuckers will pay for this! Especially yo ass Whitney!"

The officers force K.C. down the hall and into the elevator.

"Do not leave that woman alone with my wife!" K.C. screams as the elevator closes.

"I always love this." the first officer flashes his disgusting smile.

"You love what?" K.C. looks down at him.

"Catching you stupid, arrogant, black mother fuckers in some bullshit," he says, "and then ruining your fuckin' life."

"Well you won't be ruining mine," K.C. says with confidence, "I didn't touch my wife, and I'm also rich enough to buy my way out of anything. I'll be out as soon as you book me. My driver Bennie will come get me."

The officers laugh.

"Your ***driver***," the second officer says, "how does that shit feel to be that rich but have no real friends? The only mother fucker that will come bail your black ass out of jail is a dude you got on your payroll."

The truth of the officer's statement hits Keldrick Cole deeper than he'd even like to admit to himself.

Chapter 15
Cameron's Truth

(Lost)

All alone in the hospital room with a comatose Cameron, Whitney is deciding what her safest move is. Her phone begins to ring in her purse startling her instantly.

"K.C must be using his one phone call..." she smiles to herself.

It's Charlie.

She ignores the call and drops her phone back in her purse. He continues to call, and she continues to ignore the violent vibration in her purse on the floor right between her feet. After the calls become unbearable Whitney reaches down and snatches the phone out of her purse.

"Hello," she snaps, "What boy? Well if you start acting like a man, I'll treat you like one! The hell you calling me like you crazy for? You really starting to get on my nerves."

Whitney rolls her eyes as Charlie yells in her ear.

"I don't care Charlie," she yells, "thank you *again* sir for *destroying* and *hiding* a man's body *for me*; *yes,* you did cover up a crime that would have *ended* my life. But Charlie the truth is I will *never ever* run to you or *for* you, like I do for K.C. and Cameron. You're absolutely right, the three of us *do* deserve each other... or at least **two** of us do. Bye Charlie, I'm hanging up now... you can have the house I'm going to move into the mansion. Bye now."

Whit ends the call and drops her phone back down in her expensive purse that Cam bought her for her birthday. Up on her feet she walks close to Cam and takes her right hand in hers and gives way to her thoughts.

"Cameron," Whitney whispers to her unconscious lover, "look at you now girl. It's a shame really, you didn't have to hurt yourself this way, and your life didn't have to end like this. You were never built to be Kel's wife. Ever since I was sixteen years old, that title rightfully belonged and was owed to me. You knew that you little black whore but you didn't care, all your stupid ass cared about was marrying your *first*. He was mine before we ever walked in that wack ass restaurant where you were working all those years ago. I could kill you right now, and honestly if I thought I could get away with it right now I probably would. The crazy thing is I love you, I love you almost as much as I love Keldrick it's just different because he's the father of my daughter. Why couldn't I be his wife, and you... our in house slut? I also know you had sex with my Charlie before we had that orgy with him and Love. Bitch you are just the master of fucking other women's men and hiding it."

The door opens.

"Visitation is over in about an hour or so ma'am," the nurse informs her, "are you planning to stay with Mrs. Cole over night?"

"No," Whit replies, "I'm just going to sit with her for a while longer and then I'll leave."

The nurse nods and bows out of the room.

(Don't gas me up)

Still handling her uncle's car, Jaze and Josiah are riding through Orlando waiting on their instructions from him.

"We really need to stop and get gas Jaze." Josiah points towards the meter above the steering wheel."

"Yeah I know," she says, "I just checked my account again the money's not there yet."

"I got it, just find a station ASAP." Jojo says.

"There's a Hess gas station up ahead on the left." Jaze reminds him.

As they pull up to the station Jaze cuts the song on the radio up.

It's an older song. She can't remember who sings it but she knows it's one of her mom's favorite songs.

She would never admit as much out loud but she is starting to really miss her parents. After she parks near one of the pumps at the Hess gas station, Jojo jumps out to go inside and grab some chips and pay for the gas.

A brand new Infiniti pulls up on the other side of the pump Jaze is waiting at. Even though the bright red car isn't playing any music it has all of Jaze's attention, or at least the driver does.

The young Puerto Rican guy driving the car seems to be just as taken by Jaze as she is by him. He steps out of his car and makes his way to the fire engine red Camaro. His Hollister jeans fit him and his walk perfectly.

He isn't wearing a shirt, and Jaze is secretly thanking God that he isn't. His curly brown hair has a hint of blonde throughout it. His watch, ring, and bracelet are all made of impressively bright gold.

"Nice car." He says.

"Thanks," Jaze replies, "it's not mine though."

"As good as you look in that car whoever owns it should give it to you," he tells her, "this Camaro was made for you."

Jaze blushes.

"I'm Papi by the way," he says, "what's your name?"

"Hi Papi," Jaze replies with an increasingly dry throat, "I'm Jazemene."

"Nice to meet you Jazzy." he says reaching for her hand and removing his shades.

"I hate that name," Jaze says slowly looking up into the steel grayness of his eyes, "but... if you like it, I could probably get used to it."

"Yeah I like it," Papi flashes an irresistible smile, "hell I like **you** mami. So hey, why don't you give me your number so I can text you... Don't wanna get you in trouble with your **gringo**."

"My gringo?" Jaze wrinkles her brow.

"Your **white boy**." Papi smiles teasingly as he points inside the gas station towards Jojo still waiting in the shortening line.

"Oh," Jaze smiles, "Yeah, he's just my best friend. But sure you can have my number if you want it."

Papi hands her his phone, and Jaze nervously puts her number in it.

"Here you go." she hands the expensive phone back to him.

"Wait, wait," Jaze says taking the phone back, "I put my old number in there. Here I fixed it."

Papi takes the phone back.

"You sure it's the right number mami..." Papi smiles.

"Yep," Jaze confirms, "don't let it go to waste now Papi."

"A face like yours is unforgettable mamacita," Papi says on his way back to his car, "you're the only reason I came here."

"Yeah right..." Jaze mumbles to herself as he drives off without getting a drop of gas.

(Back in Miami)

As Whitney pulls back up to her house all of her demons are riding her shoulders with no intentions of letting go anytime soon. After parking the car, she grabs her purse and makes her way to the front door. From outside she can hear the T.V. on with the volume up extremely high.

She unlocks the door and walks in slamming the door behind her. Whit shakes her head in real disgust as she makes her way through the front room.

She throws her purse on the floor and her phone falls out. As the fall to the floor causes her phone's screen to light up she sees all the missed calls and ignored texts from Charlie, but doesn't take time to read them now since she's already home. She picks the phone up and throws it on the sofa along with her purse.

"Charlie," she yells with her hands on her hips, "you are such a fucking kid! No, you're not even a kid you're a fucking bitch! I can't believe you got your grown ass in here pouting and throwing a damn tantrum! I'ma stand right here until you bring your weak ass in here... *I know you hear me Charlie Breeze*!"

Tired of waiting on his response Whitney turns the loud television off and then rushes through the doorway back to her bedroom.

The door is locked. Through the door she can hear slow music playing. Whitney smiles at the satisfaction she knows she's going to feel when she catches him in the act.

She reaches up above the door and retrieves the sturdy straightened paper clip they use to unlock the bedroom door anytime they accidentally lock themselves out of it. As Whitney inserts the clip into the small hole in her bedroom door, she hesitates as new thoughts quickly creep into her mind.

(Whit)

I think I want to leave this man, but what if Keldrick still doesn't want me even after Cameron dies? Then what? I'll be all alone looking stupid. But what have I pushed this man to? I knew K.C. was always cheating on me, but I thought when Charlie looked in my eyes and swore I was the only one he was actually being honest with me. Once I open this door and see him with her...

whoever the slut is, once I see them together everything changes forever. Fuck you Charlie!

She throws the door open.

The room is empty. Whitney burst into her bathroom and then stops short near the doorway. Her eyes bulge instantly as her heart forgets how to beat.

Her screams are so incredibly loud she can't hear anything at all. Whitney's entire being feels like it's been sucked into a dark lifeless vacuum.

There's no sound, and everything seems so dim around her. The smell is almost too much for her to stand and the sight before her would unnerve the most sadistic people on the planet. On the sink she finds a letter that she slowly grabs.

"Charlie... baby," Whitney cries out as she walks towards him, "Baby, no. What did you do? Baby no... I'm so sorry; I swear I didn't mean a word of what I said. I do love you, I wanted to be with Keldrick but he doesn't love me like you do. I told you Charlie just stay... not like a dog, but like a good man who understands his woman. I just wanted you... to stay baby."

She's right beside him now. Behind what's left of his sunken in head Whitney can see the fragments of her boyfriend's brain. She tries to step closer but loses what little composure she has left and falls limp into a huge puddle of his blood on the floor clutching tightly to his letter.

De'Lure

(The Mall)

After parting ways with Jaze and Jojo again, Love and his son head to the mall for a bite to eat and a chance to catch up some more. Love is dressed in dark jeans and a burgundy shirt. K.J. has on khaki shorts and a red tank top.

"What are you in the mood for son?" Love asks.

"Chinese." K.J. says confidently.

"K.J." Love says with his head tilted slightly.

"What,' he replies, "I do, I want Chinese food dad."

"No you don't son," Love shakes his head, "I told you about that shit now. You don't have to pretend to like the things I like."

"I do dad," K.J. says looking up at his father, "we're the same; I literally like everything you like."

"Fine," Love puts both hands behind his back, "let's get Chinese."

"Fine." K.J. replies.

"And we're the same right," Love says, "we like all the same shit right?"

"That's right." K.J. confirms confidently.

"Fine," Love looks towards the Chinese restaurant, "go order for both of us."

"Wait what?" K.J. panics.

"Go order our food son," Love says, "Since we both love it *so* much, I'm sure you know what to order right..."

"No," K.J. looks over at the menu, "I mean... I'll have what you're having."

"Never do this shit again K.J.," Love instructs his son, "you're trying entirely too hard."

"I'm not dad," K.J. claims, "Chinese isn't my favorite but I don't mind eating it."

"Right," Love smiles, "see son... I don't want you to pick something you *don't mind.* If I ask you what you want to eat, that means I want you to pick what you want."

"Pizza." K.J. says.

"Perfect." Love says walking towards the pizza vendor.

They order their food and get it rather quickly as the slices just had to be reheated in the large oven behind the food display.

"I'm going to use the bathroom and grab us some napkins," Love says, "You go find us a table son."

"I'm on it." K.J. replies headed towards the crowded food court tables carrying a tray with four slices of pizza on it.

"Boy time really does fly..." a soft voice says from behind Love.

Love turns around with a temporary frown that soon fades into a pleased smile.

"Gabby..." Love hugs the full figured, caramel toned woman tightly.

She's about four inches shorter than Love with a delightful round face. Her tight fit jeans and cute black shirt seem to slim her a bit as he steps back to look at her better.

"Boy," she blushes hard reaching up to make sure her jet black hair is still in perfect position, "you better have wiped that frown off your gorgeous face... Who peed in your corn flakes this morning?"

254

"No cornflakes," he laughs with her, "but it has been a very long day."

"Why what's wrong?" she asks with her face wrinkled in genuine concern.

"Long story," he smiles, "enough about me Gabrielle Johnson **how are you**? Still pretty as hell I see."

"Still?" she asks with a sideways smile.

"You were cute back in school." Love tells her with a straight face.

"Boy," she shakes her head, "that was twenty years ago, and no I was not cute at all. But to answer your question, I'm okay. No, I'm good actually."

"Why the hesitation..." Love asks crossing his arms gently.

"Well," she exhales, "I just went through a divorce. No I just went through **the worst divorce in history** and I'm honestly just now at thirty-eight years old feeling capable of finding my true self."

"I know the feeling," Love agrees, "who were you married to? If you don't mind me asking..."

"Larry Lewis." She groans.

"Larry Lewis," Love cringes, "*Little leg* Larry Lewis?"

"Yeah that's what they called him in school," Gabby laughs, "but trust me that boy grew up and ain't nothing little bout that leg now."

"Way too much information..." Love says as they both laugh.

"I had the biggest crush in the world on you back in school Lance." Gabrielle admits.

"I know," Love sighs, "Everybody did my senior year."

"No," Gabrielle says, "Not when you got all cute Lance, before your growth spurt and the clear skin. I hated you when you were with Starlita. I still remember when you gave her that ring, and she gave it to that asshole on the basketball team, then he gave your ring to Shannon Treadwell."

"Don't remind me," Love groans, "but wait, why did you like me better when I was ugly?"

"Ugly is inside not out." She claims.

Across the food court K.J. is trying his luck with an attractive girl his age with a mouth full of shiny braces laced with colorful rubber bands. Her deep bronze skin tone drew him in instantly. K.J. has never been the type to approach girls, but with her he couldn't resist.

"So can I text you?" K.J. looks down at his feet.

"Sure," Felicity smiles, "Do you have a phone?"

"Here..." K.J. hands his phone to her.

"Who is that...?" K.J. looks off in the distance.

"Where..." Felicity turns to see what her new friend is looking at.

"My dad," K.J. says, "he's over there talking to some old fat lady."

"She's not old," Felicity scolds him, "she's not fat, and she's my Aunt. My mom died, so she takes care of me now."

"Oh, no I didn't um..." K.J. takes his phone as she hands it back to him with a seemingly permanent frown.

"I guess you deleted your number." K.J. slides his phone in his back pocket.

"No," she shakes her head, "you're very rude, and judgmental, but... you're still cute."

"Let's go son." Love rushes past K.J. and Felicity towards the mall exit.

"Wait, what happened dad?" K.J. asks following behind his father.

"Keldrick is in jail, and your mother's crazy ass needs to be dealt with." Love tells him.

"I'll call you later!" K.J. yells back to Felicity now standing close to her Aunt Gabrielle.

"We're going back to Miami?" K.J. asks his father.

"I have to get my big brother out of jail," Love heads out of the mall doors straight to Jazemene's bright blue BMW, "he can't get in touch with his driver Bennie... Ty and Jay won't answer their phones either."

Chapter 16
Secret Lovers

"It's obvious now that the police aren't looking for me." Jaze says sitting next to Josiah on an almost comfortable bench outside of a Denny's Restaurant on International Drive.

"Not yet." Jojo reminds her.

"Maybe not ever..." Jaze thinks aloud.

"How," Jojo asks, "you said Bleek's mom is going to come looking for him... and what about Roland's parents, and Scooter? Somebody is going to look for them and us too."

"And that's fine," Jaze smiles an unsettling smile, "my point is they might find you and me... but with no weapon and no bodies, there's no case against me."

"Wait," Jojo says, "No bodies? I saw the bodies in your apartment babe."

"Let me ask you a question." Jaze turns to look into the confused blueness of his tight eyes.

"What..." he replies.

"Cam's twin Megan that I told you about," Jaze starts, "whatever happened to her burned, shot, and mutilated body?"

"I don't know." He answers honestly.

"Neither does anybody else." Jaze rests her case.

Jojo smiles to himself.

"This is sick," he leans over and kisses her near the left side of her mouth, "but if I have to be a part of some sick shit I'm glad I'm doing it with your pretty ass."

"What do you mean have to?" she asks.

"Huh..." he replies.

"You keep saying **we** this and **we** that," Jaze tells him, "like we're a team. And now you just said you **have** to be here, but you really don't. And I know we had that talk the other day, but this shit is still iffy and weird as hell for me. Like, there's **no way** you just decided overnight to become my ride or die white boy."

"Jaze..." Jojo starts.

"I'm not done," she interjects, "if you really always loved me like I love you... then you wrongfully caused me so many years of pain and heartache... and for what, so you could pretend to like white girls?"

"I do like white girls..." Jojo claims.

"Yeah but you're in love with a black one." Jaze smiles at his honest discomfort.

"Let's get something to eat, I'm starving." Josiah says standing up from the bench to stretch his long tanned legs.

"Yeah, I bet," Jaze slaps him on his behind, "you enjoy changing the subject little boy."

"Only when it gets weird and cree..." Jojo starts.

"**Hell no**," Jaze interjects, "that word is **eliminated** from your vocabulary effective **immediately**. You are king creepy, Josiah Bell! You've been in love with me probably just as long as I have been with you, at least I admitted it a long time ago... your punk ass been stalking me on the low."

"I never stalked you," he claims, "well there was that one... or maybe three times I snuck through your window just to watch you sleep."

"You did what?" Jaze stops walking.

"What," Jojo laughs, "you said it, I just agreed baby."

"You **watched** me **sleep** Josiah," she steps closer to him, "this ain't no damn **Twilight**, and Bella definitely ain't black. You **watched** me **sleep**?"

"Yeah, I think we've established that..." He starts back walking towards the Burger King across the street.

"Did I look cute?" she asks finally realizing the underlying beauty of his admission.

"You were gorgeous." Josiah assures her, taking her yellow hand in his.

(Get out of Jail Free)

Several hours later K.J. and Love are waiting outside a Miami police station. They can hear the sudden frustration behind them as K.C. storms out of the front doors of the station.

"**Bro**..." Love says walking towards him.

"Thanks for getting me out." K.C. says trying to straighten his expensive newly wrinkled clothes.

"Why didn't you call me sooner?" Love asks.

"Yeah or why didn't you call me dad...?" K.J. says.

Love and K.C. both look down at the wide eyed teen.

"Because I thought you hated me," K.C. admits, "and did you just call me... ***dad***?"

K.J. looks at Love.

"It's fine." Love says with a comforting smile.

"You raised me..." K.J. says looking down at his feet as his growing dreads shield as much of his face as they possibly can.

"Look up boy," K.C. says, "I told you about looking down at your feet when you're talking to another man."

"Yes you did," K.J. says looking up into his legal guardian's eyes, "you told me a lot of things, and I know it seems like I never listened or learned but I did. I hate all the bullshit I've heard my entire life about Love, it's hurtful and embarrassing. He's my biological father, and he's a mixed up product of his fucked up childhood that I guess I blame **you** for."

"Watch your mouth son." Love says.

"No, he's fine," K.C. says, "tell me why you blame me Keldrick Jr.?"

"I just spent a night in jail something I said I would never do again," K.C. continues, "I have very important things I should be doing right now but there's honestly nothing more I'd rather do than have this conversation with you ***right*** now."

"Stop complaining," K.J. tells him, "You've done time before, what's one more night?"

"Boy," K.C. says stepping close to him, "my case took so damn long when I was in jail as a teen I did all my time… three ***damn*** years locked in a jail cell, a real cage. At least niggas in prison are free. I say I did three years in prison, but Love knows I did ***real*** hard time, locked in the damn Orange county jail. So, don't you ***ever*** tell me what should bother me and what shouldn't!"

K.J. doesn't respond.

"Don't get quiet now boy…" K.C. prods.

"Don't call him a boy K.C., he's a man." Love tells him.

"He's sixteen," K.C. replies, "if you're a man K.J., be a man and tell me to my face why you hate me and why you blame for…"

"I blame you because you are his big brother," K.J. interjects unable to stop the two defiant tears from sliding painfully down his reddened cheeks, "you saw him being abused more than once, and you never once tried to stop it. As big and strong as you are…"

"Stop it," K.C. interjects, "stop it right there. You were going to say as big and strong as I am I should have protected my little brother. That's where your hatred for me stems from, the problem is son… you're forgetting I was just a kid back then too. I didn't understand what I should have done back then, and I damn sure wasn't big enough to stop it myself."

"But you closed the door dad…" Love says with painful tears of his own welling in his broken green eyes.

K.J. looks up at Love with his forehead wrinkled tightly.

"That's right Love," K.C. hold his hand out to him, "I am your dad. I want to be that father figure, and I don't feel that it's at all too late. You ***aren't*** the only one that suffered through your tragedy Love, I cried a lot of nights too. I was in the next room, and I heard through my thin walls more than any kid should ever have to hear. But I told you the first time we spoke in my house after you got out of prison; I have your back no matter what. ***We...*** didn't have a good father in our lives coming up, but I'm the big brother and it's my job to fill the void for you. Every child ***wants*** a father, but some actually ***need*** one. Sometimes... boys that need fathers and don't have them, grow into men who still need that void filled."

Love hugs his big brother tightly as K.J. looks on with extreme emotion racing through his young mind and body.

"Do you want Whitney to disappear?" Love whispers in his big brother's left ear.

"I do." K.C. replies with a discreet whisper of his own just before breaking their much needed embrace.

"Where did you guys park," K.C. says looking out into the parking lot, "I don't see the Camaro."

As the three of them head towards the lot K.C. stops cold at the sight of the bright blue BMW.

"Jaze is here too?" he asks.

"No she's with Josiah in..." K.J. starts.

"The ***mall***," Love interjects, "Jaze and Josiah are at the mall in my car. I told Jaze I'd take ***her*** car to get an oil change and a wash."

"Right," K.C. says looking at the two of them with a furrowed brow, "So she and Josiah are talking again?"

"I guess so." Love replies.

"Now what...?" K.J. asks as they all get in the car.

"Whitney's house?" Love asks.

K.J.'s phone rings loudly.

"Hello," he answers, "Mom, mom what's wrong why are you crying?"

"***Cam is dead***..." K.C. turns around and quickly snatches K.J.'s phone from him.

"Whitney," K.C. yells into the phone, "What the hell happened? What the fuck did you do to my wife? He what... Damn. We'll be there in a minute."

K.C. hands the phone back to K.J.

"What happened bro?" Love asks starting the car up.

"Charlie shot himself in the head," K.C. says, "let's go."

"Wait," K.J. says from the backseat, "We're going to mom's house? You don't want to go check on Cam first?"

"Of course I do son," K.C. says, "but I can't go near my wife or that hospital until I get these charges dropped. Only Whitney can make that happen, because the lies all started with her."

Love speeds out of the parking lot towards Whit's house.

"Oh, I almost forgot. How much do I owe you on my bond bro?" K.C. asks pulling out his checkbook from his deep left pocket.

"Put that shit away K.C.," Love says, "and if this ever happens again... damn it, you promise me you'll call me first. That's what family is for."

De'Lure

(You're My Little Secret)

"What are we doing tonight?" Jaze asks Josiah lying across his chest in Love's hotel room.

"Are you not the least bit curious about what Osiana is up to now?" he asks.

"I tried calling her twice," Jaze looks at her phone in her hand and replies to a new text message, "no answer, but I know she's back home because I spoke to my Uncle Ty. He didn't say anything crazy... so I guess she didn't either."

"Guessing is not good enough," Jojo sits up, "something ain't right. Now, I understand that Osiana was obsessed with Love's work but to allow him to kidnap her and drive her **all** the way to **Orlando**... **hell no**, that's a bit much baby."

"I like that." Jaze grins widely as she replies to another new text.

"Huh..." Jojo replies.

"You're starting to call me baby more," she tells him, "like it's my name."

"You gotta stop getting all mushy while I'm talking about serious shit Jaze." Josiah forces her off his chest and stands up to head to the bathroom.

He closes the door behind him, and lifts the toilet seat up. He can hear Jaze laughing through the door. After flushing the toilet Josiah opens the door staring at Jaze.

"What's so funny?" he asks turning the sink on to wash his hands.

265

"Nothing," she tells him, "just a text."

"Oh yeah," Jojo says, "from who?"

"A friend," Jaze continues to type on her phone, "you don't know em."

"I don't know em," Jojo says walking towards the T.V., "is *em* a dude or a female?"

"Yeah so what are we doing tonight?" Jaze says.

"That shit is so annoying," Jojo growls grabbing a room key and heading to the door, "I'm going for a walk, you do you."

Jaze walks to the door and opens it to look out. Jojo is already out of sight. She closes the door back, sends another text with a smile on her face, and then strips naked and jumps in the shower immediately.

As the water burst forth from the shower head its cold at first, but Jaze doesn't notice because her mind is racing and her insides are boiling hot.

As she lathers her towel with soap she's picturing his smile and his perfect teeth and lips. The piercing above his left eyebrow perfectly accents his strong gray eyes.

As Jaze caresses her own taught body with her soap saturated towel, in her mind he's behind her washing her body close to his.

(Jaze)

His stomach was an unforgettable masterpiece set in bronze stone, just below his proud slightly bulging chest. The sweat dripping down into his navel looked like a precious stream of the sweetest lemonade my tongue could ever know. I think he scares me a little, because the calm yet piercing confidence in his eyes could have willed me to do anything he wanted me to, right there in that parking lot. When he made that joke about Jojo... he stuck his tongue out and revealed his double piercing in it. Damn I wanted to taste his lips and those two tiny glistening balls in his long tongue.

Jaze rinses the last bit of soap from her throbbing body and turns the shower off. After stepping out of the tub she grabs a towel and quickly dries off.

On the sofa she finds the cute red dress Josiah bought her earlier at the mall. She slips it on without bothering to put on any under garments first. Back in the bathroom with her purse open on the counter, Jaze begins to apply her makeup.

As she further perfects her face and hair with each stroke, fluff, and brush she sees a younger prettier version of her mother coming to life before her eyes again.

"Done." She whispers to herself.

After turning the light off near the bed she makes her way to the window near the second bed. She opens the curtains just a pinch to look outside to see if she can see Josiah.

There isn't a soul in the parking lot. Near the hotel room door, she slips on her sexy red heels, grabs a room key off the nearby table, and heads out the door.

Once inside her uncle's fire engine red Camaro Jaze reaches down in her purse to find her perfume.

With two light sprays of her bottle of **Radicon's Princess** perfume that her father bought her a while ago, Jaze's outfit is complete.

As she pulls out of the parking lot she lets the driver's side window down to allow some cool night air to waft in through the car to reignite the delicious sensual fragrance that's clinging tightly to her hungry body.

The GPS says that she only has three more miles to her destination. At every red light Jaze pulls down the loyal mirror above her head to check her perfection again.

She's close now and she can feel the beautiful butterflies in her athletically crafted stomach swarming around in wild anxious circles.

"You have reached your destination." The GPS says as she pulls into an open parking space.

Jaze grabs her purse and then steps out of the car. As she heads towards the entrance she presses the button on the keychain to lock the car.

Once inside the hotel she heads straight to the elevator. Her anticipation is at an all-time high now. As the elevator begins to ascend Jaze can't help but rub her thighs together as her warm wet center continues to throb in sexual angst.

The elevator door opens to an almost empty hall. Up ahead on the left as she steps out she sees a couple kissing on the wall outside a room.

The lady has a wedding veil on that the man is holding back as he kisses her softly. They're obviously newlyweds on their honeymoon, or maybe just a freaky young couple who enjoy role play and exhibitionism.

As Jaze gets closer to them she thinks about the moment some man will stand beside her before God and become her eternal soul mate.

De'Lure

That day she knows will be amazing and unforgettable. That day is the day little girl's dream about all their lives until it finally transpires. But tonight Jazemene Cole just wants to be easy and open.

She needs a release and a distraction desperately. Room 512. As she stands there at his door, she knows once she steps across this deceitful threshold there is no turning back.

With her phone clutched tightly in her left hand she smiles as she realizes in actuality she's still single and as a grown woman she is eligible to do whatever the hell she wants.

The door is open just a bit, and inside she can hear old school slow jams probably playing via the Pandora app on his phone.

Jaze takes a deep breath. She slowly pushes the door open and looks inside.

On the large round bed Jaze can see red and pink rose petals scattered everywhere beginning from a trail all the way to the door where she's standing.

She steps inside finally. The room looks and smells delightful.

As soon as her second heeled foot touches the floor he grabs hold of her pulsating body and pulls her back hard against his.

The door slams shut due to his body colliding with it. He snatches her phone from her left hand and tosses it over on the bed.

Jaze drops her purse in total submission.

"Yes..." she moans.

269

As he kisses her neck he pulls her arms down by her sides. The back of her neck is tingling from the touch of his perfectly double pierced tongue. From his pocket he pulls out a white silk blindfold.

"Do you trust me..." he whispers with his pink lips close to her left ear.

"With my body I do, but not my heart..." she whispers.

"**All I need is your body**." He interjects placing the blindfold over her eyes from behind her.

As he laces the top of her yellow back with gentle kisses he begins to pull her beautiful red dress up. Once her bottom is exposed he reaches up and pulls the top of the dress down.

Her perky breasts and firm behind are free for him to gaze upon with a lust fire neither of them has ever known before.

Squeezing both of her ample breasts from behind he begins to softly bite the sides of her neck.

Jaze arches her back a bit and pushes her ass back against him to feel all of him.

He's definitely up to the challenge that is her unquenchable sex thirst.

"Fuck me..." she whispers in a raw guttural tone.

"Not yet..." He replies grinding up against her perfect ass to the rhythm of the perfect old school beat playing throughout the room.

He can't take it anymore he needs her lips against his. He spins her around to face him.

For a satisfied moment he looks down at her rock hard nipples and then up to her pouty pink lips.

He knows how ready she must be; as he watches her blindfolded face taste her own lips so close to his.

Finally, he presses his soft lips to hers. There it is. Their first kiss, one so powerful and earth shattering neither of them will soon forget this feeling inside this very moment.

She reaches up to hold his face. He holds hers too as the kisses become deeper and more believable.

"Can you fall in... *love* with a stranger?" she whispers close to his open mouth.

"Only if she's promised to you at birth..." he says smiling as she continues to attack his mouth with her hungry tongue.

"Some loves," he continues, "are chosen for us, but designed so perfectly we would never think to mind at all."

"What does that mean?" she whispers as her heart and vagina continue to throb in perfect tandem.

"Loves have a legacy all their own..." he says picking her up into the air.

Jaze wraps her shaky legs around him.

As he walks her to the bed he forces his linen pants down as he continues to kiss her.

At the foot of the round bed he lets her step back down to the floor.

He steps out of his pants and kneels before her.

He carefully removes her heels for her, and then begins slowly massaging her feet with his hands and mouth. Then with careful precision he thoughtfully tastes each one of her tiny delicate toes one at a time.

After he's had his fill of her delicious dainty feet he stands back up.

He kisses her once, and then touches the top of her head.

She smiles and then sits back on the bed. He steps forward, and with two cool hands on his ripped stomach Jaze begins to kiss and lick on him just above his private area.

As he begins to grow she takes him in her hands.

He's ready now.

With one hand on his sack and the other holding him in place she begins to take him on. She's not quite sure if she's doing it right, but she won't stop until told to do so.

On the tips of his toes he finds his eyes fleeing to the back of their sockets in immense pleasure.

To balance himself he grabs hold of the top of her gorgeous head. The sound she's making and the excess wetness is driving him insane.

He pulls back.

Jaze turns around with her face on the bed and her bottom in the air.

He kneels down to the floor and finds the condom in his pocket.

After securing it on his long shaft he steps close behind her. Before he enters her for the first time he smiles to himself.

With real force he grabs hold of her dress wrapped around her midsection and pulls her back on him.

She moans loudly with pain laced ecstasy.

With every stroke he drives deeper and harder inside of her.

With her arms stretched out wide in front of her Jaze openly enjoys everything he has to offer.

Her phone begins to ring. She snatches off the blindfold immediately and tosses it on the bed.

As he continues to pump slowly Jaze reaches across the bed to retrieve her phone.

Jojo is calling. Jaze continues to moan as she watches her phone light up with her lover's handsome picture.

After turning around to look into Papi's powerful gray eyes she defiantly slams her phone back down on the bed face down and arches her back even more for him.

"Good girl mamacita..." Papi tells her.

"Never stop Papi," she moans, "it's all yours..."

(Whitney's House)

As Jaze's blue BMW pulls up to Whitney's house two squad cars are just driving off.

Standing there alone in the doorway is a stern-faced Whit who doesn't seem to be sad at all.

As the three Cole men step out of Jaze's car they all proceed with caution.

Whitney is still staring down the street in the direction the cop cars left in.

273

It's as if she doesn't even know they're walking towards her.

As they get a bit nearer to her she closes her eyes and turns towards them.

"She's finally lost her damn mind completely…" Love Whispers.

"Mama, are you okay?" K.J. asks.

She opens her eyes and squints at the three of them.

"Charlie's gone baby." She says.

"I know mama." K.J. hugs his mother tightly.

Whitney looks up into K.C.'s eyes.

"Keldrick," she says, "I'm so…"

"Now isn't the time," K.C. interjects, "You will fix what you've done, but right now let's just go inside and talk."

Whitney leads them inside.

As the three men take a seat in the front room, Whit makes her way into the kitchen.

"You boys want some lemonade?" she calls out.

"**Hell no** Whitney," K.C. says, "now come in here and sit your ass down."

"Are you crazy," K.C. asks as she enters the room, "your fiancé just killed himself and you wanna fix **drinks** and shit?"

"Do not talk to me like that in front of my son!" Whit demands.

"Damn that," K.C. replies, "he's heard and seen it all in his young lifetime. Whitney, you had me arrested for something you know damn well I would never do."

"I'm sorry…" Whit says looking out of the far window.

"**Hell no Whitney**," K.C. stands to his feet, "**Are you serious**? Why would you do that to me?"

"Now is not the time for this conversation Keldrick." She says.

"**Now is just as good a damn time as any**!" he fumes.

Whit takes a seat on the couch near K.J. clutching a bottle of pills she just pulled out of her pocket.

"Start talking Whit," K.C. demands, "Why would you call and make the claim that *my wife* came to you scared accusing me of abusing her?"

"I didn't say it like that…" Whit claims.

"You said it!" he explodes. "Damn it," he continues, "and you don't seem hurt at all by Charlie's death. Did you kill him Whitney?"

"No!" she screams.

"Well how would you like it if I went to the police and told them how Charlie came to me crying about the fact that he thought you were trying to kill him?" K.C. asks.

"You know damn well that's not the truth Keldrick!" Whit exclaims.

"Nope," K.C. agrees, "neither was that bullshit you told the cops about me. Tell me, why would a man like Charlie kill himself? Your cooking ain't that damn bad."

"That's not funny," Whit frowns, "and I don't know. I think he…"

"You think he what?" K.C. asks.

"Damn can I finish my statement?" Whit yells.

"Hell no," K.C. replies, "not if you keep **stuttering** and **pausing** you never will finish the lie you're trying to create."

"I don't lie." Whit says.

"Oh yes you do Whitney," K.C. laughs at her, "and you do a lot of it. Now tell me why this man killed himself."

"Because..." Whit says.

"Because what woman?" K.C. screams.

"Because he thought I was leaving him for you." She admits.

"And why the hell would he think that?" K.C. asks with a tightly furrowed brow.

"Because I was..." Whit claims.

"No the hell you were not," K.C. yells, "my wife isn't perfect, and we've hurt each other a lot emotionally and verbally... but I love Cameron and I'm never going to leave her until she leaves this earth."

"Who knows," Whit smiles, "may be sooner than you think."

"If you even look at my wife wrong Whitney Powell I'll crack your fucking head open and relieve your brain of what little sense you have left." K.C. vows.

"Real mature," she replies, "just curse me like I'm nothing, and threaten to kill me in front of my baby."

"I'm not a baby Whitney," K.J. speaks us, "stop using me as an excuse to not be dealt with accordingly."

"Cute," Whit smiles at K.C., "so you turned my baby against me too huh? Real fucking cute, Keldrick!"

"Cute my ass," K.C. says, "Now I can tell you're on some kind of prescription pills..."

"Just sleep aid pills." She claims shaking the bottle in her hands for them all to see.

"I don't give a damn what you're on," K.C. says, "go in the back and put some decent clothes on so we can get you down to the police station to fix this mess so I can see my wife."

"Yes sir..." Whit mumbles as she makes her way to her bedroom on wobbly legs."

(Papi)

Hours later Papi is lying on his back in the center of the magnificent hotel bed looking down at Jazemene who's lying on her stomach close to him.

"Where have you been all my life, Papi?" Jaze sighs.

"Well," he smiles, "I'm actually from Orlando like you, but I grew up in California after my parents got divorced."

"How did you know I was from Orlando Papi?" she asks.

"You told me..." He replies a little quicker than he meant to.

"No I didn't Papi." Jaze assures him.

"I'm sorry... I thought you did." He claims.

The new silence is awkward and almost deafening.

"So," he breaks the silence, "tell me about your mom."

"Well," Jaze sighs, "we don't talk much; we don't talk at all actually."

277

"That's not good." Papi wrinkles his brow.

"I know," she agrees, "but her name is Whitney, she lives in Miami where she owns online businesses, and she has a fiancé named Charlie Breeze."

"Fiancé," Papi frowns, "how long have they been engaged?"

"I don't really know," Jaze admits, "but she's not happy, she's settling just like I was before..."

"Before what?" Papi asks.

"I can't say Papi." Jaze admits.

"Yes you can," he replies, "you can tell Papi anything. Your secrets are my private treasures. I wouldn't share them with anyone else ever."

"I guess," Jaze smirks a bit, "I don't really know what's going on for sure, but I might be in some legal trouble very soon if anything goes wrong."

"I can get you out of the country *now*, if you want to leave," Papi claims reaching for his expensive and rare cell phone, "my family is wealthy."

"Seriously..." Jaze asks.

"Yeah." Papi confirms.

"My dad's rich too," Jaze explains, "but if he knew what I was mixed up in, he would never understand, and he definitely wouldn't help me."

"Why not?" Papi asks.

"He's a dad," Jaze laughs awkwardly; "he's just a dad. And he was right about... well *everything*."

"Like what?" Papi asks.

"He was right about school," Jaze says, "my boyfriend..."

"Your gringo right?" Papi asks with a teasing smile.

"No," Jaze smiles, "***my gringo*** has never been my actual boyfriend, just my best friend. But my dad told me to leave my ex because he was an extremely bad influence on me."

"Was he?" Papi asks.

"In less than six months," Jaze starts, "he talked me into quitting my school's basketball team, dropping out of college, and moving off campus into a busted ass little apartment with him."

"***Damn***." Papi says.

"I know right," Jaze replies, "the worst part is he was only with me because he was planning on killing my dad to get the life insurance money and my inheritance, and then he was going to kill me."

"Enough said," Papi replies, "Say the word and I'll sweep you off your pretty little feet and whisk you away to an unforgettable fantasy land that you never have to leave. You'll never have to lift a finger in ***my*** world. I do have one request though love."

"Wait," Jaze says, "first, I have a request of my own."

"Anything..." Papi replies with open ears.

"Can my best friend come with me or...?" Jaze asks with no confidence in her tone.

"Of course Jazemene," Papi replies, "um, but will you and I still be able to um...?"

"Are you freakin' kidding me," she laughs, "You are... ***This*** was ***amazing***, of course we can. Josiah has my heart but he can't do my body like you can."

"Cool." Papi lies back rubbing the top of her soft behind.

"Cool," she agrees, "So what was your request?"

"Bring your mother with you." Papi says climbing out of bed.

"My mother?" Jaze sits up to look at him.

"Yes," he replies pulling on some Polo boxer shorts, "she would love it there; you said she's unhappy right?"

"Yea, but I don't know." Jaze looks down at her phone as its starts to ring again.

"Just ask her." Papi tells her.

"I will," Jaze says fixing her dress, "but I need to get going…"

"To where," he asks, "Your gringo?"

Papi drop his boxers back down to the floor.

"You not going anywhere till after round two baby girl…" he growls.

"Come get me then Papi…" she replies pulling her dress off over her head.

Chapter 17
Miami Rush

(Jacody and Cidra)

Sitting on their sofa side by side watching an episode of ***Modern Family***, Jay and Cid don't know if they could ever be any happier than they are right now.

"Babe…" Cidra sighs.

"Wassup baby…" Jay replies.

"I'm so glad your parents came to visit last weekend." She admits.

"Yeah," he smiles, "not as glad as they are that my ass ***finally*** got married and I'm surviving in a successful relationship."

"Yeah," Cidra looks down at her gorgeous ring, "it was just good to finally spend time with them, you know…"

"Yeah I know," he leans over to kiss her ample lips twice, "and they really do like you… even if you are white."

They both laugh.

"Oh, don't get me started on my dad and what he thinks about you," Cidra continues to laugh, "and ***us***… and ***whatever***. Screw em all baby, I got you and you got me nothing else matters."

"I couldn't have said it better myself," Jay agrees, "where's my stepson I haven't seen him around in a few days?"

"I don't know baby," Cidra replies, "he's almost twenty-two years old now so he's free to come and go as he pleases."

"Yeah I know," Jay checks his watch, "but I have a listening party for one of my new artists tonight at the studio, and I thought maybe Jojo would…"

"You **don't** have to be his best friend Jacody," Cid promises him, "you've done enough. You have no idea how much it meant to him when you kept your promise to him and married me."

"Well I didn't just do it for him you know…" Jay leans in to kiss his beautiful wife again.

"Jacody," she giggles, "do not start something you do not have time to finish…"

"I always have time for my wife…" he growls close to her ear caressing her soft behind in his strong hands.

"What about the listening party babe…" Cidra moans as he slides her panties to the side and enters her warm moist body with the tip of his thumb.

"Screw em all," Jay says pulling his pants to his knees, "I got you, and you got me… and **that's all** that matters baby."

(Back at the hotel)

As Jaze inserts her room key and then opens the door she prays Josiah is still out somewhere doing his own thing.

His eyes are already locked in on her as she steps inside.

Pain and hate are both deep inside the blueness of his perfect eyes and written all over his beautifully tanned face.

Without a word he stands up and walks towards her.

Jaze's heart is pounding so loud she swears Jojo can hear it too. Everything around her is moving way too fast, even though Josiah seems to be moving in slow motion.

She never feared this man until this very second. Jaze is trying to force herself not to panic.

The power of his venomous glare is almost unbearable.

She fights the pain stricken urge to piss herself, because she knows full well he'll never let her live that down.

"I love what you've done with your hair baby," he speaks, "what is this, the sweaty sexed out sew in, or the back shot bob?"

"Josiah..." she holds her hands up to hold him back from her.

"And what's that new perfume you wearing..." he asks leaning in close to her bosom.

"Josiah." She says.

"*Smells like nuts*!" He yells.

Jaze closes her eyes tightly as his yell put more fear into her already racing heart.

"So," he continues, "have you been a hoe all this time or is this a new development? And I'm not usually the

super jealous type ***buuuut*** I thought you and I had a
fucking agreement Jazemene!"
"Oh yeah," she brushes past him, "and what was that, to
be best friends for life, like we're fucking homeboys or
best bitches?"
        "Hey," he yells following her near the bathroom,
"you agreed to it!"
        "Maybe I changed my mind." She shrugs.
Jojo grabs her by her face and pushes her back hard
against the mirror on the front of the hotel closet doors.
"You don't get that option!" he growls.
"Let go of me Josiah Bell!" Jaze screams.
"No." he replies.
"Get the fuck off of me or ***I'll tell my Uncle to kill you and
eat your pale ass body***!" she yells.
He lets her go instantly.
Her phone rings in her purse.
She clutches the bag tight to her chest, but not quite tight
enough.
Josiah quickly snatches her purse away from her and
empties it out on the floor in front of her.
As the phone hits the floor, they both watch it slide to a
stop by the wall as it continues to ring.
"You want it so bad get it." Jaze says stripping naked.
Leaving Jojo alone with the phone Jaze walks into the
bathroom and turns the shower on closing the door
behind her.
Jojo picks the phone up off the floor. There's a notification
on her screen for a new text message.
Josiah opens it hastily.

De'Lure

**Papi: Did you make it back safe Mamacita... Hey, if you
fuck your Gringo tonight make sure you close your
beautiful eyes and fantasize about me...**

Jojo throws the phone across the room and then snatches
his shirt off. Next he rips his sweatpants, boxers, and socks
off as well and throws them as far as their weights will
allow them to fly across the room.

Jojo then snatches open the bathroom door and steps in
slamming the door behind him.

After stepping inside the steaming hot shower he grabs
Jaze by her neck and pulls her back to him.

She quickly turns around with wide eyes overflowing with
real fear.

Jojo picks Jazemene up in the air with new strength that
even momentarily surprises him.

As she wraps her legs around him, and he enters her body
naked without a care in the world.

Next he turns around and leans her back against the back
shower wall.

He knows from a late night game of **Truth or Dare** this is
her favorite position.

As he strokes deep inside her he begins to kiss her more
passionately than he ever has before.

"Get down." He growls.

She obeys.

Standing there with the water to his back Jaze waits on his
instruction.

Jojo turns her around and faces her towards the water.

With her hands on her knees Jaze readies herself for his
pleasant intrusion.

The hot water is beating down on her neck and upper back now. She doesn't give a damn about her hair at this point. She decides she'll just deal with the ugly frizzy aftermath later on.

He slides in slowly from the back, and then immediately quickens his pace.

Jaze looks from one side to the other; the flimsy white shower curtain on her left hand side is rippling freely due to the commanding force in which Josiah is handling her from behind.

On her right the off white shower wall speckled with almost golden flakes is her only hope for stability as she tries to withstand his powerful thrusts.

With her left hand on the silver tub faucet and her right hand positioned on the wall in a forward angle she pushes herself back against him as his strokes are now helping her to maintain her overall balance.

This position is becoming more comfortable by the second.

"Yes…" she cries.

"Yeah!" he yells.

"Hell yeah baby," Jazemene moans loudly, "right there baby… fuck me *just like that.*"

"He said close your eyes and think about him…" Jojo growls.

"What baby?" Jaze moans.

"That Mexican prick you're cheating on me with," Jojo says between more powerful strokes, "his text said *if you fuck your gringo tonight… close your beautiful eyes and fantasize about me!*"

286

De'Lure

Jaze closes her eyes and begins to bite her bottom lip as this doesn't sound like the worst idea she's ever heard. When she doesn't respond, Josiah leans to his left to better see Jaze's face.

"Open your fucking eyes!" he demands smacking her hard on her bottom.

"Don't you ever think about him," he growls thrusting even harder now to Jaze's delight, "don't you think about him or **any other man** while you're with me. You ain't going nowhere, you're mine!"

"Okay baby." She moans as she looks up into the never more beautiful light above her head that continues to feed both of their hungry bodies with raw sexual power.

(Back at the station)

Keldrick Jermaine Cole Sr. storms back inside the same local Miami police station he was incarcerated in just hours ago; this time he's not handcuffed or without back up.

"Aye," he yells, "where the hell are those two punk ass officers that were harassing me based on that bogus ass tip they got?"

"I'm sorry sir," a young Spanish lady near the front desk says, "can you please lower your voice?"

"Man I'm not lowering a damn thing!" K.C. assures her.

"Okay," the lady replies in her thick accent, "I'm going to have to ask you to..."

287

"**You don't have to ask me to do a mother fuckin' thing**," K.C. exclaims, "I'm usually a nice guy, but two of your officers arrested me falsely and I want justice…"

"Okay," she says grabbing a pen and pad, "What were their names?"

K.C. looks past her with a deadly glare.

"Those two assholes right there." He points.

"Oh you back already superstar?" one of the officers says with a smug smile.

"Did you actually kill your wife this time," the second one asks, "or did you just punch her in the back of the head a few **more** times?"

Love's eyes begin to darken as he reaches in the back of his pants. His big brother sees him, and quickly grabs his arm before he makes a huge mistake.

"No." K.C. tells Love.

Then he looks down at Whitney as the officers come within arm's length.

"Tell them what you did Whitney." K.C. demands.

"I lied." She mumbles.

"Louder Whitney, louder!" K.C. exclaims.

"I lied," she screams out, "I was the one who called down here and made the accusation that Keldrick Cole beat his wife and caused her stroke."

The officers can feel the panic on their reddening faces.

"Oh and by the way," K.C. pulls his phone out of his pocket, "my phone was recording during my arrest so all that bullshit you two idiots said, is right here on my phone."

"Yeah right." The first officer laughs.

K.C. presses play on his phone's screen.

The recording:

Officer one: "I always love this."

K.C.: "You love what?"

Officer one: "Catching you stupid, arrogant, black mother fuckers in some bullshit, and then ruining your fuckin' life."

K.C.: "Well you won't be ruining mine; I didn't touch my wife..."

K.C. stops the recording.

"Do you need to hear more or..." K.C. asks them.

"You can't use that in court," the second officer says, "and besides that could be anybody's voice."

"Oh no," K.C. replies, "It's you two assholes. And no, I can't use it in court, but I can take it to the local news stations. I'm sure they'd all love to do a story on you two and me."

"That's just childish and unnecessary Mr. Cole," the first officer says, "Now we apologized, there's no reason for you to jeopardize our jobs like that. We both have families to feed."

"Oh now I'm **Mr. Cole**," K.C. laughs, "First off, you did not apologize. But, I'll tell you assholes what; if you don't go have somebody call the judge, or get on one of these old ass computers in this musty ass office and get those charges against me dropped you'll lose more than just your meaningless ass jobs!"

(305)

The fire engine red Camaro pulls up to the large McDonald's on Sandlake Drive. Jaze parks the car and then runs inside. Jojo remains in the passenger seat.

As soon as Jaze enters the sliding doors of the restaurant she begins searching for his eyes.

Nothing yet.

Jaze knows, and she can feel that whenever she's in his presence he can feel her, and his eyes lock onto her like a heat seeking missile.

Walking deeper inside the restaurant she scans the crowd to her left. There he is, sitting at the very last table; stunning gray eyes irresistible lips and all.

As she makes her way towards him she can't stop herself from smiling and her stomach is doing whatever the hell it wants to.

"Hello gorgeous…" he speaks.

"Wassup Papi?" she smiles.

"So you're leaving now?" he asks.

"Yeah like *right* now." She confirms.

"Come here." He says opening his arms.

Jaze hugs him tightly and kisses him twice.

"Why do you look sad, this isn't goodbye," Papi says, "I'll see you again soon my love."

Jaze leaves out of the McDonald's with more than she can handle on her young mind.

After drifting into the briefly friendly traffic Jaze heads towards the interstate. The calm flow of the traffic is serving as a peaceful get away for her cluttered young mind. Everything is not okay, but in the coming moments nothing else can go wrong. All she has to do is drive, and allow the flow of the traffic to soothe her mind as it propels her forward towards her supposed final earthly destination.

Jaze can see a white and green Orange County Sheriff car a couple of lanes over and immediately taps Josiah's knee.

"What's wrong...?" Jojo asks.

"I think shit's about to get real." She replies.

"Wait what?" Jojo turns around to look just in time to see the Sheriff drift in their lane right behind them.

"Fuck!" Jojo exclaims.

"Don't panic babe," Jaze says, "I got it... we're fine."

"No the hell we're not fine..." Jojo says trying to use the passenger side rearview mirror to watch the Sheriff.

"Yes we are." Jaze says turning the music up a bit.

"There are so many other lanes and other cars that mother fucker could be behind... but he's not. He's behind us!" Jojo says.

"Very astute Jojo," Jaze smiles at him, "baby please calm down, I told you we're fine. He hasn't turned his light on or anything..."

WHOOP WHOOP!!

"Now what Wonder Girl," Jojo screams, "*you glass half full hippy minded mother fucker you*, I told you! God damn it!"

291

"Now what..." Jaze says as she pulls off to the side of the road near the interstate entrance.

"Now you wanna ask," Jojo says, "Don't panic, we're fine babe. What the hell Jaze. They found us, it's over now. You're going to prison forever for murder, and I'm going to jail for public nudity. That crap is gonna look so bad on my background. Damn it!"

"Jojo shut the hell up," Jaze says, "neither one of us are going to jail."

"No," he agrees, "I'm going to jail, you're going to prison."

"No I'm not," she says checking her mirrors, "Okay, its two officers... one each side. Should I drive off now, or take my chances?"

"You already stopped now." Jojo reminds her.

"Yeah, you don't watch a lot of T.V. do you," Jaze asks, "look... if he mentions what we did behind that building or what happened in Miami at my apartment, I'm taking off."

"Are you serious," Jojo asks, "and what are they doing behind the car? What's taking them so long to come up here?"

"I don't know," Jaze checks her mirror again, "but I told you what the plan is so be ready."

"This is so messed up." Jojo shakes his blonde head.

"Yep," Jaze says, "these assholes are gonna have to beat me to Miami, cuz that's where I'm headed."

A tall dark skinned Sheriff knocks on Jaze's window. His partner is on Josiah's side looking in the back of the car.

Jaze lets her window down with a breathtaking smile.

"Hello sir, how are you?" Jaze greets him.

"I'm doing," the Sheriff replies, "do you know why I pulled you over?"

"See that's the thing," Jaze smiles even brighter, "I honestly have no idea what I could have possibly done wrong."

"You have a tail light out," he tells her, "do you have your license and registration?"

"Well," Jaze says, "that's the thing this isn't exactly my car... per se."

"Then who's car is this per se...?" the Sheriff asks folding his arms.

"No, it's not like that sir," Jaze laughs as her face reddens instantly, "it's my uncle's car, he has mine."

"Why?" he asks.

"That's not really your business officer." Jaze says as polite as she possibly can.

"License and registration please." The Sheriff says holding his hand out.

Jaze reaches behind her seat and finds her wallet deep inside her purse.

"And you're sure this is only about the tail light right?" she asks hesitantly handing him her I.D.

Jojo nudges her arm.

"Why do you ask?" the Sheriff searches her eyes.

"No, I was just asking." Jaze lies.

"Drive off Jaze..." Jojo whispers to Jaze.

"Go now..." he continues, "I'm ready."

"I pulled you over because of the light," the Sheriff claims, "but I'm going to go run your name and if anything comes back, then I'll have to deal with that accordingly..."

"Oh," Jaze replies, "of course. You're just doing your job."

"I am," he says looking down at the I.D., "wait Jazemene Cole... are you, is your father Kool Hands?"

"The one and only." Jaze smiles.

"You know I thought I recognized her..." the Sheriff says over the top of the car to the other Sheriff near Josiah's window.

"What happened?" the second Sheriff asks.

"This is Kool Hands Cole's baby girl." He tells his partner.

"Are you serious," the second Sheriff asks, "that man is the best receiver the league will probably ever see."

"When you're right, you're right Jackson," the first Sheriff says handing Jaze her I.D. back, "I apologize about this misunderstanding Ms. Cole. If you don't mind... if I can just get you to sign something for me, you and this young man can be on your way."

"Like an autograph?" Jaze asks.

"Uh, let's call it a favor for a favor." The officer smiles handing her his pen and a pad.

"That'll work." Jaze says happily signing her name with the best penmanship her hands have ever known.

"Thanks," he says taking his pad and pen back, "what happened with you playing ball at the U? You were supposed to be must see T.V. all season long. Or at least that's the way they were advertising you all over the news a while back."

"Life happened," she says honestly, "but thanks for giving me a break sir. I really have to..."

"No, its fine," the officer interjects, "go ahead get out of here, just get that light fixed. And drive safely Ms. Cole; there are a lot of crazy people on the road these days."

"You have no idea." Jazemene whispers as she pulls back into the steady traffic once again.

(Miami)

(Love and K.J.)

In the front yard of K.C.'s mansion, Love and his biological son are playing catch with one of K.C.'s many footballs.

"You know I can't lie to you son." Love says throwing a decent pass to his son.

"So don't." K.J. replies catching the ball.

"I really wanna get your mother for continuing to mess with Keldrick." Love admits throwing the ball to K.J.

"I know." K.J. replies catching a pass.

"It really sucks to have such a fucked up lady for a mom." K.J. continues tossing the ball back.

"You don't know the half kid," Love reminds him, "Your mom was causing trouble and trying to ruin people's lives long before you were ever even a thought."

"I believe that," K.J. admits throwing a slightly too high pass to his dad, "but at the end of the day she's still my mom, she gave me life."

"And your Mama Cole was my mom," Love throws the ball back to K.J., "shit happens son."

"You're right but..." K.J. pauses holding onto the ball.

"No buts son," Love says, "when bad people refuse to change and stop hurting the people you love, you take things into your own capable hands, and you handle their asses. Whitney will be my last kill... well hopefully."

"Don't kill my mom, dad," K.J. throws the ball back, "Just scare the hell out of her or something."

"Why not..." Love asks.

"Because dad," K.J. really looks at him, "I'm asking you not to."

"Fine," Love replies, "for you, I'll let her live."

"So what time are we meeting with...?" K.J. looks around.

"I'll let you know," Love says, "now go long."

(Star Crossed)

"Josiah." Jaze says as they near the Miami city limits.

"Yeah baby." He yawns.

"First off," she laughs, "wake yo tired ass up it's not even 8 p.m. yet."

"I'm up." he straightens his posture to look out of the window and try to figure out his exact whereabouts.

296

"How would you take it," Jaze pauses, "if I said I might be…? I don't know. If maybe, I might be…"

"Might be what," he interjects irritated by her pauses, "gay, HIV positive… what? Why do you keep pausing?"

"Calm down boy," she says, "nothing like that."

"Then what is it," he asks, "You're scaring the shit outta me?"

"How would it sit with you if I told you I'm in love with someone else?" Jaze spits the question out quickly.

"If you what," Jojo sits forward to look at her, "I would have rather you told me you were gay or dying."

"Well damn." Jaze says with a tightly wrinkled brow.

"How would it sit with me," Jojo repeats part of her question, "that shit wouldn't sit well with me at all. And I think that's some real selfish crap to say. And to be honest it really pissed me off."

"Why baby?" Jaze laughs.

"This is not funny," Jojo assures her, "I got all emotional and told you how much I… *whatever* and then you just say some dumb shit like that."

"It's not dumb," Jaze continues to amuse herself, "it was a real and honest question."

"Okay so you're saying its real?" he asks.

"What?" Jaze squints at the road ahead.

"That you are in love with another man?" Josiah asks.

"Because if you are," he continues before she can reply, "you can just take me straight to my mom's crib **now**."

"Right now I'm about to meet my uncle." She replies.

"Whatever Jaze," Jojo leans back, "just stop talking, you said enough already."

"I never said it was actually the case Josiah," she looks at him while waiting at a stop light, "I said how would you feel *if* that was how I felt."

"You really wanna know how I would feel?" he asks.

"I really do." Jaze admits.

"Okay fuck it," Josiah replies, "I love you. I love the shit out of you! And honestly... if I believed, really believed another man had a chance to take you away from me I would probably... do something I have no business doing!"

"Like what Josiah," Jaze turns the radio down even lower than it was, "I can't read your mind boy."

"Jazemene if I thought I was losing you for good," he says, "I would do the same thing I would do if you died."

"Cry?" she asks.

"Cry," he laughs, "hell no! Well yeah, at first probably but then I would kill myself."

"So if you can't have me," Jaze smiles a sick beautiful smile, "you'll actually kill yourself?"

"Well not exactly," he explains, "the only way I'm leaving this earth is with you. So, if you decide to love another man, on some Romeo and Juliet shit I'm going to kill us both."

"That's not quite how that story went..." Jaze tells him.

"I don't give a damn," Josiah says with confidence, "that's exactly how our story would end. I would drive you and me off a mountain or some shit down into a deep ass ocean... deep as the soul shaking love I feel for you. Once we crashed into the water I wouldn't allow either one of us to survive I promise you that."

Ten minutes and several turns later, Jaze and a still quietly angry Josiah meet back up with Love and K.J.

"I can't believe you." Jojo mumbles.

"Josiah what the hell are you talking about now? Damn." Jaze pouts.

"You fell in love with that dude in Orlando." Jojo says.

Love steps out of his car and motions for his niece to come to him.

Jaze leans over and kisses Josiah's cheek and then rushes over to her uncle.

"Hey Unc." Jaze speaks as she hugs her uncle tightly.

"I uh, got a call from your Auntie Osiana." Love explains.

"Bad news?" Jaze's panic explodes openly on her face for her uncle to see.

"The parents are asking a lot of questions Jaze," Love explains, "we need to do something drastic and fast."

"Damn it!" Jaze says.

"No, now baby girl we knew this was coming sooner or later," Love puts his hands on her shoulders softly, "you have a lot of me in you. Take that for what it's worth good and bad... but in a situation like yours that's a damn good thing little girl."

"No, I know it is," she agrees trying to fight the tears, "but I'm not you Uncle Love I can't survive prison."

"Yes you can," he says, "and you will if it comes to that."

"No!" she screams.

"Jaze calm down..." he says.

"No," she yells again, "those dirty prison bitches are going to destroy my ass!"

"No they won't." Love shakes his head.

"Yes they will!" Jaze contends.

"I won't let them." Her uncle vows.

"You can't protect me on the inside Uncle Love." Jaze cries.

"Listen to me Jazzy..." he says after turning to look in the car at K.J.

"I'm listening." She cries.

"I know everybody says I'm crazy as hell," he admits, "but every crazy person has a stroke of genius in them. Now when I say what I'm going to say... look at it on as many levels as you possibly can. I don't know who's watching us or following you or anything like that so..."

"Uncle Love," Jaze cries, "please just spit it out!"

"Do you love that young man sitting over there in my car?" Love asks.

"Who Josiah?" she cries.

"Who else," he wrinkles his brow, "yes Josiah, *do you love him*?"

"So much it scares me." Jaze admits.

"The kinda love little girls dream about right," he asks, "no matter how long or short your life may be you wanna spend every second of it with him…"

"Yes Uncle Love," she whines, "what is your point? You're scaring me now, because Josiah was already talking crazy about killing me and himself."

"Bingo," her uncle smiles, "Life is a cage my love… we never become more free than when we pass away. If you die now, together with Josiah, your souls will be connected… intertwined, if you will forever."

Love pulls out his gun. Then he leans in close to his only brother's, only child and whispers very deadly words.

Jaze snatches away from him and runs full speed back towards the red Camaro.

Two shots ring out.

Josiah and K.J. although in two separate cars both sit forward as their eyes bulge out of their heads in justified terror.

(Ty's house)

Jaze rings the doorbell at her Uncle Ty's house but has no idea what to expect once the door opens. After waiting several minutes Jaze contemplates ruining everything by running back to her BMW and driving to the hospital. The door opens. Osiana looks down at her red faced niece and can't even pretend to be angry with her.

"Come in Jazemene." She says.

"Where's Uncle Ty," Jaze asks following her inside, "I thought I saw both of his cars outside?"

"You did," Osiana confirms, "he's sleeping. What happened to your…"

"I'm fine," Jaze assures her, "can I see Uncle Ty please?"

"Jaze you are not fine!" Osiana raises her voice.

"I'm fine Auntie." Jaze repeats.

"I don't like this at all," Osiana admits, "whatever this is."

"Can I see my uncle please?" Jaze asks.

"He's very tired baby…" Osiana shakes her head.

"I won't wake him," Jaze promises, "I just want to see him… one last time."

"One last time," Osiana repeats, "running off to Mexico huh?"

"I wish." Jaze says following Osiana to one of the many bedrooms to look at her Uncle's tired face once more. Jaze walks over to Ty and kisses him on his warm wrinkled forehead. After leaving the room she checks her watch as she follows Osiana back towards the front.

"Um I really should get going." Jaze says.

"I would love to stop you my love," Osiana admits, "But you're a grown woman now Jaze so this decision is yours."

"I know Auntie," Jaze fakes a smile as her tears become more obvious; "I love you."

"I love you too hun." Osiana hugs Jaze and then watches her run awkwardly back to her car.

Jojo is holding his nose when Jaze gets back inside the car. She's still crying as she pulls away from Osiana's house in her blue BMW. Jaze is grinding her hands into her steering wheel as she speeds down the street.

"Are you okay?" Jojo asks. "I can drive if you want me too." He continues.

"No!" She screams. "I want you to make it so that I don't have to do this," she fumes, "Can you do that?"

"You know I can't do that Jazemene," he shakes his blonde head, "but don't you think deep down it will be epic to go out like Romeo and Juliet?"

"Did you ever read that story," Jaze yells, "Juliet never had to do this!"

"You're still bleeding pretty bad Jaze," Josiah notices, "Do you want me to drive?"

"No Josiah I want you to shut the hell up!" she cries out.

"Fine," he crosses his arms and leans back, "hell, I'm not the one who shot you."

Jaze looks over at her lover with obvious regret.

She's never wanted to apologize so badly in her life. It doesn't matter because she can't find the words to do so anyway.

"God Bleek's body stinks." Jaze says as she looks in her rearview mirror.

"Just drive Jaze." Josiah says.

"Romeo and Juliet huh…" she smiles through her tears.

"Hell no," Jojo smiles, "we're better than them… what we have is way deeper."

"So, you ready to die baby?" she asks.

"Do I look nervous?" he asks with unwavering eyes. "As long as you're the one killing me I was born ready to die."

Chapter 18
Love Me to Death

As Keldrick ventures out of the elevator on the floor his wife is now being kept on he can hear nothing outside of his thoughts.

(K.C.)

I swear I hate hospitals more than any damn thing on earth. I know damn well they're created to, and are supposed to help save people's lives. But I always hear about more dying than saving. Somebody better save my baby mama, because if God himself doesn't touch my heart soon her ass is gonna be dying too, but it won't be in a hospital or because she's physically ill. The bitch is bipolar and dangerous as hell. If I had the balls, I'd kill her ass my damnself for all the dumb shit she put me through since I was a teenager. But I don't have to do a damn thing I know my baby brother will put her ass on ice real quick.

As Keldrick Jermaine Cole Sr. walks into his wife's hospital room all of the fleeting thoughts swirling around his brain fall deathly silent.

The woman downstairs said that this was the room he would find his wife in. There is a woman in the room, but she's definitely not the woman K.C. married.

Even from the door he can tell her skin is pale and scaly. Her eyes are swollen and closed completely. She looks deathly thin beneath the sheet that's been laid on top of her.

The biggest give away that this woman can't be Cameron Candice Jiles Cole is the alarming fact that she's almost completely bald.

"***Mr. Kool Hands Cole***." The voice says startling K.C. from behind.

K.C. turns to look at the familiar doctor's face.

"I'd like to apologize to you Mr. Cole," the doctor continues to talk to a silent K.C., "when you got arrested before I was only doing my job staying out of the way…"

"Doc, who the hell is that in my wife's bed?" K.C. asks.

"I'm sorry," the doctor frowns, "I don't understand the question."

"It's a simple question Doctor!" K.C. contends angrily.

"Um, yeah it is a ***very*** simple question Mr. Cole," the doctor agrees, "It's just not a very good one."

"Damn it do not make me angry," K.C. fumes, "who the hell is that bald headed, ashy, mother fucker lying down in ***my*** wife's bed?"

"Well," the doctor says, "she is very sick, but part of her rough physical appearance is due to adverse reactions she had to some of the medicines we had her on. But to be honest she didn't look well when she came in sir."

"That's not my wife!" K.C. exclaims.

"Please lower your voice Mr. Cole, she **can** hear you." The doctor points behind him towards Cameron's open eyes.

K.C. slowly turns around to find his wife staring at him through half open lids. He quickly rushes to her.

"Baby, I'm so…" K.C. starts.

"Do not apologize, Keldrick," she smiles, "I know how bad I must look to you. I'm the one who needs to apologize. If I had known, you were coming I would have had one of the nice nurses to put my hair on for me."

"Your skin," he cries, "What happened to it… What, why do you look so pale baby…"

"I'll leave you two alone." The doctor says heading back out of the door.

"I'm sick Keldrick… I've had cancer for some time now." She falls headfirst into a dangerous coughing spell.

"I never noticed your skin was so…" K.C. pauses unsure how to word his concern.

"My skin looks that bad huh," Cam coughs a bit more, "well I can honestly say the makeup helped hide it, but this is the first time in years I remember you actually looking at me Keldrick."

"That's not true." He contends.

"Yes it's very true." She tells him.

"*I was so lost… and angry about Kelmeron*." K.C. admits.

"I know… I know," Cam cries, "and I am… **eternally** sorry for the stupid, sick, psychotic shit I did that day."

"Sorry won't…" K.C. can't fight his inevitable tears.

"No," Cam interjects as every word seems to take all of her strength to form, "Sorry won't fix it, or bring our son back... but *sorry* is *all* I have left Keldrick. I'm tired... I'm so tired and I'm dying. So after I'm gone you can marry Whitney. I'm sure she would still leave Charlie in a heartbeat for you."

"Charlie's dead." K.C. takes a seat in the chair across from Cam's bed.

"What do you mean?" Cam asks weakly.

"He's gone," K.C. confirms, "shot himself in the head."

"I thought," Cam pauses to give way to phlegm filled coughs again, "I thought you were going to tell me your brother killed him."

"No," K.C. wipes his tired eyes, "Love didn't kill Charlie, but I can't say the same for your triflin' ass girlfriend."

"He killed my Whitney?" Cam gasps holding back more disgustingly hard coughs.

"First of all," K.C. says, "you don't have a **Whitney**, and no she ain't dead yet."

"Love is not killing my Whitney." Cam wipes her mouth and then coughs some more.

"I am so glad she was never able to brainwash me like she's done you," K.C. shakes his head, "she was planning to take you out in this hospital Cameron."

"What are you talking about," Cam wrinkles her peeling forehead, "what do you mean she was planning to take me out?"

"She doesn't love you baby," K.C. tells her, "Whit is, and has always been obsessed with the idea of being my wife. Now, she will steal, kill, and destroy anything in her path to do just that. You are not going to die, I'm going to get you the best treatments money can buy, and I'm gonna get you out of here and healthy... but you have to promise to stay the hell away from Whitney."

"I can't do that baby." Cam admits.

"You can and you will." K.C. tells her.

Chapter 19
Fallin' Till the End

(Jaze)

Have you ever been in love? No, I mean have you ever truly been in love beyond yourself to the point that person... the one you love matters more than your own well-being? Have you ever been a part of a soul shattering connection to another person's heart and life, to the point neither one of you can exist without the other? Would you die with or for that person? Would they do the same for you?

Free falling off of a huge bridge that was built for you, by you into a perceived but unknown end that will hurt and break a lot of people's lives even if only for a little while. Love takes on a life of its own and sometimes you just don't even try to stop it. Who's to say love doesn't know best?

As a woman, if you are lucky enough to meet and exist happily with a man who would actually die for and with you... would you not be foolish enough to take him up on that offer and join him? Every woman wants a fairytale relationship, marriage, and life... that "till death do us part" kinda love. So if you have that kind of love; and you can choose when and how you and your lover can leave the world of the living together, why not? They'll miss us, but not forever, true love never dies so we will be with our loved ones again one day. I'm completely aware of how crazy that sounds, but isn't that what we all truly want? A love… a real love that can stand the tests of time, trial, and turmoil. We want a love that can last beyond death, one that feels so good it can't be wrong. Love should exist forever, never being destroyed by outside sources. Does love drive you crazy? Of course it does, or at least it can. But who would fight a pure love that reaches deep inside your chest and grabs firm hold of your heart, reroutes it and ties it around your soul and then smashes it beautifully and perfectly together with the heart and soul of the only person you're living to exist in this world with? One man, one woman, in a world where nothing else matters beyond each other… and even when we die… together, our young pure love can and will live on forevermore. If that's not what you're searching for, then what you're looking for is not real love.

Chapter 20
Father I need Thee

(K.C.)

K.J. isn't my biological son, and there were always silent questions in the back of my head about my deceased son Kelmeron as to whether or not he was biologically mine. But one child who has never been in question is my beautiful baby girl Jazemene. I knew from the moment I laid eyes on my tiny princess she was mine. I always had love for Jazemene, but I was young and so lost without football... my injury back in high school changed and ruined everything! When I got locked up and lost those precious years with my daughter, I knew damn well eventually that would set in motion the unstable relationship we'd possibly have when she became a woman. My baby... My baby girl is gone. I'll never get to... walk her down the aisle or hold her children. I'll never get to see her beautiful face ever again. And when they found her remains her body and face were burned and mutilated so badly she was almost unrecognizable. The remaining particles of her clothes were a dead giveaway though. Cameron passed out as soon as she saw the car. Jaze's blue BMW was almost all black from the collision and fire. I can't even pretend like I want to keep living now. I've never been the suicidal type, but to know that my baby chose that black ass idiot Bleek over me and then died with him over something probably as simple as a petty argument, I can't fucking take it! I'm losing what's left of my mind. And I can't understand for the life of me what Josiah Bell was doing in the car with them. None of it makes any sense. Josiah's mother Cidra identified his wallet and shoes so there was no mistake as to who the poor third charred body belonged to. There are still two other young adults, Melody Scooter Speights, and Roland Dansby who are missing. The police continue to search for them just hoping they're still alive. Something's not right though; I can feel it in my aging bones. Nonetheless, may my baby rest in blissful paradise.

(Pastor White)

There's an almost spooky calm over the large group gathered around the fresh graves in the familiar cemetery. No one can believe Josiah Bell and Jazemene Cole are really gone. Their old classmates are all standing around in complete shock and confusion.

"I am saddened today," Pastor White speaks, "because almost eleven years ago today I buried one of these young people's grandmothers. Jazemene Cole stood up here with me and cried her little eyes out begging for her grandmother's tormented soul to be saved. I remember telling her that in my eyes her love alone should have been sufficient enough to save Mama Cole's soul. But, today Jazemene has gone to the other side to meet and be with her beloved grandmother for eternity and she has with her a young man she used to talk my ears off about after Sunday school many, many years ago."

The crowd laughs softly.

"Yes," Pastor White continues, "Jazemene Cole loved that white boy ever since she was just a little girl, and I am more than sure that real love between the two of them lives on deep inside God's heavenly gates. Young love that ends tragically has a way of living on in spirit. Think of how long the popularity of the Shakespearian play, **Romeo and Juliet** has lasted. Maybe one day some storyteller as great as Shakespeare will come along and write the star-crossed love story of Jazemene Cole and Josiah Bell. Lord, I have no understanding today of the reason these two souls and lives were taken, but I will not question you and your ways. I have to believe in my heart that just maybe you were in need of a couple more obedient angels inside your Heavenly realm. These two will serve you well Father. Jazemene was well versed in Your Word. Forgive me everyone I just want to take a second and reflect on who little Jazemene Cole was and what she meant to me and my church. She was so passionate about the Lord at a very early age. The Coles weren't at church every Sunday, but when they were there, and early enough for Sunday school, young Jazemene would at times lead her Sunday school class herself. I remember... that, on the days she taught teenagers and young adults would sit in and listen to her teach. As she got older, she didn't come around as much, but I never feared that she was losing her way permanently. She simply finished high school, and got busy with college classes and sports. Our little Jazemene had become a beautiful, talented... and very busy young woman. And that's okay, children have to grow up and out, and go through changes. It's the changes... ***our own*** personal changes that make us who and what we are as adults. Jazemene had to stumble, she was supposed to, but I knew she would eventually find her way home."

(The Pain)

Days after the service, no one connected to the tragedy has even begun to move on. On the front lawn of the Keldrick Cole Miami mansion hundreds of people came with lit candles, dressed in all black, some carrying flowers as they stood in silence remembering Josiah and Jazemene. It's not often that the iron gates of the Cole mansion are opened to complete strangers, but at this point in his forty plus year existence, Mr. ***Kool Hands*** thinks it's high time he starts opening up before he explodes from the inside out. The people who came to join in the candlelit post funeral vigil didn't pay much attention to the T.V. and news cameras. Most of them refused to be interviewed proving they were truly there to pay their respects and remember two vibrant young adults who lost their lives entirely too soon.

After the last candle holder hugged K.C., Josiah's mother and stepfather, and then Cameron he left the yard with his head and shoulders low. Now faced with a sea of neatly laid flowers before them K.C., a sickly Cameron, Jacody, Tyrone, Osiana, Love, K.J., and Cidra Bell all stand in confused silence.

"Keldrick," Tyrone says hugging his big brother tightly, "man I don't know what the hell to say, and I don't know if I ever will but my heart is dying for you man. ***If I***

ever lost a child... man I don't know bro, I just don't
know."

"Thanks Ty." K.C. hugs him back.

After their hug is broken Jacody takes his place
with his best friend.

"I know you have everything fam," Jacody says,
"but man you already know if you ever, ever need
anything I got you fam. I love you; you are my family no
matter what. That little girl of yours was my child too. All
that bullshit between us, it's dead, we'll never speak of it
again man."

"Okay Jay..." K.C. starts.

"Got damn it!" Jacody breaks down hard while
hugging Keldrick tightly.

"No, no, no Jazzy," Jay cries, "Come back baby girl.
Unc ain't been around enough. I been busy running this
damn record label... god damn it!"

K.C. hugs Jacody tighter.

"This ain't your fault Jay," K.C. assures him in a
strong comforting tone, "my baby was confused. I was
contacted by the police a couple days ago, there was
already an open investigation involving her. There's a lot
we still don't know, but this is not your fault."

Cidra hugs Jacody from the back and gently pulls
him away from K.C. as he turns to hug her now. Love hugs
K.C. and whispers words of his own to his big brother.

"I'm so sorry," Jacody cries in Cidra Bell's ear, "I am
so damn sorry. That boy, our son needed a real man in his
life. And I... I played that role when it was convenient, but I

didn't do nearly as much as I could have. Damn it baby I'm so sorry."

"I love you Jacody," Cidra cries, "and my son did too. I don't think you were playing a role at all."

"Yes I was Cid," he admits, "the most important thing on my mind was my company and having a beautiful wife and family. I wasn't focused on actual relationships at all."

"It's okay baby." Cidra cries on his chest.

"No its not," Jay holds her back from him to look down in her eyes, "this is my fault... I married you, I should have..."

"Yes baby," Cid interjects, "you did marry me, and that made Josiah very, very happy. It was not your job to save my son, Jacody. I won't let you tell that lie to yourself, you can't carry that burden, and this is all hard enough as it is. I miss my baby so much, but I need you to be strong right now, you can't fold baby."

"I'll never fold," Jacody assures her reaching down to rub her full belly, "but he'll never get to meet his baby sister..."

"Yes he will," Cidra cries pulling Jay back close to her, "he's talking to her right now from above."

"Where is Whitney?" K.C. asks.

Cameron tries to respond but instead starts coughing for the first time in an hour or so.

"Baby you should be laying down." K.C. pulls her close to him.

"I'm exactly where I should be." Cam assures him.

De'Lure

"Lying in that smelly cold hospital bed day in and day out," she continues, "ain't gonna help me live any longer."

She coughs again a little harder this time.

"You're not dying Cameron." K.C. rubs her sore back and kisses her forehead gently.

"Not tonight," she tries to smile, "but as far as Whit... I called her hours ago."

"No answer?" K.C. asks.

"Yeah she answered," Cam replies, "but she wasn't anywhere close to being in her right mind."

"Drunk?" Jacody asks.

"No," Cam shakes her tired wig covered head, "she's on some kind of medication. Said she's been on it since Charlie passed. It makes her extremely drowsy. One second we were on the phone, the next she hung up and hasn't answered or called back since."

"Sleeping pills." K.C. says.

"Whitney is fine," Love says, "We'll all be dead in our graves and Whitney Powell will still be right here on this earth causing hell."

"Yeah I think you're right bro." Kel agrees.

"*Damn it*," Cidra exclaims, "*I'm so sorry everybody*!"

"I am so sorry," she continues, crying in full force for the first time since the funeral, "*I'm trying to be strong but I can't... I just can't! This is not fair I want my son back! God please bring me my baby back!*"

She falls to her knees on the mansion's well-manicured front lawn.

K.C. has had enough of all the emotions surrounding him in his front yard. After hugging everyone once more he heads inside and leaves Cameron to say her goodbye's and walk everyone to their cars.

Once inside K.C. heads upstairs but not to his room. Not yet. Instead at the top of the stairs K.C. hangs a right and heads to a room he's rarely set foot in since that day. The hallway in front of him looks a mile long, inside he wishes it was, he never wants to make it where he's headed, and he never wants to feel what that place will undoubtedly make him feel.

(K.C.)

Standing here at this door brings back everything in full force. I still feel the pain, the harsh, permanent scar worthy pain that feels as if it will always be at the guarded forefront of my mind. I also still remember and feel the love I had for him... for you. Son... Kelmeron, in my heart you will never die son. Daddy loves you more than you'll ever know. I want so desperately to open this door and find you lying in your bed fast asleep. I want to walk in your room and tuck your small warm body in your bed right now, wearing some colorful super hero pajamas, and your tiny wave cap. I still remember you wanted your waves to swirl around your head just like daddy. Damn it Kelmeron... damn it baby. It was my job; it was my damn job to protect you. You were my true legacy and heir. I should have never left you alone with your mother, she was very sick son. I am so, so sorry. If daddy could take it back, I would baby boy. I miss you so damn much; I swear to Jesus I hope you know that son. I would die if could... just for you to come back and live a beautiful full life in my place. You didn't... nobody deserves what you went through... the way you... died, is just... tragically unforgettable, and eternally unforgivable. You were... taken from us, or me way too soon Kel. You were... not a burden to me... or anybody else. When she... took you, away from me I harbored so much hatred for your mother. She isn't well, she's dying now, and I can't help but believe that maybe this is God's way of punishing her for... doing what she did to you. Damn it, I can say it... she... she killed... your mother murdered you son. It was no accident, I have watched it over and over, and over again on film. I'm so sorry son, god damn it! And I had no relationship with your big sister Jazemene at all, I'm trying son... I have tried everything I know, but nothing works. I want so badly to have a bond with her before I pass away one day leaving her with so many pains and earthly regrets... I love..."

The front door slams shut downstairs.

K.C. lets go of his son's bedroom doorknob without ever even turning it, and heads to his own room with his head held low.

Every step he takes now feels as if it's the last he can bear. Part of him wishes he could physically die right now, since he's already dead emotionally. He wishes he could take Cam's sickness and pain on with his own body. If he could, Keldrick Cole Sr. would gladly do it and quickly succumb to the disease so that he could bow out from the cold world he has been trapped in as of late. Inside his room K.C. heads for his bathroom sanctuary. Locked inside of it now, K.C. pulls his pants down and takes an almost comfortable seat on his thrown. He needs to use the bathroom badly but he can't.

(K.C.)

"Fix it Jesus," he mumbles, "fix it Lord…. Fix this. Lord God, Jesus Christ please… please fix, this for me. I don't want it. I do not want this pain, or this life. Take it all Lord you can have everything just give me Kelmeron, Jazzy, and Cameron. We won't need anything else in this world but your love and guidance. Give me my children and a healthy wife Lord, I don't need a dime. Take every single worldly treasure I've ever had or could ever have and just give me my family back whole… in good health Jesus. But I know you can't… or won't do that for me. I don't deserve it or you. I have been… you have blessed me with so much. I never took the time to properly thank you or reach out to my fans and tell them of the glorious things you've done in my life. If they could all hear me now… I don't know what I would say, but I do know I would tell them you can make all the money man can print, but if you lose the people who matter the most to you that cash and all the things you can obtain because of your riches lose their value. Lord I can't lose Cameron now…"

"You'll never lose me." Cam's voice strains from the other side of the door.

"Cam…" K.C. cries.

"Yes baby…" she replies with her face to the locked door.

320

"You okay baby?" he asks.

"I've never been better," she lies, "I'll be in bed waiting for you when you come out."

K.C. drops his handsome head deep in his large chocolate hands. He feels chills running along his spine. His body is gently shaking, but no longer from his cries. From above his head he can see a bright white light breaking through everything.

"My son," Keldrick hears a strong voice speak to him from the light, **"nothing is what it seems. You are not being punished at all. True, you have not been very kind to the people you claim to love the most. You have hurt them all in ways you will never understand. But you are not dead Keldrick, so you have time to right your wrongs and to love the ones closest to you ferociously for the rest of your days. Never take another second of your life for granted Keldrick. This feeling... this pain, this too shall pass. I love you with all My heart."**

K.C. stands up unsure what to do next. Standing in front of his toilet he feels a cool breeze across his behind and immediately looks down to see his pants still around his ankles.

He turns around to flush the empty toilet stool and then makes his way to the bathroom door. With everything inside of him, K.C. hopes Cam is still listening at the door. He hopes she heard the Lord speak to him as well, so he can know he's not completely insane.

He unlocks the door. Then he opens it slowly.

As he looks through the crack in the door he can see Cam lying in bed facing him, waiting for him as she said

321

she would. Lost instantly in her stare it no longer matters to Keldrick if he's crazy or not, as long as he can be crazy with Cam.

"Are you okay?" she asks with what little strength she has.

"I think so," he smiles as he roughly wipes away old tears, "I think we're gonna make it my love."

"I believe that." Cam says with a soft smile.

"I don't," he admits, "I want to, and I'm going to try hard for you. But my spirit is definitely broken.

K.C. climbs into bed and snuggles up close to his wife wrapping her in his strong arms. He smells like caramel oils and to him she smells like crushed fruits blended perfectly together.

K.C. gently nudges Cam's less than perfect nose with his. After calmly locking eyes with the pure chestnut windows to her soul K.C finds Cameron's lips and licks them twice to wet them before kissing her genuinely for the first time in a long time.

"This is nice..." Cameron moans against his lips.

"Yes," he agrees, "it is. But we have some work to do."

"Do we?" she asks holding back her painful inopportune coughs.

"We do," he confirms, "we have been broke, and now we are richer than anyone we know. We've had it all, but what does it matter now? Both of or children are gone. We have no need for all of this stuff, these cars, this ridiculously big house..."

"So what are you saying baby?" Cam looks deep in his eyes as he searches her soul.

K.C. gently removes her wig and really looks at her. She closes her eyes as tears form. K.C. smiles and then kisses her with soft concentrated passion. Cam opens her eyes to his handsome smile.

"What were you saying before baby...?" Cam whispers.

"I'm saying," he pauses to stroke her almost bald head, "I'm saying... I'm moving you back home to Orlando, and I'm going to do my best to nurse you back to full health."

"What?" she replies.

"If that's okay with you my queen..." he kisses her again.

"I'll follow you anywhere," she admits, "all of this we have... everything you've worked for is very nice, but honestly all I've ever wanted was you and your love Keldrick Cole."

The temporarily happy couple lay face to face lost in conversation for the better part of twenty minutes. As Cam continues to confess her undying love for K.C., he begins to kiss her neck intensely.

Her words are slowly melting into moans. As he continues to lick and bite on her chocolate neck K.C. reaches behind her and grips her soft behind.

Cam opens her legs for him to slide in between them. He declines and rolls her over on her stomach softly.

Lying completely flat on her stomach Cameron remains still as K.C. removes all of her clothing. As her last standing article of clothing, her pink lace panties hit the floor, Cam knows it's about to get real.

K.C. starts removing his own clothing quickly as his arousal is at its full potential now. It takes a few extra seconds to get his pants off as his enormous erection is in the way of him pulling his pants down.

He finally frees himself from bondage and briefly smiles down at the perfect large hardness of himself. Leaning forward almost in push up position K.C. gently turns Cameron's head to the side so he can taste her lips some more from behind now.

As they kiss he allows his shaft to hang down and graze lightly against her buttocks and lower back. As the kisses grow wetter and deeper Cam can't help but to arch her back and raise her body up towards him. At the height of her lust filled lift she can feel his still ripped six pack abs plush against her ass.

"I love you Keldrick Cole..." Cam moans against his hungry lips.

"I love you too Cameron Cole." He replies entering her from behind slowly with two strong fingers.

"*I love you baby*..." Cam moans much louder this time as he removes his busy fingers.

"I love you too." He growls as he enters her fully from the back simultaneously plunging his tongue deep in her mouth.

"*Yes!*!!" she cries.

"Ba... aaaa... by," she cries out, "baaa... aaa... by, oh I missed you Keldrick!"

"I never left you..." he moans.

"Yeeeesss you diiiid…" she moans gripping the sheets with all her might.

"Well I'm back now." K.C. says with an extra powerful downward stroke.

As Cam blindly throws her soft ass back to him, Keldrick is quickly finding the perfect rhythm.

Cam's sweet love nectar is flowing from her wet center more frequently with every stroke.

"Ooh…" she moans and smiles at the pleasant almost raunchy sounds of their love making.

The excess air being forced out of her wetness is growing louder and louder. To K.C.'s delight she pushes back even more on him.

"Right there baby?" K.C. moans.

"Yes baby," she cries, "do it… do it riiight there…"

With her neck now gripped tightly by his left hand K.C. holds Cam's hips steady with his right hand.

He has perfect control now, as he swings her much smaller body back and forth against his. The sweat from his forehead is seeping into his eyes, but the burning sensation is not unbearable enough to make him stop.

K.C. flexes his still tight muscles as he begins to pull her harder, and drive himself a little deeper inside of her.

After they finish making passionate love K.C. soon falls asleep inside the body of his slow breathing, almost content, still very beautiful wife.

(Date Night)

Back in Miami Love and K.J. are in route to their dinner date with Felicity Johnson and her aunt Gabrielle. Love is driving calmly with his mind on his niece Jazemene and a million other things that are completely out of his reach.

He realizes that he's psychotic and because of the fact he obsesses over things... *a lot*. He doesn't mind much, because he believes his obsessive compulsive behavior is just a part of his genius. He's done a lot of terrible things over the past ten years but he's still free as a bird, and will remain that way because he's fashioned himself into the perfect criminal. He's a survivor and he's yet to meet a force outside of himself that can sensitize him or come close to outwitting him.

"Dad..." K.C. breaks the silence to voice some thoughts of his own.

"Yeah son..." Love replies still trapped deep in his cluttered mind.

"If Jaze..." K.J. starts.

"Damn it!" Love slams on breaks in the middle of traffic forcing the vehicles behind him to recklessly swerve around him.

"I told you we do not talk about your sister... *ever*!" Love sternly reminds his wide eyed son.

"Sorry." K.J. mumbles.

"Do not let it..." Love glares at him.

"It won't happen again." K.J. interjects.

Love briefly checks his rearview mirror as if he ever gave a damn about the other drivers he is inconveniencing. Then he quickly speeds off joining back in with the flow of the steady traffic. After reaching beneath his seat, Love begins to look in the other cars, secretly hoping one of the drivers near him catches a deadly case of road rage or so much as gives him a dirty look. Lucky for them none of them have been caught looking in Love's direction at all.

"So…" K.J. speaks again.

"Damn it boy!" Love screams.

"It's not about Jaze, dad," K.J. claims, "God, I was just going to ask what I should talk about tonight… **with Felicity**."

Love smiles.

"My bad boy." Love apologizes sincerely.

"Don't call me boy dad," K.J. speaks up, "I've heard enough of your stories to know I don't wanna be called a boy. I'm a man… even at sixteen years old I'm a man dad, just like you told K.C."

"Yes you are K.J.," Love agrees, "but I do apologize for going off on you. You know how I am; I don't like to talk… about certain things. I'm… very meticulous that way and…"

"Dad," K.J. interjects, "what do I say to Felicity?"

"That I can't tell you son," Love admits, "the more I try to teach you how to talk to the ladies the more you'll mess up. We are two different people son, you have to find your niche… just be yourself and find your own comfort zone. Figure out, what the two of you have in common."

"Okay." K.J. stares blankly out of the front of the car.

"Your dreads are getting long son." Love takes one of his son's locks in his right hand.

"Yeah, but how do I start the convo dad?" K.J. asks.

"You don't," Love says turning onto Gabrielle and Felicity's street, "you don't. You let her start the convo. If she can't, then you just start simple. Find out her birthday, favorite color, favorite movie, favorite music artist, and food. And if you really like her, which I'm guessing you do because every time you're on Instagram or Facebook you're on her page... which is okay, but if you like her that much do not forget the answers to those five questions they can carry you a very long way with any woman son."

"You ready?" Love asks pulling into the driveway.

"Nope," K.J. admits, "but I'll be cool."

"Come on," Love says opening his door, "just follow my lead son."

K.J. pulls the mirror down in the sun visor above his head. As he looks deep into the greenness off his wide eyes he knows fully that he has no clue who he is, but with his father he's happy so nothing else really matters. After stepping out of the car himself, K.J. meets his father near the front of the car. They check each other out and then head towards the door.

"Aye dad," K.J. frowns, "How come you have flowers and I don't?"

"Because you're a kid," Love smiles down at him, "take it slow son."

"Right... slow." K.J. whispers to himself as his father knocks on the door.

"Coming..." Gabrielle yells from inside.

Moments later the vibrant full figured woman answers the door with a breathtakingly infectious smile.

"Well aren't you two just as handsome as can be." Gabrielle says.

"Thanks gorgeous..." Love replies handing her the flowers as K.J. tries not to blush.

"For me," Gabrielle smells the rare roses, "thank you Lance."

K.J. looks up at his dad and waits.

His father says nothing.

K.J.'s jaw drops at the fact that his father allowed this woman to call him that name. The name he openly dreads and would kill over.

"What's wrong with you K.J.?" Gabrielle asks.

"Nothing," he says quickly, "is Felicity..."

"Yeah she's upstairs playing the game..." Gabrielle steps back to allow them both to come inside.

"No way," K.J. lights up, "she didn't tell me she plays video games."

"Well did you ask her?" Gabrielle asks with another pleasant grin.

"No, I guess not." K.J. recollects.

"Well, yes baby she loves her video games," Gabrielle assures K.J., "she also does dreads... so if the two of you are looking for a new stylist, she's really very good."

"Perfect," K.J. mumbles, "um, do you know what game she's playing?"

"The new Grand Theft something another," Gabrielle laughs at her lack of video game knowledge, "child I don't know. You can go upstairs, turn left and it's the only door on that side."

"**Grand Theft Auto**," K.J. gushes, "I'm gone. See ya dad."

Love smiles as he and Gabrielle watch his son bound up the stairs as his nerves seem to have completely melted away.

"Kids." Love laughs.

"Tell me about it." Gabrielle laughs with him as she leads him to the kitchen.

"Oh I meant to ask you," Love starts taking a seat at her kitchen table, "did you and **Little Leg,** have any kids?"

"**Larry** and I," Gabrielle smiles with a hand on each hip, "have a son. His name is Marcus."

"Great," Love says, "where is he I'd like to meet him..."

"Marcus is with his father." Gabrielle sighs as she stirs the contents in one of the larger pots on her stove.

"Why?" Love inquires.

"Because," Gabrielle pauses to open her oven, "apparently I'm an unfit mother, and my son turned twelve and decided he didn't want to live with me anymore."

"So, the courts gave **Little**, I mean Larry custody," Love asks, "That's some rare shit. The only time I hear about fathers getting custody is if the mother is crazy, or locked up... or if the father is rich and famous."

330

"Yeah well," Gabrielle sighs again speaking now with less volume in her voice, "they didn't give my son to Larry, my son chose to go and live with his father. But, if he hadn't they probably would have given him to Larry anyway."

"But why," Love asks, "am I missing something here?"

"Lance Cole," she turns and smiles at him with new tears in her eyes, "now you came here to eat and enjoy my company while we catch up on the past decade or so. We are not here to talk about my wreck of a life."

"Oh no Gabby," Love stands up and makes his way close to her, "you're crying. Why are you crying?"

"Because I'm a female." She laughs through her real tears as Love wraps his arms around her round soft body.

"Look," Love says, "whatever it is, I swear it's going to be fine."

"No actually it's not." She contends.

"It will be." Love says hugging her tighter.

"No it won't Lance," Gabby cries, "I lost my job two months ago, my savings are spent, food stamps are almost gone... my son can't live here with me because I'm about to be homeless."

"Damn Gabby." Love pulls back to look at her.

"The worst part is my niece doesn't even know yet." Gabrielle admits.

"You haven't told Felicity?" Love asks lowering his voice considerably.

"No," Gabrielle confirms, "I don't know how Lance."

"Here," Love takes her by the hand, "sit down and talk to me."

Love pulls a chair out for her, and then sits across from her in the chair he was sitting in before.

"I do not want to bother you with my problems Lance," she cries, "I'm just happy you came to see me, it really means a lot to a single mom like me."

"And why is that?" Love looks intently at her.

"Well," she laughs wiping more tears, "if you haven't noticed I'm fat as hell, I'm not exactly getting the lion's share of dating offers. I'm not stupid Lance; I realize men just don't look for women like me that often."

"I'm looking." Love says without hesitation.

"Are you?" she says void of emotion.

"Yeah I'm looking right at you," he takes her hand in his, "and I see what you obviously don't see. You are not fat you are divinely built. And you have always been a pretty girl to me, I was just too lost in my own world and new found popularity our last year of high school to really notice. That was my fault. Now I've had my share of thin women, thick women, and women of all races but right now I think you're exactly what I'm looking for Gabrielle."

"Don't play with me Lance Orlandis." Gabrielle says wiping more tears away.

"Does it look like I'm playing with you girl?" he asks still holding her hand.

"No, but..." she looks away.

"No buts," he interjects, "now I know this is forward of me, and I'll completely understand if you say no..."

"Oh my God Lance," she covers her mouth with her free hand, "are you proposing to me? Because if you are I'll know you're crazy as hell, because it's way too soon and I'll have to ask you to leave..."

"Girl hush," he laughs, "I'm proposing something but its damn sure not marriage, and I am crazy but that has nothing to do with this conversation."

"Your pretty ass *is not* crazy." Gabrielle gushes.

"Okay," Love replies, "Well, like I was saying... if you don't mind, I was planning on moving my son back here permanently, and rather than search for a house..."

Gabrielle doesn't speak.

"I mean feel free to say no," Love lets go of her hand, "but that looks like a decent sized guest bedroom over there near that hall closet. I could help get you back on track financially, and help with the upkeep of the property."

"Are you seriously asking to move in with me Lance Cole," Gabrielle squints at his face, "because you actually sound like you're serious?"

"Well," Love hesitates, "I uh..."

"Because if you're serious," Gabrielle interjects, "I would love it if you moved in with me. And your son is welcome too. I know; I know this is some crazy shit going on and I shouldn't be opening my home to you so soon, but I am really in an impossible situation..."

"No need to explain," Love smiles, "We'll be helping each other."

"Great." Gabrielle smiles as her tears have finally faded away.

(Upstairs in Felicity's room)

"So you like legit play videos games," K.J. looks on with wide eyes, "and you're actually good? This is crazy."

"Why?" Felicity asks never taking her eyes off the screen.

"I don't know it's just weird." K.J. replies.

"Did you just call me weird?" she looks at him.

"Well yeah," he confirms, "but in a really good way."

"I love your dreads," she says handing him the video game control, "here sit on the floor I wanna play with your hair."

"Okay." He says taking her place on the floor in front of the bed as she begins braiding his dreads.

"So," he says, "when's your birthday, what's your favorite movie, color, singer, and food?"

"Damn," she laughs, "what is this, twenty-one questions?"

"No just five." He replies playing the game fiercely.

"It was a joke," she says leaning forward to smell his hair, "damn your hair smells good."

"Thanks," he replies, "now answer my questions... please."

"Why?" she asks.

"Because I like you," he admits, "so if I know all that, and I remember it... it'll take me real far with you."

"Oh really," Felicity continues to braid his hair, "and who told you that?"

"My dad..." K.J. confesses.

"Well," she blushes, "I think I like your dad already."

Felicity smiles down at the back of K.J.'s head as she continues to work her scalp soothing magic.

Epilogue

As K.C. pulls up to his church he can't help but feel overcome by déjà vu. He remembers going to seek his pastor back home in Orlando many years ago when his life was falling apart at the seams. Other than the fact that he's wealthy K.C. feels no different today than he did that day. He can't find the bright side no matter how hard he tries.

K.C. parks near the back door of the church, cuts the car off and sighs deeply. As he heads towards the door he readies himself for whatever will come from this much needed conference with his trusted pastor.

K.C. reaches to knock, before he touches the door it opens from the inside.

"I was waiting for you," Pastor White smiles, "I saw you when you pulled up Keldrick. Come on in son, how you holding up?"

"Not too good honestly..." K.C. says following the pastor inside.

"I know son," Pastor White replies, "it's written all over your face."

"Is it?" K.C. asks reaching up to rub his face as if he can erase the obvious stress from its deep chocolate surface.

"Yes son it is," the preacher confirms, "no one can blame you though. You have been through more in your forty-two years than I have in all of mine, and I am a very old man now Keldrick."

"You're just as young as you ever were Pastor," K.C. pats him gently on his old back, "and I gotta keep you around for years to come. You keep me straight man."

"I'm indebted to you for life son." The Pastor says.

"Don't mention it Pastor, but where are we going," K.C. asks, "your office is down that hall?"

"Oh we're not going to my office son," the pastor continues to walk, "we're going straight to the sanctuary."

"Why?" K.C. asks.

"Why not?" The pastor smiles back at him still in full stride.

As they enter in through the sanctuary's beautiful shiny wooden double doors and begin to take in the rare biblically inspired artistic beauty of the place for a moment K.C. forgets why he came.

As they walk K.C. can feel the power in the church seeping into his very bones.

Pastor White walks right up into his pulpit.

K.C. stands from the floor looking up at him.

"Come on up son," the pastor beckons to him, "you built the church you can go wherever you please."

"This is your church Pastor," K.C. forces a smile, "I just footed the bill to have it constructed."

"Son, do you ever wonder why I'm always here?" Pastor White asks.

"Actually I do Pastor." K.C. admits.

"I wondered the same thing about my pastor Reverend Kennibrew when I was a child, "the pastor admits, "When I was a boy, in my mind churches meant two things… sad funerals and sappy weddings. Church was not somewhere I wanted to be as a child."

"Are you serious Pastor White?" K.C. asks.

"Yes I am," the old man replies, "I hated going to church, **could not stand the thought**. I found out later on that the real reason I hated coming… was because God was calling me, He was pulling me to the church with so much power as a boy all I wanted to do was go the opposite direction."

"Makes sense." K.C. says taking a seat in the pulpit next to the pastor.

"But Keldrick," the pastor starts, "I'm always here because there is no deeper peace I have ever known than being all alone inside the walls of a church. The peace a man can find alone inside these beautiful walls is priceless."

"I want that peace." K.C. admits desperately.

"I know you do son," Pastor White replies, "and it's yours for the taking. All you need is alone time in here to talk to God."

The pastor stands up from his seat and walks close to his podium.

"You know son," he says, "When I stand up here every Sunday and preach the Word, I know that God is speaking through me to my congregation. These people need me just as much as I need them. I am the messenger, but without them I would have no one to deliver the message to."

"That's deep Pastor White." K.C. stands to his own feet.

"It's not deep at all," Pastor White turns to look at K.C., "but it's very true. Now I'm going to leave you in here to talk to God."

"I thought **you** were going to talk to me Pastor White," K.C. frowns up, "I can actually **see** you."

"Keldrick," the old man says, "I could do that. I could sit in here and talk to you until both of our faces turn blue."

"Then do it." K.C. replies.

"I told you years ago at your wedding," Pastor starts, "I am not your God, I'm just a man. You don't have to see God to know He's here. He's here son, trust me. And... He has already spoken to you."

K.C. looks away from Pastor White.

"That's crazy pastor, what are you talking about?" K.C. asks.

"You heard the voice of God didn't you," the old man walks close to K.C., "I can see it in your eyes son."

"No you don't," K.C. replies, "and no I did not hear God speak to me."

"You'll be fine son." Pastor White hugs K.C. tightly and then heads for the exit back out towards the church's lobby.

Alone in the presence of an always invisible God K.C. falls to his knees to pray.

(K.C.)

"Jesus... I'm all yours," K.C. says aloud, "take me Lord, break me, make me, and mold me into whatever you would have me be. I'm so tired of finding you and then losing you, time and time again. I will seek your face

339

from now until the end of my meaningless existence. And after I pass away I will know fully that I'll be spending eternity with you in Heaven. I believe you created me, and have saved my sorry ass time and time again for whatever reason. It's time for me to reach out to other men and women who have lost their way, I know that because of all the things you've blessed me with they will all listen to me... This is my purpose now. Please protect my wife Lord, that's all I ask. No matter what, when she is away from me, please always keep a hedge of protection around her. In Jesus name I pray Amen."

Bonus chapter

K.C. wakes up early the next morning and decides to take a walk. Before passing his mailbox he remembers the fact that he didn't check it the day before. He opens it and finds all bills. After throwing it all in the nearby trash barrel he notices the envelope on the bottom is pink.

K.C.'s never seen a bill in an envelope quite that pink. He quickly retrieves the envelope and feels tears on his face before he even knows he's crying.

He rips the envelope open and rushes inside the house to find Cam.

"Baby!" he yells.

"I'm in here..." Cam calls from the bedroom.

K.C. makes his way into the room crying and smiling in excellent proportion.

He unfolds the paper and begins to read aloud.

"Hey dad, I guess I'm writing this letter to let you know I'm alive. I wasn't in my car when it crashed. Honestly, I did kill two of the people whose scarce remains were probably found in my car though. Roland Dansby tried to rape me and Bleek's been raping me for years mentally and emotionally. I didn't kill the girl, Scooter. But I would have if I could do it all over again. Uncle Love is a genius by the way. He shot me again... but it was just a flesh wound this time and it's being tended to well here, I'll be fine. He did what he had to do to protect me, I know that now. My blood had to be in the car. I'm free now, but I do miss my beautiful BMW. So

basically, if what I'm saying now still isn't clear, Unc hid all three of the dead bodies found in the crash until I could escape the country. Then he altered them so no D.N.A. specialist on the planet could definitively identify their bodies, and he put them all inside of my car before he sent it over that bridge. Oh wow! Dad, Josiah just proposed to me! He literally just proposed to me while I'm writing this letter. Of course I said yes. And dad, I apologize for giving you so much hell, but we hurt each other and I'm sorry for everything I said or did. I'm doing okay now. I guess as soon as we set a date and get everything arranged I have to get everybody here for my exotic island wedding. It's so beautiful here dad, Jojo and I literally can get married and have our honeymoon right here in the same place. Enough about me give K.J., Uncle Love, and Cam a kiss for me please. I love you dad, and I'm truly sorry I didn't quite turn out the way you wanted me to.

Love,

Jazemene Argelle Cole-Bell

p.s.

Dad, please don't mention my being alive to anyone not named in this letter. I already made all the right people believe I was in my car the day it crashed. I love you daddy, talk to you soon.

(On the Island)

In the room next door to where Jaze and Josiah are, Whitney is sleeping hard and has been for the past thirteen hours due to her high-powered prescription sleeping pills.

"Thank you for bringing Whitney back to me Papi." Dr. Carlos Sanchez says watching over Whitney as she sleeps.

"You're welcome father," Papi replies, "it wasn't hard she was like this when we picked her up. But why is she chained to her bed?"

"Never mind that," Dr. Sanchez tells him, "but you did well son."

"Thank you," Papi replies, "but father may I ask you another question?"

"Anything son." He replies with his hands behind his back.

"Why... didn't any of these people know you had a son?" Papi asks.

"Learn to only tell people the things they need to know to help you and nothing else." His father instructs him.

"I understand," Papi looks out of the nearby window, "father... you do realize you made me fall in love with this girl don't you? You showed me pictures and raved about how God created her to be my wife. You manipulate and control everything around you father... your words shape people's minds eternally."

"Papi..." Dr. Sanchez speaks.

343

"I am in love with her," Papi head admits, "you made me love a woman I barely even know, just so that you could get her mother back."

"I told you son," Dr. Sanchez takes his eyes off Whitney to look at his son, "Loves have a legacy all their own, **this**... this **love** you feel for Jazemene Cole may have been inspired by my words, but it was designed **for you** nonetheless. You'll see."

"Yes sir," Papi replies, "well, I guess I'll leave you two alone now."

"Good boy." Carlos flashes a devilish grin.

The End

Take My Breath Away 4
-The Final Chapter-
Prologue

Anyone who tricks a man and plays him for his weaknesses deserves nothing less than destruction. Violence has a tangential relationship with psychotic disorders. And even though I believe fully that my current mental state is largely something I inherited, I also know there are things people can say or do to other people to enhance their state of psychosis. It's far more than just the assholes around you that can drive you over the edge of course. I read that approximately twenty percent of patients that suffer from violent psychosis are directly motivated by their delusions or hallucinations. It is also well documented and believed fully by experts that people with schizophrenia have an increased risk of committing violent crimes including homicide. I don't think a doctor alive has dealt with a head case like me before. I know full well my level of psychosis has elevated to a level far beyond return. My aunt Osiana tricked my father back into his original psychotic state; I'm going to end her. Because of what she did, my legal father Keldrick Cole Sr. is having my biological father Lance Orlandis Vinson Cole, committed to a nut house. But yet he's a billionaire now living in a tiny house back in Orlando with his half dead wife Cameron, where he spends every day searching for my missing mother, whose fiancé just blew his own head off a few months back because she's still in love with K.C. If you ask me they're all crazy. So fuck it, my girlfriend Felicity and I will kill them all and then run away to Dr. Sanchez's island to live with my sister and her fiancé Josiah. No, I'm just kidding everything's really good. My dad is finally really happy. He and Ms. Gabrielle are really great together. Dad and I moved into their house with them. The house isn't far from where K.C. and Cameron live now in Mama Cole's old house. We all go to church together almost every Sunday, and we sit together on the front pew at Pastor's White's old church. I don't know where my mom is, but I have a feeling we're going to find her when we fly out to the island in a few months for Jaze's wedding. Life isn't perfect, but what is? I'm learning to just live life as I expect and accept the moments that take my breath away...

Chapter 1
Rich Blood

As Josiah Bell walks down the beautiful beach he revisits his past life back in the states, and the daily torment of wanting to spend every second with a woman he denied since he was a kid. It was so hard to just give in and admit he had in fact fallen even harder than her. All the years he called her a creep, he was definitely the creepier of the two. And she's everything he ever imagined she would be as his woman and much, much more. The sex is great but almost unnecessary; the bond between them is priceless. In a world on this island where nothing in a day is mandatory he and Jaze are free to focus on intertwining their soul love destined hearts closer together with a blissful vengeance. The island is perfect, but Josiah does secretly wish he was back in the states, maybe holding down a couple jobs, paying bills, and struggling at times to take care of his woman. Here on the island thus far everything has just been given to them free of charge. He wants friends, and hobbies, and real life experiences in the real hard world. Jaze has a new best friend. When she's not with Josiah she's always with Papi. Josiah never complains because he's sure the friendship is pure, and Papi did save Jaze's life for whatever reason. He also realizes now that Jaze is his woman; he can't expect to still be her best and only friend as well. He could, but Jaze obviously has other plans on the matter.

This morning Josiah woke in bed and rolled over to kiss his gorgeous fiancé, but she was gone.

In her place was a beautiful hand written note lying beside him. He smiled as he picked it up, pure passion rushed through his body before he read a single word of it. In the letter she thanked Josiah for everything he has been to her and asked him to meet her in the small cave on the beach.

After brushing his teeth, washing his face, and slipping on some cargo shorts and sandals Jojo's been walking ever since.

He can see the cave up ahead now.

He puts his hands in his pockets and smiles down at the sand as he gets closer to the spot where he'll find his destiny. True equally reciprocated love is a rare blessing that most humans will never know, but Jazemene Cole and Josiah Bell live inside of just that every single day. As he steps inside the mouth of the cave he sees her standing there with her back turned to him. She appears to be crying. Josiah rushes towards her.

"Baby what's wrong?" he asks touching her shoulder.

When she's turns around he realizes it's not Jazemene at all. Jojo stands there face to face with one of the younger house keepers.

His face begins to itch as his heart begins to race.

Behind him Josiah can hear footsteps. As he turns around, the site before him freezes every drop of blood in his veins.

Standing side by side, hand in hand are Papi and Jazemene. Papi is aiming a powerful handgun at Josiah's head.

"What the hell is this?" Jojo asks.

"How could you Josiah?" Jaze cries.

"How could I what," Jojo turns to look at the smiling maid, "wait, you think I came down here to meet her? I thought the note was from you?"

"Shut up Josiah, just shut the hell up!" Jaze cries.

"I came down here to meet you," he screams, "what the hell kind of game are you two playing?"

Papi cocks his gun. Josiah closes his eyes and begins to whisper the Lord's Prayer.

2-14-2017

Characters

Jazemene Argelle Cole

Keldrick Jermaine Cole Jr. "K.J."

Cameron Candice Jiles "Cam"

Keldrick Jermaine "K.C." Cole

Whitney Michelle Powell "Suga Mama"

Lance Orlandis Vinson "Love"

Carlos Luis Sanchez "Dr. Sanchez"

Jacody "Jay" Miller

Tyrone "Tyboonie" Carter

Osiana Blue

Josiah "JB" Bell

Cidra Denise Bell

Gabrielle Johnson

Felicity Johnson

"MY PRAYER"
I pray that you all love and enjoy my characters as well as their stories. Know that all things are possible through Christ who strengthens us, and we can do nothing that matters without Him.

In Jesus name I pray Amen.

M. De'Lure

About the Author

De'Lure is a dreamer who writes with his heart and a very realistic imagination. His first passion was acting, but from that love spawned an even deeper passion for the art of writing. The imagery he uses to create stories is packed with all the components of legendary writing careers. Expect great things from De'Lure.

If you enjoyed this novel you should check out these other *AMAZING* titles by De'Lure

Onyx Cielo: Book 1 -The Tree of Transformation- (Fantasy)
Take My Breath Away: Orlando Nights – RELOADED- (Realistic Romance/ Drama)
Take My Breath Away 2: When Love Calls (Realistic Romance/ Drama)
Passion Absolute –Radicon's Princess- (Realistic Romance/ Drama/Erotica)
De'Lure Shorts & Poem (Poetry/Drama/Short Stories)
De'Lure Shorts & Poems 2 (Poetry/Drama/Short Stories)
He Without Sin (Realistic/Romance/Drama)
The Art of Beauty (Realistic/ Island Romance/ Drama)
Mental Apex -Invisible Pyramids- (Deep Poetic Perfection)
Kissed (Murder Mystery/Suspense/Romance)

Available through Infinitypublishing.com, Amazon.com, Barnes&noble.com, and many other retailers. Signed copies can also be ordered directly from the author.

Email: ceom.love@gmail.com

FB: Published De'Lure